HOMELESSNESS
AMID
AFFLUENCE

HOMELESSNESS
AMID
AFFLUENCE

Structure and Paradox
in the
American Political Economy

MICHAEL H. LANG

PRAEGER

New York
Westport, Connecticut
London

Library of Congress Cataloging-in-Publication Data

Lang, Michael H.
    Homelessness amid affluence : structure and paradox in the
American political economy / Michael H. Lang.
      p.   cm.
    Bibliography: p.
    Includes index.
    ISBN 0-275-93167-6 (alk. paper)
    1. Housing policy—United States. 2. Homelessness—United States.
3. Poor—Housing—United States. 4. Urban policy—United States.
I. Title.
HD7293.L27   1989
363.5'1'0973—dc20   89-32271

Library of Congress Catalog Card Number: 89-32271
ISBN: 0-275-93167-6

First published in 1989

Praeger Publishers, One Madison Avenue, New York, NY 10010
An imprint of Greenwood Publishing Group, Inc.

Printed in the United States of America

∞

The paper used in this book complies with the
Permanent Paper Standard issued by the National
Information Standards Organization (Z39.48-1984).

10 9 8 7 6 5 4 3 2

To Catherine and Abigail

Contents

Preface

Homelessness in America is a gut-wrenching problem for all concerned citizens. Homelessness represents the next to the last stop on the downward trajectory from initial economic stability through poverty to absolute destitution. Except for death from exposure and starvation, no worse calamity awaits one after the descent to homelessness; one has truly hit bottom.

As a result of the psychological impact of witnessing the growing phenomenon of urban homelessness, many people have become involved in some aspect of the search for a solution to this national scourge. This book was the result of my personal involvement in assessing one small aspect of shelter policy for the homeless in Camden, New Jersey, an involvement that quickly grew into a desire to understand how widespread homelessness came to be tolerated in our society.

Specifically, I was asked by local housing activists to assist in seeking a resolution to an impasse in the local policymaking process in Camden County, New Jersey. The impasse arose due to the inability of local policymakers to agree on how best to shelter the homeless in the county. Initially, the county had embarked on a policy of providing temporary shelter for the county's homeless in a large facility in the City of Camden. There was intense community debate over the wisdom and justice of centralizing the homeless in a large and somewhat institutional shelter. Sensitive to the public pressure by local housing advocates, the county authorized a review of this policy. That study, while it appears to have met its goal of resolving the size/locational aspect of local shelter policy, also served to raise larger policy questions about how the problem of homelessness arose and how long-term permanent housing could be secured (Lang

1988). While the results of the study are reported here, it is these latter questions that form the central focus of the book.

This book would not have been written without the support and encouragement of a host of dedicated social policy activists in Camden County, New Jersey. These activists are affiliated with the Community Planning and Advocacy Council, the Human Services Coalition, the Emergency Housing Consortium, and the Camden Shelter Coalition. They are: Catherine A. DeCheser, Pat Bolden, Joel Bethany, Jack Abbott, Tom Knoche, Father Edward Walsh, Rev. Sam Appel, Rev. Don Dudley, Fontaine Fulghum, Papas Das, Dawn Fayer, Eleanor Vine, Wolfgang Hertz-Lane, Wenllian Stallings, Andi Rauer, Jerrothia Riggs, Joyce Williams, John Williams, Rev. J. Allen Nimmo, Clem Carney, and Stephen Tobias. Mr. Peter J. O'Connor and the Rev. Robert Shaffer of the Fair Share Housing Corporation are working at the provision of low cost housing from a different but equally important perspective. Their advice and counsel were extremely useful in the development of this project. The Reverend Al Wilson was instrumental in providing professional assistance as well as unstinting encouragement throughout the duration of this project.

Camden, New Jersey, is fortunate in having a concerned local political delegation that has responded to the crisis of homelessness with commendable vigor. Among those particularly active were State Senator Walter Rand, State Assemblyman Wayne Bryant, Assemblyman Joseph Roberts, and Mayor Randy Primas. I am also grateful for the support of the local elected and appointed officials in Camden County whose dedication to the principle of being their brother's keeper stands in stark contrast to the less generous motivations that often prevail in our society: Robert Andrews, Lewis Bezich, and Joe Carroll.

Some of the concepts for assisting the homeless mentioned here were raised at a symposium on homelessness at the annual meeting of American Orthopsychological Association in Chicago during the Spring of 1985 where I benefited from an exchange of views with Professors Madeline Stoner, Ann Abbott, John Simpson, Ezra Susser, Paul Colson, and Morris Klass. Some of the policy issues involved in dealing with the homeless were further developed for presentation at a regional conference on homelessness held at Rutgers University, Camden, New Jersey, in the Fall of 1986. Dr. Ann Abbott and Doreen Brager of the Rutgers–Camden social work department, and Jane Malone and Chris Sprowal of the Philadelphia Committee for the Homeless provided a wealth of information and referrals to programs and professionals dealing with the homeless.

Much of the information in the case study which forms the basis for Chapter 8 came from input developed by an expert panel. This panel was made up of professionals who work with the homeless in different parts of the country and whose support and enthusiasm for the project were invaluable. Panel members were Woody Widrow, Edward Rager, Dr. Edward Kaplan, Greg Wilderman, Terry Lynch, Peggy Raferty, Patrick Walsh, Sister Jane Stewart, Fr. Edward Tinsley, Philip Starr, Tim Hager, and Joseph Houston. Valuable technical assistance for this study was provided by Professors Phyllis Kaniss of the University of Pennsylvania and Robert A. Beauregard of Rutgers University–New Brunswick.

Colleagues at the Rutgers–Camden Department of Urban Studies and Community Development and the Rutgers–Camden Forum for Policy Research and Public Service were instrumental in encouraging me to broaden my initial case study and were helpful in reviewing early drafts of some chapters, in particular, Dorrie Margolin, and Professors Jon Van Til and Jay Sigler. Many fine graduate research students helped with the development of this book: Lorena Camphor, Jacqui Collins-Parker, Eugene Wisnosky, Larry Gregorio, and Steven Zerbe. Lisa Hobbs-Fernie provided the legal analysis upon which Chapter 9 is based while Joanne Harkins was instrumental in framing portions of Chapter 7. Other individuals who were instrumental in providing professional input to this project were Dr. Edward Kaplan of Yale University; Dr. Russell Schutt, University of Massachusetts at Boston; David Sciarra, Department of the Public Advocate, Trenton, N.J.; Mr. Karl Bertrand, Executive Director, The Sharing Community Inc., Yonkers, N.Y.; and Mr. John H. Knight, attorney for the Coalition for the Homeless of Westchester, White Plains, N.Y. I also wish to acknowledge the fine word processing assistance I received from Mrs. Nancy Brooks. Finally, I wish to thank my family who put up with my single-minded preoccupation with the task of writing this book.

HOMELESSNESS
AMID
AFFLUENCE

Introduction

Homelessness is a societal problem that is quickly assuming major proportions throughout the United States. In its cities, towns, suburbs, and
rural communities, the growing specter of homelessness has become a
gripping reminder of the fragility of our sociopolitical fabric. Confronting
urban homelessness is becoming unavoidable as increasing numbers of
destitute individuals can be seen huddled over steam vents in full view of
passersby. They cruise along our downtown streets rifling through garbage
receptacles in search of food scraps. Often they can be seen using curbside
hydrants as bathroom sinks and the storm drains as toilets. Many suffer
from extreme deprivation due to hunger and exposure (Collins-Parker
1986). Many of these individuals are clothed in filthy rags and keep their
few possessions in a tattered shopping bag. Most of us turn away rather
than confront this sad reality. Volunteers and social workers attempt to
feed and shelter these individuals, particularly in the colder months when
there is a real risk of death. Indeed, during the winters of 1985–86 in
Philadelphia alone some forty-two homeless individuals perished from
exposure (Loeb 1987).

The homeless that we see are but a fraction of the total number of
homeless who are scattered throughout the city. Many squat in abandoned
buildings, some live in their cars, others utilize public waiting rooms, while
some prefer local soup kitchens or special shelters that exist in some
localities (Wiegard 1985). Most of the visible homeless are men but a
significant and increasing proportion are women and children (Peuquet
and Leland 1988). Many have had a history of mental instability or
substance abuse but an increasing number are single parent families who

are homeless due to the lack of low cost housing and meaningful job opportunities (W. Wilson 1987; Clay 1987; Dolbeare 1987; Fox 1985).

The homeless are found throughout the country. The major concentrations are in our large cities, but suburban and rural areas also have their own homeless. Often these nonurban homeless are forced to migrate to the city in order to find publicly provided shelter and food services which their locality is unable or unwilling to provide (Lang 1987).

Urban homelessness in the United States is increasing and it is affecting individuals and families that were heretofore untouched by this most tragic of economic conditions (Erickson and Wilhelm 1986; Redburn and Buss 1986; Hope and Young 1986a; Wiegard 1985; Hopper and Hamberg 1984; P. Smith 1987; Clay 1987; Dolbeare 1987). Homelessness is emerging as a central domestic policy problem of the 1980s. It claims this centrality because homelessness stands as stark evidence of the extremes of wealth and poverty tolerated in our affluent society. It is the visibility of homelessness in affluent urban areas that provides a new and unsettling dimension to what is, after all, a continuing dichotomy between rich and poor in the United States. The reemergence of this low rung on the ladder of opportunity has jolted a response out of the media and public officials.

Much good work on meeting the immediate needs of the homeless has been done at the local level by dedicated individuals and groups; yet few successful programs or policies to combat the increase in homelessness have been established (Hope and Young 1986b). As a result, most authorities anticipate the problem getting worse in the foreseeable future.

One of the characteristics of the homeless problem today is its multifaceted nature (Hopper and Hamberg 1984; Erickson and Wilhelm 1986). There are many different kinds of homeless people who are homeless for many different reasons. This makes the study of the homeless problem extremely difficult. However, some general facts about the homeless are relatively clear; for instance, the number of homeless has become significant. Nationwide, estimates of the total number of homeless vary widely from a low of 192,000 to a high of 3 million (Hope and Young, 1986a, 17). Large cities are forced to shelter increasing numbers of the homeless; Philadelphia reports 12,500 homeless (Wiegand 1988); Boston has about 2,500 (Johnson 1986); New York has over 50,000 (Barbanel 1987). Similar numbers are reported from cities throughout the United States (National Coalition for the Homeless 1987b). Suburban and rural areas also report increasing numbers of homeless families and find themselves hard pressed to shelter them within their jurisdiction. One central fact that stands out is that the total number of homeless people is rising. Here again the rate of increase varies by wide margins, from a low of 10% in Memphis to a high of 50% in El Paso, but in most cases there is a significant increase (Smith 1987, 31; National Coalition for the Homeless 1987b). As a result, emergency shelter resources are severely taxed, and new resources must be created (P. Smith 1987, 6).

There is a large and growing literature on the subject of homelessness. Much of it attempts to describe and categorize homelessness and its causal factors. For instance, there are many excellent studies based on in-depth interviews with the homeless that attempt to isolate those factors that led to their condition (Baxter and Hopper 1981; Kozol 1988; Kates 1985; H. Murray 1986; Coleman 1986). There is also a sizable body of literature on local service delivery aspects, often focused on the needs of particular subgroups among the homeless such as the mentally ill (Dear and Wolch 1987; Lamb 1984). Some studies have tried to grapple with the practical implications of homelessness most often by analyzing social welfare policies (Hope and Young 1986a; Bingham, Green, and White 1987; Stoner 1986; Stone 1986; Phillips, Kronenfeld, and Jeter 1987).

This book approaches the subject of homelessness from a public policy perspective. In so doing it will touch on the contributions of a number of separate academic disciplines. This entails the risk of offending those proponents of each discipline who may feel that insufficient attention was paid to a particular approach or a particular study. The benefit of the public policy approach is that it affords a more fulsome analysis of the problem of homelessness which may lead to a more profound understanding of the various social, economic, and political factors that give rise to the problem. Policies and programs to alleviate the condition can then be assessed. The benefits of such an approach outweigh the risk. In any case, the problem of homelessness is so profound and troubling that it calls for efforts that may help identify meaningful long-term solutions that could lead to the elimination of the embarrassment of homelessness from this country.

Thus, this book begins with an acknowledgement of all those who have viewed the problems of poverty and homelessness from the vantage point of their particular discipline. There is a wealth of relevant academic literature and applied research based in the disciplines of sociology, social work, community development, planning, public policy, law, urban economics, and political theory. Indeed, relevant information is often found in subfields or specializations within these major disciplines. The fields of housing policy, social stratification, and social justice bear mention. This book is based on an attempt to tie some of the salient contributions of these respective disciplines together thereby leading to an increased understanding of the policymaking context from which a solution to the problem of widespread homelessness must emerge. At times this task appears daunting. There are so many theoretical trails to follow. Many appear at first to be relevant but once followed, lead one down long and eventually obscure intellectual paths. At the same time their contextual contribution can be significant. The issue is how to find the right mix; how to place the proper emphasis so as to avoid being overwhelmed by the sheer profusion of empirical data and academic theory.

For instance, the most cursory review of the literature indicates that an array of causative factors can lead to homelessness. Specifically, homelessness is most often a problem caused by the lack of affordable shelter or adequate income (Governor's Task Force on Homelessness 1985, 1), but this may be due to a dizzying constellation of secondary causative factors such as welfare cuts, loss of entry level blue collar jobs, poor educational opportunities, discrimination, transportation barriers to job opportunities, deinstitutionalization, substance abuse, urban gentrification, and displacement (Hope and Young 1986a; Kozol 1988; Hopper and Hamberg 1984).

Selecting a policy framework with which to view these causative factors is of great importance. There are many that could be devised and utilized. For instance, one framework can be devised by analyzing recent federal, state, and local approaches to urban policy (Hope and Young 1986a; Meyers 1986). Another by analyzing the functioning of urban labor markets in capitalist societies undergoing a shift from manufacturing to a service-based economy (M. P. Smith 1984; Goodman 1979; Fainstein et al. 1986; W. J. Wilson 1987; Auletta 1982). Yet another, by studying the supposed failings of our inner-city educational system (National Commission on Excellence in Education 1983). Clearly, the task of devising and applying a meaningful framework is not an easy one, but to look at just one causal element such as the supply of low cost housing is to risk missing the true systemic nature of the phenomenon of homelessness. As a result, this book will look at the broader theoretical aspects of housing and urban community development policy in our political economy in the hope of identifying interrelationships and tendencies that foster lasting poverty, inequality, and homelessness. It is hoped that such an approach will also identify approaches to policy development and implementation that have potential for achieving true systemic change; change that could free us from the horror of living in an affluent society that countenances the existence of a large and growing corps of homeless individuals.

The immediate problem can be defined in three parts: in the short term, how best to provide services to the homeless which encourage a stabilization of their lifestyle; in the mid term, how to devise public policies that ensure we move toward the creation of a society that delivers sufficient low cost housing matched with access to adequate employment and/or income so as to end all homelessness; and in the long term, what approach to policy implementation stands the best chance of achieving meaningful results.

The answer to the first problem can be found in the development of a suitable service delivery system on the local level that is capable of responding to the needs of the homeless (Hope and Young 1986a; Ferrell 1985; Philadelphia Committee for the Homeless 1985; Dear and Wolch 1987). The answer to the second problem lies in advocacy of change in the policies and programs on the local and national levels that have an impact on homelessness: welfare, minimum wage laws, job creation, community development, and most centrally, government-supported low income housing (Hope and Young 1986a; Hopper and Hamberg 1984; Kozol 1988). The answer to the third problem lies in fashioning a policy approach that is based on an appreciation of the complexity of the policy implementation process in general and the tension that exists between local and national policymaking process in this country in particular. Such an approach must recognize the real barriers to reforms of our political economy (Lindblom 1980).

In attempting to grapple with these complex and interrelated issues, this book has been divided into five parts. The first, "Understanding Homelessness," provides a conceptual overview. Accordingly, Chapter 1 reviews the history of homelessness in this country and looks at present day circumstances affecting the problem. It examines the causes of homelessness today and looks at the size and composition of the problem. Chapter 2 provides a theoretical approach to homelessness and its companion conditions, unemployment/lack of income. This chapter reviews Marxist and regulated market views on the subject. Particular stress is given to the role of the so-called safety net in regulated market economies. The discussion includes a hard look at the various theoretical approaches to policymaking in our market-dominated democratic society. Also explored are cyclical factors that might favor the reemergence of a broadbased spirit of altruism capable of influencing the development of national public policies for the homeless.

The second part, "The Urban Policy Context," deals with the context from which a solution to homelessness must emerge. Thus, Chapter 3 looks at the development of urban policy and programs from an intergovernmental context. This analysis highlights the real dysfunctions inherent in the policymaking context. These dysfunctions become an issue whenever there is a need to fashion comprehensive approaches to significant socioeconomic problems in our society. Chapter 4 reviews the struggle for a national housing policy in the United States. This chapter examines the history of public and subsidized housing programs and assesses the potential for increased involvement by governmental and nonprofit entities in this area. Particular emphasis is placed on an analysis of the growing shortage of low cost housing.

The third part is "Policy Initiatives to Produce Low Cost Housing." Chapter 5 reviews local-level programs which deliver so-called affordable housing. The majority of affordable housing programs attempt to modify the private market and government regulatory maze that affects the housing market in this country. The implications of these programs for the homeless will be discussed. Chapter 6 reviews the history of the failed efforts to open up suburban communities to low income households by means of the local "fair share" housing program. Federal involvement with this policy is also reviewed. The impact of fair housing legislation is also analyzed. The case for a national fair share low income housing policy and its relationship to the problem of homelessness is examined.

The fourth part, "Policy Initiatives to Assist the Homeless," deals with the specific policies and programs developed in response to the needs of the homeless population. Chapter 7 reviews the existing federal, state, and local measures to combat homelessness. The contention by housing advocates that federal level efforts are insufficient and place an unfair burden on the state and local levels is examined. Chapter 8 analyzes the problems that have greeted the efforts of Camden County, New Jersey, to shelter a large and growing number of its homeless people.

The fifth part, "Real Policy Reform—The Impossible Dream?" analyzes some new policy approaches that advocates claim hold the promise of resolving homelessness and poverty. It ends with an assessment of the more likely policies to emerge from the continuing policy debate over this issue. Accordingly, Chapter 9 reviews proposals for a national right to housing law that many housing advocates feel may serve to engender a stronger federal role in the delivery of low cost housing in this country. Chapter 10 provides the concluding analysis. It stresses the ramifications of current governmental policy regarding the phenomenon of homelessness. The chapter examines the likelihood that the policies discussed in the earlier chapters or something akin to them can be fashioned into a coherent national policy for eliminating homelessness.

Part I

UNDERSTANDING HOMELESSNESS

1

Homelessness, Past and Present

Homelessness in the United States is not a new phenomenon nor are the visible manifestations of the problem particularly new. Historically, there have always been homeless people in our society; there were homeless among our first settlers, indeed many of the homeless in Europe were sentenced to exile in the American colonies. Not that these colonies were any more compassionate; most quickly enacted anti-vagrancy laws by 1650. Only New York City offered assistance to its homeless by opening the first almshouse (Erickson and Wilhelm 1986; Coll 1971; Hoch 1987).

The industrial revolution during the second half of the nineteenth century is considered the origin of much modern day homelessness. Most of these homeless were workers laid off from construction jobs on the railroads and in the cities that boomed during this era (Erickson and Wilhelm 1986; Hoch 1987). Also prevalent in the post-Civil War era were the bums, hobos, or knights of the road chronicled by Jack London and others (London 1977, 4; Stone 1965; Anderson 1923; Bahr 1973). Most such knights of the road were Civil War veterans and industrial workers left jobless due to the depression of 1873–79 when some 2 million workers (13% of the work force) were left unemployed. Many resorted to a migrant life on the rails in a constant search for temporary agricultural jobs. There exist few records of the extent of homelessness in this period but evidence from Philadelphia puts at 60,000 (5% of the total population) the number of transients in that city in 1874. In response to a rise in homelessness in New York City, several charitable shelters were opened there in that year (Erickson and Wilhelm 1986; Coll 1971; Schneider 1986; Hoch 1987).

In this period the basic shelter and service needs of these individuals were being met by the formation of the skid row district in many American cities. These districts provided the lodging houses, single room occupancy

(SRO) or welfare hotels, as well as the missions, bars, and other services required by transient workers and the unemployed. The population of skid row waxed and waned along with the business cycles of the economy. Strictly speaking, the skid row population, while at the bottom of the economic ladder, was not homeless. Only when the population swelled beyond its capacity did overt homelessness occur. For instance, during the depression that followed the panic of 1893 the numbers of homeless were such that in 1896 New York City, using a waterfront barge, opened the first publicly supported emergency housing. Middle-class charitable efforts by groups such as the Charity Organization Society of New York helped establish almshouses which provided a less repressive response to the homeless problem (Erickson and Wilhelm 1986; Coll 1971; Bogue 1986; Dear and Wolch 1987). The police were also a large part of the institutional framework of skid row because it was their job to enforce the laws against public intoxication and vagrancy. In so doing they ensured that a significant proportion of the homeless were temporarily sheltered in city "drunk tanks" and jails. By 1890, the New York police were providing some 150,000 such lodgings annually (Hoch 1987; Cuomo 1987; N. Anderson 1923; Bahr 1973).

In the 1900s increased mechanization on farms and in industry resulted in falling demand for seasonal manual workers. As a result, the population of skid row began to decline as the temporarily unemployed migrant workers were replaced by a smaller number of hard core "odd jobbers, day workers, the handicapped and societal misfits" (Erickson and Wilhelm 1986; Schneider 1986).

The Great Depression of the 1930s provided the next period of homelessness. Hundreds of thousands of unemployed workers were joined by tens of thousands of evicted and foreclosed families to form the large pool of homeless that existed during this period. Squatters were living in shantytowns in the most debased conditions on the outskirts of the cities. By 1932, various agencies in 60 cities with populations over 50,000 were sheltering 400,000 individuals each night. Pressure on the federal government resulted in the establishment of the Federal Transient Program by the Federal Emergency Relief Administration in 1933. By 1935, the program was assisting over 373,000 homeless per month. With the advent of World War II, and resultant full employment, homelessness almost vanished (Erickson and Wilhelm 1986; Coll 1971; Schneider 1986; Hoch 1987; Reitman 1937).

After World War II, the continuing economic expansion served to keep the population of the skid rows fairly low. By 1960, these areas had declined in size and were now less oriented toward the marginally employed and more oriented toward an older, alcoholic, welfare dependent population of (usually white) men. The negative effects of periods of unemployment were lessened by such programs as unemployment insurance and Social Security initiated during the New Deal (Erickson and Wilhelm 1986; Hoch 1987). Depending on local economic conditions, between one third and one half of skid row men had held menial jobs. By the 1970s these skid row areas had largely disappeared due to public and private renewal efforts. Part of the reason for this was the general economic prosperity of the time and the availability of affordable housing. Between 1950 and 1970, real median family incomes almost doubled due in part to significant wage increases gained by those in unionized industrial jobs. Simultaneously, there was a significant growth in programs for the poor resulting in a period of maximum income equality (Hopper and Hamberg 1984; Schneider 1986).

At the same time housing conditions were undergoing a rapid improvement, supply grew by some 50% and outpaced household formation. This allowed for a decreased prevalence of overcrowded conditions. Federal housing programs were aimed at encouraging increased homeownership by means of federally insured mortgages and infrastructure support for low cost suburban housing. These policies were successful since the rate of homeownership increased from 43.6% in 1940 to 61.9% in 1960 (Hopper and Hamberg 1984).

Success in housing policy can also be measured in terms of decreased substandard conditions achieved by the demolition of unfit units or their renovation. A measure of success in the postwar era can be seen from the fact that in 1940 45% of all units lacked complete plumbing but this had dropped to just 7% by 1970. In similar fashion, poor structural conditions declined from 18% in 1940 to 5% in 1970. The improvement stemmed from the effects of several simultaneous trends in government policies and the robust urban economy. First, rural to urban migration allowed many rural shacks to be demolished as their occupants moved into improved urban units. Urban renewal and urban highway programs cleared some of the worst inner city housing. Federal law ensured that those displaced had the right to be relocated to suitable accommodations elsewhere. Finally, postwar suburbanization provided plentiful affordable housing that allowed for the decanting of the overcrowded cities and the freeing up of sufficient units for the newcomers (Hopper and Hamberg 1984; Sternlieb and Hughes 1983).

It is important to note that all this was done without the need to spend any more individual disposable income on housing. A 1950 renter household paid an average of 19% of its income for housing and this rate stayed the same or declined slightly over the next two decades (Hopper and Hamberg 1984). While governmental housing policy was chiefly aimed at increasing the rates of homeownership, there was a small but successful federal public housing program that served low income households. The 1960s saw additional housing programs aimed at the renovation or construction of units for those of moderate income.

The result of this confluence of forces was to produce housing conditions that are enviable today. While there were the poor who had to resort to skid row accommodations, and inadequate housing conditions were still a problem for many in our cities and rural areas, there is no denying the real improvements that were accomplished in this period. Most important was that while some were poorly housed, they *were* housed (Sternlieb and Hughes 1983).

Today we confront a very different situation. To begin to gain an understanding of the distinctions between historical patterns of homelessness and contemporary homelessness, it is necessary to look at causal factors.

CURRENT CAUSAL FACTORS CONTRIBUTING TO HOMELESSNESS

Understanding the range and varying characteristics of these causal factors is necessary because they were precursors to the development and application of remedial policies. Today's homeless population is variegated. It can no longer be described by reference to the stereotypical Bowery bum whose alcoholism has led him to his sorry condition or the transient worker existing on the margins of society, a victim of the ups and downs of the national economy. This greater variegation differs from earlier years, when homelessness was chiefly a product of cyclical conditions in the economy and affected male laborers. Today, however, there are other causative factors at work such as significant shifts in labor demand, welfare policy, lack of affordable housing, and the decline of the extended family (Erickson and Wilhelm 1986; Hoch 1987; Jahiel 1987; Stefl 1987; Wright 1988). As a result, homelessness is not apt to be solved by a return to economic growth.

Changes in family structure comprise one factor often related to homelessness. Specifically, the declining number of intact families in this country has led to the increasing feminization of poverty (Moynihan 1986; Ellwood 1987; W. J. Wilson 1987). Many analysts have noted that separation and divorce are quick paths to poverty for many female-headed households. In 1983, there were 3.5 million female-headed households and 7 million children in poverty. Also related to this is an increase in spouse abuse. Domestic violence often leads to homelessness. Victims of spousal abuse form a sizable group of homeless individuals requiring specialized services (Fox 1985; Hagen 1987; Sullivan and Damrosch 1987).

Federal cutbacks for a variety of social support programs such as AFDC, Food Stamps, and Child Nutrition are a related causal factor (Joe and Rodgers 1985; Burt and Pittman 1986; Hope and Young 1986a; Hoch 1987). These changes have contributed to the increase in the number of homeless families with children. Currently, children are the largest single group among the homeless in some regions, a particularly disturbing demographic trend (Kaufman and Harris 1983; Fox 1985; Gioglio and Jacobsen 1986).

Women and children represent as much as 30% of the population in single room occupancy (SRO) accommodations. In New York, over half the total homeless are families. These patterns show that increasing numbers of women and children are joining the ranks of the homeless (Hopper and Hamberg 1984; H. Rodgers 1986; Sidel 1986; Hagen 1987; Sullivan and Damrosch 1987).

Another factor is welfare reform which swept many states during the early years of the Reagan administration. In this case, welfare reform meant cutbacks in payments to so-called employable males, which increased the number of young males who were truly destitute (Fox 1985; Hopper and Hamberg 1984; Magill 1986; Abramovitz 1986; H. Rodgers 1988; Sidel 1986; Joe and Rodgers 1985).

Another factor related to homelessness concerns the reform of mental health policy that has led to the deinstitutionalization of mental patients who would have been housed in mental institutions. Much homelessness is indirectly due to this policy of deinstitutionalization. These individuals were to be released into community-based facilities under a policy of maximum "normalization" for those patients who could function in society with the aid of psychotropic drugs and outpatient care. In some instances, these former patients were not adequately served by a community-based system. In other instances, facilities existed but often were not designed so as to ensure a patient's successful transition to a more independent existence. In a few cases, patients were released who would in all likelihood never function very well without a level of care not easily delivered in a community setting. The overall result was that significant numbers of former mental patients were reduced to roaming the streets of our cities in search of food and shelter (Fox 1985; Hopper and Hamberg 1984; Hope and Young 1986b; Lamb 1984; Dear and Wolch 1987). Yet, it should be stressed that the prevalence of mental illness among the homeless is significant, but not pervasive (Snow et al. 1986).

Discrimination remains a potent element contributing to homelessness. For instance, racial discrimination in housing persists and serves to limit the supply of affordable housing (First, Roth, and Arewa 1988; Bowser 1985; Jefferson 1986; Wilhelm 1986; Aiken 1985).

3) Substance abuse is another major causal factor leading to homelessness. Indeed, substance abusers are heavily represented among the homeless. This group includes both drug and alcohol abusers. Many experts debate the extent to which the horror of homelessness occasions such abuse or exacerbates a preexisting condition. In any case, these individuals require professional supervision which is often in short supply (Bruner and Cosby 1985; Kozol 1988; Hope and Young 1986a; Montgomery County Government 1985).

Advances in the area of human rights can be unintended secondary causative factors. Specifically, the striking down of local anti-vagrancy laws has meant that vagrants are no longer routinely arrested and allowed to sleep in the local "drunk tank." When they have no access to low cost accommodation, these individuals add to the growing numbers of homeless (Hopper and Hamberg 1984).

Homelessness caused by the deliberate action of the homeless must also be considered. Such "intentional homelessness" is a category that is very controversial and hard to define. It implies that homelessness is artificially caused by individuals who make themselves homeless in order to partake of the programs available for the homeless (Main 1983b). A common example would be someone who is living in crowded quarters with a friend or relative. The existence of a local shelter or government-provided motel accommodation might presumably attract a few such individuals who would view such housing as preferable to their current cramped and tense living arrangements. The specter of massive intentional homelessness is often raised by local politicians who fear if they provide a local shelter for the homeless, they will create a demand for more shelters. This possibility was also alluded to in statements by the Attorney General of the United States when he implied that those in line at shelters and soup kitchens were there only because it was preferable to having to pay for their own bed and board (Hopper and Hamberg 1984). By implication, homelessness is a function of the supply of shelters rather than external causal factors (Main 1983a, 1983b). Many authorities feel such a category of homelessness does not exist because, in reality, shelter living is an existence so crowded, inhospitable, and even dangerous that it is inconceivable that anyone would choose it in preference to something else. Some social service workers do claim that there is an incentive for some individuals to claim homelessness in the hope of eventually securing a referral to low cost public or private housing. To the extent that this does occur, it is reflective of the abysmal housing conditions and lack of alternatives that the poor must suffer in this country.

④ There are other causative factors that must be considered. In recent years, the structure of our economy has undergone profound changes. These changes have resulted in a massive decline in the number of blue-collar manufacturing jobs which has had a profoundly negative effect on the opportunity structure in this country. These lost jobs have been counterbalanced by the expansion of the economy in new technologically oriented areas, but these jobs require a high level of education. An increase in entry level service jobs has also occurred, but these are poor replacements for the highly paid unionized jobs that were lost. These service jobs are usually minimum wage jobs with little opportunity for meaningful advancement. In many areas of the country it is simply not possible to live on such salaries even in two wage earner households. It is also true that many of these jobs are marginal and are apt to disappear first during a recession (Hopper and Hamberg 1984; W. J. Wilson 1987; Auletta 1982; Goodman 1979; Bluestone and Harrison 1982).

Access to entry level jobs is also important particularly for economically marginal households. However, America's postwar community development process has produced an increasingly segregated housing/employment pattern that limits such access. Inner city poor find it difficult to reach new service jobs in the suburbs and nonmetropolitan areas. This produces the paradox of rampant unemployment in the cities and labor shortages in our developing suburbs.

It is important to note that all the causative factors listed above have been present in our economy at other times and often have been more pronounced than at present. For instance, significant poverty, hunger, unemployment, deinstitutionalization, and migration have predated the advent of the recent surge in homelessness. For example, while 35.3 million people or 11% of the population were considered poor in 1983, in 1959 39.5 million or 22.4% of the population were considered poor. In addition, welfare benefits were much more limited in the past. Unemployment reached a high of 10.8% in late 1982 but it had been above 9% during the recession of 1974–75. Most deinstitutionalization occurred in the late 1960s and early 1970s but it was not until the 1980s that the homeless mentally ill became a common sight in our central cities. Likewise, major interregional migration peaks have frequently occurred. The most recent was the population shift in the 1970s to the southwestern states, but significant homelessness there did not appear until the mid 1980s (Hopper and Hamberg 1984). Hopper and Hamberg argue persuasively that we have reached a critical confluence of sociopolitical factors in our economy that have reacted so as to create the homelessness we currently see:

The suspicion is unavoidable that boundary conditions have changed, that the operating set of limits and tolerances that determines a social order's capacity to absorb surplus population has been materially altered. Somewhere a threshold was crossed.

THE SHORTAGE OF AFFORDABLE HOUSING

While all of these factors are important, the primary cause of homelessness is the national shortage of affordable housing. Today, there is simply not enough affordable housing for the lower income groups in our society. There has been a real decline in the numbers of available units in some areas at the same time as there has been an increase in demand for such units. The loss of low income housing has been traced, in part, to the effects of the Reagan administration's cuts in domestic spending that are now almost a decade old (Meyers 1986). There have been no low cost public or assisted housing programs under his administration; indeed, the repair of existing public units has not been fully funded leading to an absolute decline in units in some localities (Downs 1983; Dolbeare 1987; Clay 1987; National Housing Task Force 1988; Apgar and Brown 1988; Carliner 1987).

Subsidized housing programs have been cut for all groups of recipients, even the heretofore favored elderly. Cuts in the Community Development Block Grant Program have made it impossible for local governments to take up the slack left by the federal pull out from low cost housing. Some states have tried to fund such housing by the use of revenue bonds, but even this strategy was severely curtailed by recent federal tax reform that restricts the issuance of tax-free instruments. Local nonprofit housing corporations have tried to construct or rehabilitate housing and have achieved some notable success but the numbers of units involved are just too small to be meaningful (Meyers 1986; Atlas and Dreier 1988). Too much affordable housing is constantly being lost for these efforts to make any headway. All of these cutbacks ensured that the supply of new affordable housing would decrease and it has. Production of federally assisted low and moderate cost housing units has declined from 350,000 in 1980 to some 200,000 in 1985 (Meyers 1986). A recent study by Philip Clay, funded by Neighborhood Reinvestment Corporation (Clay 1987), foresees over 18.7 million Americans being unable to secure affordable housing as a result of ongoing losses of low cost housing stock. The report indicates that more than 3.5 million low cost rental units, those costing $325 or less per month, are expected to be lost by the year 2003 reducing the total number to 9.4 million from the current 12.9 million. At the same time, the number of people needing such units is expected to climb from 11.9 million to 17.2 million.

Some government-supported housing programs do exist but many benefit the middle class. For instance, many states offer below market rate mortgages for lower income groups. However, participation in such programs is limited to those who have a secure source of income and few credit problems (M. H. Lang 1985). In short, the truly needy cannot hope to be accepted. The biggest federal housing program is directed at the middle class in the form of tax relief for homeowners on their first and second homes. The amount of revenue foregone by the Treasury under this program of tax relief exceeds all current low income housing programs combined (Dolbeare 1987).

Concurrent with the decrease in new affordable housing has been the decrease in existing older rental units. This decrease is often very traumatic since it often leads to outright homelessness. Many factors have contributed to this decrease. Perhaps the greatest cause for the decline in low income units is the abandonment of old, decaying units by their owners. Many of these units are in blighted inner city housing markets where the rate of return does not match alternative investment opportunities elsewhere. These buildings cannot be sold to new owners unless there is a chance to initiate a complete renovation in order to attract an affluent clientele. In either case, abandonment or renovation, the original low income tenants are evicted. Their only hope is that there is sufficient vacancy among the remaining low cost units. If there is not, as is increasingly the case, they may well end up homeless if they cannot double up with a friend or relative (Downs 1983; Lipton 1980; Sternlieb and Hughes 1980).

Of particular concern has been the loss of single room occupancy (SRO) housing units (Kasinitz 1986). These units are low cost efficiency apartments catering to the very poor in our urban areas. The danger is the loss of these units due to the revitalization of the local housing market. Many of these SROs are of very poor quality and house individuals with an array of physical and mental problems. They are particularly important since they provide a measure of privacy so crucial to the mental health of these often vulnerable individuals (Siegal 1978). Usually, SROs are concentrated in certain transitional areas that have gained a reputation for catering to the down-and-out (Dear and Wolch 1987). George Orwell wrote eloquently about how major cities cater to the down-and-out by providing basic low cost sheltering services in the core area (Orwell 1933). These skid row areas—New York's Bowery, Philadelphia's Tenderloin, and San Francisco's Yerba Buena—have all been revitalized out of existence or are under growing pressure from developers. Because their political clout was small and their cause unpopular, no relocation plans were set up for the displaced residents. As a result, their destiny was left to the vagaries of the local housing market.

While many reformers are against SRO housing in principle, to some it is the quality and management of particular buildings rather than the type of housing per se to which they object. They feel such housing, if provided in a clean and efficient manner, must be carefully safeguarded as it is a crucial part of the housing continuum that ranges from emergency food and shelter to permanent low cost housing. New York has passed laws to make it harder for owners to evict sitting SRO tenants in order to convert the units to upper income accommodation; however, a recent court ruling has overturned this restriction (Hopper and Hamberg 1984; Hartman 1974; Hope and Young 1986b; Kasinitz 1986).

One ramification of the loss of low cost housing is the increase in overcrowding in the remaining units. There is no accurate information on the extent of this problem because it is an illegal situation and therefore all parties have a vested interest in keeping the information from housing inspectors and census takers (Hughes and Sternlieb 1987). However, anecdotal reports by public housing authority officials confirm that it is an increasing problem (Hopper and Hamberg 1984).

Often homelessness is created by both public and private urban revitalization activities. Urban revitalization refers to a physical renewal process whereby older cities attempt to recapture some of the economic vitality they enjoyed at the height of industrialization when they were the site of most of the nation's shops, offices, and factories. Unfortunately, publicly funded urban revitalization often entails the wholesale clearance of blighted housing in order to have sufficient open space to lure commercial interests attuned to low rise suburban land use patterns. In clearing these areas, city officials often overlook the fact that what was lost was low income housing. While enjoined to relocate those displaced, many studies show that this is not done with sufficient care to achieve replacement level housing. Either the residents are worse off or they have to pay significantly more for their new unit. The result is a real and continuing decline in the number of low income units available in our central cities (Gans 1962, 1965; J. Q. Wilson 1966; M. Anderson 1964).

In recent years, much attention has been given to the effects of privately funded urban revitalization, often referred to as gentrification. In many cities, gentrification has resulted in a decline of low cost housing units (Kasinitz 1986). Gentrification is the name given to the functioning of the private housing market whereby the middle class becomes predominant in formerly low income areas of the city. Gentrification is one of the most dynamic forces reshaping old central city neighborhoods in the United States. The term refers to the economic and cultural ascendancy of affluent young individuals and households in former low income areas. It is a widespread phenomenon occurring in most large cities and recently in smaller ones as well (Levy 1978; Clay 1987; Laska and Spain 1980; Carliner 1987). Gentrification results in a significant positive impact since, as newcomers arrive, these neighborhoods undergo a rapid socioeconomic change that affects the area visually and functionally (M. H. Lang 1982, 1989).

There are many positive socioeconomic aspects associated with gentrification but there are negative aspects as well. Displacement is one of the negative side effects of gentrification; it refers to the involuntary relocation of those inhabitants who predated the arrival of gentrification. These low income communities that have a high proportion of renters are clearly at risk due to rapidly rising rents or outright eviction. Eviction, it should be stressed, is the most cited reason for homelessness in many areas (M. H. Lang 1987). Thus, at its most extreme, gentrification can precipitate outright homelessness. Often renters are forced to make multiple moves, forced out repeatedly as gentrification proceeds apace. Often, the impact of displacement on a neighborhood is a gradual rather than a cataclysmic event thereby lessening its immediate political implications, but this in no way lessens its catastrophic consequences for those displaced. Clearly, the availability of low cost housing is a crucial element in forestalling homelessness, yet housing policy in the United States often ignores this basic reality. A more detailed analysis of our housing policy is contained in Chapter 4 (Hartman, Keating, and LeGates 1982).

DEMOGRAPHICS

It is very difficult to get a reliable fix on the size of the homeless population at either the national or local level. There is widespread disagreement even within the federal government concerning the magnitude of homelessness. In 1983, the Department of Health and Human Services found that some 2 million individuals were homeless. Soon after, the Department of Housing and Urban Development placed the figure at between 250,000 and 350,000 based on their study of the problem.

Another study that found a relatively low incidence of homelessness was Rossi's study of Chicago. Advocates for the homeless contested both studies as grossly inaccurate and, in the former instance, accused the government of covering up the true size of the problem. They cited a figure of between 1.5 million and 3 million as being more accurate (National Coalition for the Homeless 1987). A serious debate continues regarding these figures as well as the methodology employed by various researchers (Hope and Young 1986a; Coughlin 1988). Independent academicians agree that the homeless are a very difficult group to count and that it is likely that there will be continued debate on the true size of the problem (Wiegard 1985; Peroff 1987).

There are a number of reasons that the homeless are difficult to count. First, they tend to be mobile, often moving from city to city in search of jobs or a warmer climate such as migrant laborers who get left behind in the rotation between seasonal agricultural jobs (Hopper and Hamberg 1984). Such individuals have no fixed address and have not been part of formal enumerations, although an attempt will be made to count them in the upcoming census. Figures for the homeless are often derived from counts at local social service agencies serving their needs. Such records are clearly inaccurate, since false names can be given and individuals may be registered at several agencies in a given day. Many homeless, on the other hand, are invisible, they avoid all contact with agencies and exist in abandoned buildings or sleep on the streets. Some local surveys have attempted to find and count these homeless, but again can only hope to approximate the number sleeping "rough." It is also problematic whether or not to label those who live in severely crowded conditions as homeless. Most estimates of the total number of homeless do not attempt to gauge the number of such individuals (Peroff 1987). There is general agreement by all parties that the number of the homeless is large and it is growing rapidly. Some agencies report an annual increase on the order of 67% (Wiegard 1985; P. Smith 1987; Redburn and Buss 1986; National Coalition for the Homeless 1987b; Peroff 1987).

DISCUSSION

For our older citizens, today's homelessness is a horrifying reminder of the widespread homelessness created by the Great Depression in the 1930s. For the rest of us, the very term homelessness seems foreign to our ears. Most people prefer never to think about homelessness. To the extent they do, many associate it with the housing problems of poor under-developed countries. As a society, we might accept the fact that we have some poor people but there is a feeling that various existing governmental assistance programs prevent true destitution. Thus, the sight of people sleeping outdoors over heating vents has been profoundly shocking to most Americans. The existence of widespread homelessness in the United States is a difficult concept for the public to grasp but reluctantly it has begun to do so.

The next chapter provides both a theoretical framework for analyzing homelessness and a glimpse of the reality facing those who hope for the development of ameliorative policies.

2

Homelessness and Unemployment: Theoretical Aspects

A cursory perusal of the political history of the United States provides evidence that many of the programs and policies needed to forestall homelessness have long been discussed in local municipalities, state legislatures, Congress and in the executive branch of government. The question of why so few of these programs have been enacted and why more recent efforts to alleviate homelessness have been so unsuccessful remains. Obviously, there are a host of reasons. Some are specific to particular attempts to provide programmatic assistance. Others are more profound and relate to both the biases as well as the limitations of the policymaking process in this country when it addresses issues of justice and equity. This chapter will stress these latter aspects.

One component of a framework for explaining the existence and perseverance of contemporary poverty and homelessness comes from understanding the theory of housing production and employment in our regulated market economy and the Marxist critique. Housing production is reviewed because of its central importance to the question of available shelter options. Employment is reviewed because access to shelter is regulated by income in market economies.

To suggest that there is a debate between Marxists on the one hand and defenders of regulated market economies on the other is somewhat artificial. It must be stressed that utilizing this concise bipolar theoretical alignment is an analytical expedient. Rather, there exist many different schools of thought that fit uneasily into these two paradigms. For instance,

Medcalf and Dolbeare (1985), looking at the existing spectrum of American political theory identify eight distinct schools of thought: liberalism, neoliberalism, particularistic reform movements, economic democracy, democratic socialism, neoconservatism, conservatism, and the new right. For the sake of simplicity, all of these, save democratic socialism which has Marxist elements, will be considered variants of the regulated market school of thought. It is also recognized that to consider Marxism as a unitary category is a simplification since to do so hides the rich diversity of thought in the literature of socialism and communism. Nonetheless, this simplification will aid the analysis of the distinct approaches to housing and employment policy inherent in these two major contending theoretical paradigms. While this is not the place for an extensive analysis of these paradigms, a brief review serves to highlight their relevance to the foregoing discussion. Only those aspects relevant to that discussion and the issue of homelessness will be presented here (Lindblom 1977; Wilber 1983; Hanson 1983).

A MARXIAN PRIMER—
THE LOW COST HOUSING SHORTAGE

While housing policy is not a central theme in Marxian analysis, it was the deplorable conditions endured by the inhabitants of British slums in the nineteenth century that helped form the political views of Friedrich Engels (Castells 1977, 3). More recently, urbanists both here and abroad have begun to develop a structural Marxist theory that provides a fresh perspective on urban development and its attendant problems (Castells 1977; M. P. Smith 1984; Tabb and Sawyers 1978; Bluestone and Harrison 1982; Fainstein et al. 1986; Kantor 1987; Badcock 1984). Previously, leftist urban analysts tended to concentrate on what Zukin has called "radical empiricism" whereby urban scholars enumerated the particular problems affecting the poor in our cities. These studies tended to propose new social programs as solutions, thereby accepting the liberal democratic state as agent of social reform (Perry 1984). Structural Marxists view cities and their problems from a different and broader viewpoint. M. P. Smith describes this viewpoint:

For structural Marxists economic logic is the primary determinant of class inequality. The logic of private capital accumulation, as mediated by the state and modified by the social conflict engendered by the accumulation process, are the basic causes of urban development. The "urban" realm is a by-product of economic organization; the political and cultural spheres are only "relatively autonomous" from the economic (M. P. Smith 1984, 12).

There is much ferment among proponents of structuralism; in particular, there is intense debate over the role of groups and individuals in the structuralist paradigm (Beauregard 1984; Perry 1984).

All Marxist analysis is based on viewing the free market economy as meeting the interests of the capitalist class by ensuring the subservient position of the working class (Edwards, Reich, and Weisskopf 1986; M. P. Smith 1984; Schultze 1985). Marxists would ascribe the rise of homelessness to the failure of our housing delivery system which is based on a free market ideology. This free housing market serves the class interests of those in power. The bulk of the population functions as passive consumers, a resource to be manipulated to further the profitmaking ends of the capitalist class. In such markets, expensive new housing is constructed for the affluent and older housing is supposed to become available to the less affluent since it will drop in price as the increasing supply of new housing lessens its desirability (N. Smith 1975; Grigsby 1973). In essence, housing is competed for like any other good and the poor get the aging slums that are left over. In a free housing market, housing is viewed as a commodity to be sold to the highest bidder and the issues of equity or justice are largely ignored. Indeed, housing is viewed as an investment more than as a means of shelter. This has led to severe underoccupation of housing, the profusion of second and third homes for affluent families and empty inner city shell properties owned chiefly for speculative reasons. The capitalist system is typified by stark contrasts: huge opulent homes that bear little relation to the housing needs of their rich inhabitants on the one hand and decrepit urban slums and rural shacks that do not meet local housing codes on the other (Hartman 1983; Bratt, Hartman, and Meyerson 1986; Marcuse 1988).

Indeed, the provision of housing in a capitalist system provides an excellent example of the system at work since it forces the poor to live in slums surrounded by the most deplorable conditions. These slums will exist so long as their owners can make a profit on the units. They will attempt to cram people in these slums and charge the highest possible rents in order to increase their profits. Landlords will fight any attempts by authorities to regulate their business and are steadfast against the introduction of building codes and rent control laws—a battle that continues to this day in many of our cities. If, during conditions of housing surplus, they no longer can make a profit on a building, they abandon it. Many private units in urban submarkets are lost annually when the cost of repairs to older units cannot be recouped via higher rents or sales prices. In such cases, the units are seen as a bad investment and are abandoned. Frequently, conditions of market disequilibrium occur when a condition of excess housing supply exists simultaneously with a shortage of low cost housing. When there are not enough slums to house the rising numbers of the poor, a phenomenon common to many of our older urban areas today, then the final indignity of homelessness results (Achtenberg and Marcuse 1983; Hartman, Keating, and LeGates 1982).

All our older cities have large and mounting inventories of abandoned housing units that all told could easily shelter the nation's homeless. They are not utilized because it is not profitable for the private owners to make them available. Paradoxically, city governments often come to own these abandoned houses due to tax foreclosure, and many find their way into government-financed housing programs that aim to rehabilitate these units for low income households. The problem is that the rate of publicly supported rehabilitation is greatly exceeded by the rate of continued private abandonment of other units. Not enough public money is appropriated to repair these units at a sufficient rate so as to ensure that all the poor can find safe shelter (Grigsby and Carl 1983; National Housing Task Force 1988).

Thus it is the shortage of low income housing due to the reliance on the free market in housing that has occasioned homelessness. In this view, homelessness, particularly in cities saddled with large inventories of abandoned housing, is proof of the failure of many postindustrial societies to adequately protect their citizens from the cruelties of market capitalism. Indeed, Marxists argue that the provision of publicly supported shelters for the homeless should be resisted since it only serves to paper over the fundamental problems of capitalism which should see the light of day and thereby influence public opinion (Hopper and Hamberg 1984). They think opinion should be influenced to the point that the public demands that adequate housing become a government provided right rather than a private sector commodity. In the Marxist view, low cost public housing should be provided by the central government so all citizens would be guaranteed access to decent and affordable housing. Private ownership of land and housing would be severely restricted. Housing should be seen as providing shelter rather than as a private financial investment instrument. Such housing could be provided in a number of ways. Public rental housing or subsidized owner-occupied housing could be provided throughout the country in sufficient quantity and at such a price or rent as to ensure the goal of adequate shelter for all. Resale restrictions, for example, could ensure that owners receive a predetermined return on their investment thereby eliminating the windfall profits so characteristic of much of the free market in housing (Achtenberg and Marcuse 1983).

A Marxist critique of the free market in housing would also include a strong denunciation of the tendency of large corporations to dominate the agenda for the revitalization of our older cities. Specifically, these corporations usually support a type of revitalization of the central areas that eliminates the existing low cost housing and replaces it with commercial buildings or upper income housing. Central city revitalization often serves to "cream off" more affluent residents from outlying older urban neighborhoods, destroying their socioeconomic balance. Indeed, studies of central city revitalization show that many of the newcomers to these areas are former residents of urban neighborhoods and not suburbanites returning to the city. Thus, in these areas owner-occupiers move out and are replaced by lower income renters. Building maintenance slips and the area begins to cycle downwards. At the final stages, renters are evicted from these units as landlords finally walk away. Once again homelessness characterizes the final stage. The losers in this kind of revitalization program are the central area residents actually displaced as well as those citizens in peripheral urban neighborhoods. This is because reinvestment in these latter areas is not similarly encouraged; instead, the buildings and general infrastructure are allowed to decline (Hartman, Keating, and LeGates 1982).

The Marxists also link neighborhood decline to the actions of large banks and corporations. Specifically, it has been shown that many banks withdraw capital from older inner city neighborhoods at the first sign of economic change, thereby sealing the area's fate. While continuing to take deposits from residents, they often refuse to lend money or grant mortgages. As a result, housing conditions deteriorate as investment falls off. The end of the process for the residents is wholesale housing deterioration and abandonment. Marxists claim this so-called "red lining" is done not for sound economic reasons as is claimed by the banks, but rather so as to be able to create new markets for their services in the future. Viewed from this perspective, older urban areas have been fertile territory for investors, since money is made on all phases of its life cycle: birth, growth, maturity, decline, and eventual rebirth through redevelopment. This pattern of infusion and withdrawal of capital funds ensures that the neighborhood goes through cycles of boom and bust that typify the capitalist system. The fact that "red lining" leads to the loss of low cost housing and precipitates homelessness is what is important here. The Marxist critique stresses the impotence of the individual and the neighborhood in the face of the countervailing corporate agenda. This impotence stems from the basic inequities inherent in free market capitalism which treats citizens as depersonalized consumers to be manipulated by entrepreneurs so as to maximize profits (Castells 1977; Hartman, Keating, and LeGates 1982; Lang 1985a; Taggert 1974).

A particular concern of Marxian analysts is the type of self-serving redevelopment which occurs after older urban neighborhoods have suffered a period of disinvestment and are then redeveloped to meet the needs of large corporations. They argue that when corporate investors become involved in older neighborhoods, it is only to further their own interests at the expense of the local community. An example of this occurred in the Poletown section of Detroit, Michigan, where General Motors Corporation leveled large areas of a working-class community in order to build a new car plant. It is a measure of the economic depression gripping these older cities that such a plan garnered political support on the strength of the promised jobs. For Marxists, this type of corporate economic blackmail is the essence of free market capitalism. In fact, there were many dispossessed households without a member employed by General Motors. For these people the plan was a no win situation that could be the first step toward homelessness since affordable replacement housing was in short supply (Hartman, Keating, and LeGates 1982).

Another important aspect of the housing issue for Marxists is the geographical location of low income areas and the poor and homeless populations. In the United States, the inner city has long functioned as the zone for transitional and/or slum housing as well as for the social services that cater to the poor and homeless. The minimal governmental efforts to provide low income housing and remedial social programs have also been concentrated in the core cities. This is because the suburbs were established by the corporate elite to function as the preserve of the middle and upper classes and as separate governmental entities, able to enact laws to ensure that low income classes are excluded. Marxists point to the resulting disequilibrium that forces impoverished cities to care for the preponderant share of the nation's poor and needy while the affluent suburbs avoid such responsibility. Thus, corporate interests devised the mechanism that has fostered the creation of the stereotypical black and minority dominated city surrounded by the "white suburban noose" (Warner 1968; Gottdiener 1977; Perin 1977; Danielson 1976; Dear and Wolch 1987).

In actuality, this pattern is always shifting somewhat as some older inner city areas revitalize and become more affluent. Today, some central city districts are the preserve of the affluent young who are eager to sample the cultural enticements of the city. Many will leave when it becomes time to educate their offspring, however, thus ensuring that this urban revitalization will remain limited in impact. More important than this small scale revitalization process is the fact that the suburbs have not allowed the production of any significant amounts of low cost housing to enable them to accommodate their fair share of the poor or minority population. The segregation of the poor and minority groups denies them access to plentiful suburban educational and economic resources that nurture advancement. Such inequality remains a salient product of housing patterns in the United States thereby furthering the interests of the dominant economic class who are content to live in their "suburban foxholes" (Schultze 1985; Polikoff 1978).

A further refinement of this critique has been advanced by Castells who suggests that capitalist development has served to separate the locus of social interaction and human development from that of economic organization and political power. Castells worries that the need to contest the local implications of spatial and employment dislocations engendered by new capitalist modes of production will force local social movements to cut from their agendas more important issues concerning government responsibility for the needs of the working classes. This concept is in many ways an extension of Webber's more positive view of a communications-based urban structure (Webber 1965; M. P. Smith 1984; Castells 1984).

A MARXIAN PRIMER ON JOBS/INCOMES SHORTFALL

Income generated by meaningful employment is a crucial determinant of one's ability to obtain shelter. A Marxist view of employment is based on an analysis similar to that of housing. Again, labor is viewed as a resource to be used as required by the capitalist class. Thus, by definition unemployment is tolerated since capitalists require a reserve army of cheap labor ready to meet their short-term needs. There will also be periods of greater unemployment when less labor is required due to shifts in market demand or changes in production processes. Of course, job opportunities might be available elsewhere and labor is expected to pack up and go seek them. Each individual is on his own in this search. Constant insecurity prevails as do significant and lasting income disparities. There is no commitment between laborer and capitalist, since that would interfere with the profit motive of the latter. So it is the inherent structural aspects of the system that force the capitalist to adopt this attitude, for to do otherwise would risk being crushed by competitors not so kindly disposed. In addition, racism and the economic precariousness of life for minorities who form a disproportionate share of the lower classes results in a psychological pressure cooker that destroys many minority individuals and their families (Staples 1987). It is this dehumanizing aspect of free market capitalism that Marxists find so abhorrent. Labor unions, while initially very helpful in collectivizing the power of the labor movement, are not a sufficient counterforce to capital in today's global economy since there is always the threat that production will be moved elsewhere in order to find a cheap labor market. Such structural realities force the state and local governments to be active participants in this process by assisting in the internecine competition to attract jobs (Edwards, Reich, and Weisskopf 1986; Kennedy 1984; Belcher and Singer 1988; Goodman 1979; Judd and Ready 1986).

In recent years this country has experienced high rates of unemployment reaching 10% for significant periods of time. This figure is recognized as an undercount since it does not include those discouraged jobseekers who have dropped out of the market. The rate also obscures the fact that certain populations are disproportionately affected. Minorities have significantly higher rates of unemployment, particularly young inner city blacks who often have rates of unemployment approaching 50%. Lack of adequate education is a causative factor as is the loss of traditional entry and middle level manual or blue-collar jobs in many areas caused by the restructuring of the job supply (Sassen-Koob 1984). In some areas, there has been considerable growth in higher paying professional job categories and in the low paying service sector job categories. However, many of these new service sector jobs offer little hope for advancement and do not pay enough to cover reasonable living expenses even when two family members work (W. Wilson 1987; Sassen-Koob 1984).

Financial restructuring unrelated to the production process also exerts a toll on labor. Particularly galling is when profitable local operations become pawns in a corporate takeover game in which investors milk the assets of the local operation in order to fuel further corporate takeovers. The end result of such mismanagement can be plant closings and more unemployment. The Marxist alternative is for the people acting through a strong central government to replace the private sector and to make the necessary contract with labor to plan jointly for the wider needs of the economy and labor as a whole. Since competition will no longer exist, the will of the wider community will prevail over the selfish needs of the individual capitalist (Bluestone and Harrison 1982; Goodman 1979).

Marxists also criticize the tendency of capitalist societies to foster severe and lasting regional economic inequalities that lead to conditions of local high unemployment. These inequalities result from the manipulation of capital by monopoly interests that seek more favorable returns available in certain geographic areas. Thus, many parts of the country find themselves cut off from lending streams that are available elsewhere. A good example of this tendency is the movement of capital, industry, and jobs to the Sunbelt in the mid-1970s. Economists have long been concerned with the detrimental impact such volatility fosters, such as local inflationary pressures and overdevelopment in the expanding areas and depression and decay in the abandoned regions. Much of the rationale behind such wrenching dislocations is the search for cost advantages by investors, in particular, labor cost savings. That these advantages will inevitably erode, forcing another round of dislocation with all the attendant costs, is irrelevant to the individual decisionmaker who must abide by the market's imperative to minimize costs and maximize profits in the short run.

The reaction of President Reagan to the plight of those people adversely affected by these dislocations was that of a classic market supporter. He counseled the "get on your bike" approach that would have the unemployed abandon their homes and community in order to seek employment elsewhere. The resultant negative impact on those who are left behind because they will not or cannot relocate does not count in this calculation, needless to say. The young are the most able to pull up roots and relocate. Those left behind are those older and less skilled individuals who have little likelihood of finding new jobs and now must rely on an increasingly impoverished local community for assistance (Castells 1984; Belcher and Singer 1988). The result is local economic depression with increased social deprivation and homelessness (Bluestone and Harrison 1982; Sawyers and Tabb 1984; Smith and Judd 1984; Goodman 1979). Marxists reject as simplistic the view that these phenomena are not manifestations of free market capitalism but the result of the expansion of knowledge and therefore purely technological in nature (Castells 1984).

This brief review of some of the relevant aspects of Marxian analysis is not intended to be exhaustive. Rather, those aspects of Marxist thought relevant to the occurrence of widespread homelessness were included. Much more could be said about the market disequilibrium caused by monopoly capital and the role of local and national elites to name but a few of the important concepts in the rich field of Marxian analysis (Sawyers and Tabb 1984; Hill 1984).

To some extent, the Marxist view of market economies is based on a nonregulated model of the classic free market economy. It is probably accurate to assume that none of the original Marxist critics of free market-based societies ever imagined that the capitalist powers in these countries would allow the type of market regulation that was to develop over time (Goodman 1979). Today, all market-oriented liberal democratic societies have complex market regulations based on the authority of their governments for taxation, commerce, and administration. While these regulations do much to dampen the volatility of free market capitalism and cushion many of its negative socioeconomic effects, few would claim that this regulatory system has been perfected, particularly in the United States (Piven and Cloward 1971). As a result, it is important to review the theoretical aspects of regulated market housing production and employment.

A REGULATED MARKET PRIMER—
THE LOW COST HOUSING SHORTAGE

Porter and others who support the free market housing system make their case on more than just aggregate housing output. Specifically, they argue that the so-called filtering process in a free market housing system ensures that both rich and poor will be able to find suitable accommodation. The filtering process is predicated on a stage or cyclical view of housing market dynamics in a free housing market. In such a situation the market caters to the potent demand for the highest priced housing since this will result in the most effective housing production schedule and the highest profits for the industry. The construction of such housing for the wealthy also results in improved housing opportunities for the middle and lower income groups since for every top-priced home built, an extended series of moves (the multiplier effect) is initiated back down through the categories of lower-priced homes. This occurs because the new top-priced homes lessen the effective demand for former top-priced homes by siphoning off some of their potential consumers. In short, the aging process puts former top-priced housing at a competitive disadvantage; they are not as up to date or prestigious as the newest housing. House prices fall, first in the category of homes that were formerly top-priced and eventually rippling down through all housing categories. As a result, many households opt to move up into homes that are now more affordable to them. All of these moves entail a distinct improvement in the families' living conditions (Porter 1976; Grigsby 1963; Olsen 1973; Lowry 1960).

Supporters of the filtering process point out that as households move up into newer housing, they will also be moving into newer communities. As a result, they will be likely to benefit from improved municipal services and community infrastructure.

According to its supporters, the only real problem inherent in the filtering process is that it is dependent on the health of the economy in general and interest rate fluctuations in particular. Sufficient funds for housing construction and mortgage lending must be available at reasonable rates through primary and secondary financial markets. This liquidity is essential to the maintenance of sufficient demand to maintain housing production and thereby the filtering process. Free market supporters urge that housing policy be centered on the maintenance by the Federal Reserve Bank of a supportive financial environment for housing production (Sternlieb and Hughes 1983).

Empirical tests of the multiplier effect have provided evidence that the filtering process does work to a degree in some situations. In other situations, it does not work in any uniform way and, perversely, it can even hasten the decline of an area. For instance, there is no way to control the geographic aspects of filtering. Filtering may well result in the availability of additional units of housing, but these units may not be in the area of greatest need. Similarly, filtering can be truncated if households in the middle of the process decide to spread out and consume more housing in their initial location. Additionally, rent control and zoning restrictions as well as other factors that have an impact on market operations can adversely affect the filtering process (W. Smith 1975; Lansing, Clifton, and Morgan 1973).

Proponents of the regulated market see homelessness as simply the result of mismanaged social welfare and housing policies and not a fundamental flaw in the market-based housing delivery system. Regulated market supporters tend to view the problem of homelessness as one caused more by a shortfall in incomes rather than in a shortage of housing units. They justify this viewpoint by pointing out the sheer number of housing units built since World War II in this country and the concomitant increase in the housing standards enjoyed by the vast majority of the population, standards which are the envy of the world (Porter 1976; Weicher 1984; Sternlieb and Hughes 1983; President's Commission on Housing 1982).

At the same time, they would acknowledge the existence of real hardship at the bottom tier of certain urban and rural housing markets: households unable to locate affordable housing and others living in overcrowded conditions in below-standard units. In these cases, they would call for job training and employment programs. These programs would help the poor to better themselves by improving access to employment, thereby providing the income necessary to obtain decent housing. In cases where employment is not an option, they would call for government-supported income maintenance programs. An alternative or combined approach, which is less favored, would be for the government to fund low cost housing programs which deliver adequate supplies of low cost housing to enable those who are on welfare or otherwise on very low incomes to find adequate housing. Such programs would be considered crucial components of the so-called safety net that ensures that the poorest in our free market society are looked after by the rest (Moynihan 1986; Thurow 1980; Etzioni 1983; Nenno and Brophy 1983).

Proponents of a regulated market would claim that significant housing problems in our society are largely confined to certain housing submarkets in our older urban areas. Looking at the desolation that characterizes so many of our inner city neighborhoods, they draw very different conclusions than the Marxists would. To market proponents, the presence of abandoned units in our central cities is proof that the majority of the former inhabitants of these cities have moved up and out to newer and better quality housing in the burgeoning suburban areas. They would cite numerous surveys that show an urban locale is least favored, while a small town or suburban locale is most favored by consumers. They would also mention the postwar decline in the populations of our large cities as further proof of this desire on the part of the public. Their view is that inner city housing is old and obsolete, a legacy of the industrial era "gritty city." It was built in another era for people with vastly different lifestyles than those of today. As a result, most urban row houses or apartments are cramped and inefficient; they were built at a high density with little surrounding public or private open space or parking facilities. Those who can afford to move out, do so at the earliest opportunity which is a positive function of the vast choice in housing available to the public in a free market system (Porter 1976; Sternlieb and Hughes 1983; Hinshaw and Allott 1973).

Market proponents agree that the problem of disposing of the housing units when they have cycled through to the end of their useful economic life is one that is not easily solved. This is because old neighborhoods do not decline in a uniformly predictable way (Firey 1947). Units that are clearly beyond repair sit side by side with units that are well kept. Many units that remain occupied are below standard, however. The fact that some old neighborhoods have gone through cycles of revitalization and renewal confounds those who predicted the demise of most old inner city residential areas (Forrester 1969; Birch 1972; Norton 1979; Rust 1975). Nonetheless, market proponents claim that most older inner city areas need to be closed out and their remaining residents relocated to newer areas. This should be done in a timely fashion so as to lessen the pain involved. This policy is based on the "triage" approach since it denies help to those areas that cannot be revitalized and gives it to those that have a realistic chance. They recognize that triage is very unpopular among many housing advocates who support the right of people to remain in their old areas (Perry 1984). Unfortunately, given the prevailing economic structure, such a policy ensures that many poor households must suffer substandard accommodation in blighted areas that are continuing to decline. If their building is condemned or the owner cannot make basic repairs, these people could easily join the ranks of the homeless; either way, displacement and redevelopment would be inevitable (Starr 1978; Schwartz 1977; Holcomb and Beauregard 1981).

Market proponents claim urban neighborhood decline is due to technological forces working in the fertile environment of a regulated free market, namely the revolution in transportation, communication technology, and the service economy that has lessened the advantages hitherto enjoyed by the cities. Simply put, the car, the telephone, and more recently, the computer, have all functioned to deemphasize the need for the frequent and easy face-to-face contact which cities facilitated. In a service economy more and more services are not place-oriented but can be produced anywhere. As a result, the city has lost its dominant function as locus for employment and production of goods and services (Webber 1965; Friedlen 1983; Logan 1983; Ostrum 1983). The weakening of the economic primacy of the city has led to the decline in the quality of its housing stock that no amount of money can forestall. Units in many older sections will age, decay, and be abandoned as they no longer have an economic function. Indeed, to attempt to reverse neighborhood decline by the inclusion of publicly funded housing rehabilitations is doomed to failure since the value of the resultant rehabilitations will be dragged down by the prevailing depressed market conditions. Instead, public policy should be aimed at ensuring an orderly market-led transition rather than trying to prop up uneconomic housing (Starr 1978; Bradbury, Downs, and Small 1981).

One market-oriented urban theorist ties urban decline to the aging of cities and their physical infrastructure. Thought to be too highly deterministic by some, the theory holds that as cities age they go through cycles of growth, maturity, and decline ending in abandonment of the commercial and residential structure of the city. While the existence of exceptions to this rule are granted, they are considered to be few and small in impact (Forrester 1969).

Other market-oriented analysts tie the decline of American cities to the post-World War II governmental policies that set up a massive program of government-insured, low cost mortgages for veterans that specifically excluded their use in urban areas. This effectively shunted much of the postwar housing growth out to the suburbs and made necessary the costly system of expressways designed to allow these far-flung areas to grow. This anti-urban tilt persisted in all federal spending programs until the mid-1970s when the Carter administration made a concerted effort to eradicate it, but by that time the damage had been long done (Muller 1981).

Other governmental policies and programs have been blamed for fostering inner city housing decline. Reliance by local governments on the property tax as a source of revenue has been cited as a causal factor in housing decline and abandonment. Much has been written on the often inequitable market distortions occasioned by this method of raising revenue, particularly the negative impact of this tax on older urban neighborhoods. Some market proponents argue for a shift toward greater use of a uniform, progressive income tax system to generate local revenues as is done in much of Europe. Others suggest greater use of tax rebates and caps for selected populations and areas (Aronson and Hilley 1986; Meyers 1986; Donnison and Ungerson 1982).

Much attention has also been given to the influence of social tension that resulted from the ebb and flow of population groups, particularly in urban neighborhoods. For instance, the Chicago school of urban sociology developed theories of "invasion and succession" that focused on the social and economic changes that resulted from the arrival of new ethnic and racial groups in particular neighborhoods. Urban decline was often identified with so-called "zones of transition" which accommodated a high percentage of such lower-class newcomers to the city. Urban decline was ascribed to the inability of some newly arrived groups to ensure that their properties were maintained or in some instances, to their lack of familiarity with homeownership and its responsibilities. In any case, broadly conceived patterns of socioeconomic housing stratification were linked to urban residential blight and decay due to conditions of unequal access to services (Hill 1984; Castells 1977; Pickvane 1984).

Market proponents would also argue that homelessness in urban submarkets has been worsened in part because of local opposition to a rational housing policy built on the principle of triage. They feel it is not the free market in housing that has occasioned problems but rather the misguided disruption of market forces by local political interests bent on protecting existing residents at all costs. Some would agree that the homeless situation has been exacerbated by the drastic cutbacks in low cost housing programs instituted by the Reagan administration and that the solution lies in the restoration of these cuts. These funds would allow the hard-pressed cities to begin to refurbish vacant public housing units, build new scattered site units, and most important, begin to rehabilitate the vast array of abandoned housing units that exist in our older cities. But increasingly, housing experts are insisting on the need to utilize the triage concept in order to redevelop large areas of our older cities along the low density pattern so popular in our suburbs. In this way, they reason, cities will have a chance to compete on more equal terms with the newer suburbs

(President's Commission for a National Agenda for the Eighties 1980; Starr 1978; Downs 1977; Hanson 1983).

A REGULATED MARKET PRIMER—UNEMPLOYMENT

Proponents of the regulated market view unemployment as a regrettable but necessary result of a dynamically changing economy that is moving through periods of growth and transformation due to innovation. These transformations often lead to unemployment which, while painful, cannot and should not be prevented. At the same time, it is the government's responsibility to ensure that these unemployed individuals receive sufficient income to tide them over until they find new employment. It is also the responsibility of the government to support adequate retraining programs so as to ensure that the unemployed can be rehired in newly emerging fields. In recent years, the U.S. economy has produced a prodigious number of new jobs. The problem has been that they are different from the bulk of existing and now declining job types (Sassen-Koob 1984). This growth and change in job categories is due to the working of a healthy and innovative market-oriented society, adherents would claim. Innovation in a consumer-oriented world market and the need to nurture the entrepreneurial spirit that is its necessary medium is the fundamental *raison d'être* of free market capitalism. Supporters point to the superiority of the capitalist democracies in producing unparalleled prosperity for the majority of their citizens. The system also nurtures the creative spirit in science, medicine, and the arts. The way to maintain these beneficial outcomes is to ensure that the government's role must be limited to that of safety net provider for those who are adversely affected by the market's changing priorities. A central debate in U.S. politics concerns the size and role of the federal government as it goes about fulfilling this role (Gilder 1981; Lindblom 1977; Hanson 1983).

Regulated market proponents would agree that postwar development patterns have made it more difficult for the inner city poor to have access to entry level jobs in the suburbs. Most would address this problem by aggressively enforcing fair housing laws so as to ensure access to all housing for people of all racial and ethnic backgrounds. Nonetheless, they would eschew policies that would ensure similar access for the poor who are an economic minority (Gilder 1981).

Currently, the free market economies have weathered a difficult period of adjustment as they have evolved into postindustrial service economies. In so doing, many jobs of long standing have been lost due to market dislocations. Many careers have been destroyed. Workers have been forced to adapt to the reality that the types of jobs that they held for so long are no longer available. It is true that other jobs have been created but they require new skills, particularly the ability to communicate and calculate effectively. Lost are the blue-collar jobs in the steel mills and manufacturing plants; newly created are the "white coat" jobs in the high technology and service sector. Older workers are hardest hit, but the need to make adaptations also affects the young and minorities (Harrington 1984; Gilder 1981; Costa, Dustin, and Shanahan 1987; W. J. Wilson 1987; Richman 1987).

Related to this problem of employment dislocation are broader questions concerning the high rate of individual failure within our socioeconomic system. Many educators trace such failure to low success rates for students in many of our urban school districts. Such students are often condemned to lead lives on the margins of a society increasingly oriented to high technology. Such individuals often lose their tenuous place in society due to local or national recessions that are so frequent in a free market economy. One cause of this problem is the poor quality of segments of our educational system and its inability to prepare students for a future based on rapid technological change. These changes may require an ability to switch careers several times during one's lifetime. Such career paths would be quite different from the single sector employment expectations of third generation steel, rubber, and mine workers. Responding to the training needs of this dynamic and constantly evolving economy is seen as a major task facing the leaders of market-oriented societies in the future. Failure in this area may lead to mounting numbers of American citizens who are unable to secure and hold jobs that allow them to maintain the kind of lifestyle Americans have enjoyed for so long. Put more starkly, as more Americans become downwardly mobile, more will join those who have bottomed out and are now counted among the homeless in our society. Supporters of a regulated market would attempt to solve such problems with appropriate training programs and temporary economic support oriented toward reintroducing workers into the free market. They feel that only free enterprise coupled with social and economic support programs to cushion the impact of rapid dislocations caused by this market can produce innovations necessary to tackle the numerous problems facing society (Gilder 1981, 1984; C. Murray 1984; Hanson 1983; President's National Urban Policy Report 1980). Naturally, the prospect of such an insecure, strung-out society is odious to Marxists who feel it reflects the complete capitulation of government to the increasingly disruptive demands of capital interests (Castells 1984; Fainstein et al. 1986).

While this situation may be seen as a rough description of what prevails in periods of prosperity, it is recognized that free market economies are subject to swings or cycles of expansion and decline. Here again a regulatory approach to the market has evolved. In the market downswing, there is clearly a need for increased governmental intervention to rekindle growth. Likewise in periods of expansion, credit restrictions serve to dampen inflationary pressures. Such macroeconomic regulations based on Keynesian economic theory are now an accepted part of the market system. This regulatory intervention has been the basic guiding philosophy that has fueled our postwar prosperity. Thus, there is a need for a regulated economy responsive to macro-level market cycles as well as micro-level dislocations. All told, these and other regulatory interventions guide and control the performance of the market. The aim is to preserve the ability of the market mechanism to allocate goods and services in an efficient and timely manner while providing a safety cushion for those individuals adversely affected by the dislocations inherent in all dynamic markets (Lindblom 1977; C. Murray 1984; Weicher 1984; Hanson 1983; President's National Urban Policy Report 1980).

DISCUSSION

In most instances, Marxists and market-oriented urbanists ascribe different root causes to the same phenomena. For example, market proponents would agree with Marxists that our disjointed pattern of local governments impoverishes our older urban jurisdictions and thereby contributes to urban housing decline and abandonment. They would agree that this is reprehensible and therefore should be subject to reform. They would cite attempts at regional local government reform in Dade County, Florida and elsewhere. Where Marxists differ is that they argue that such reformist measures are doomed to failure since they inevitably come up against resistance from the same societal forces that produced the problem in the first place.

Many, such as Dahl, specifically reject the arguments of structural Marxists and point to factors such as technology and the division of labor as exerting influence independent of the capitalist mode of production (Pickvane 1984). Bensman has called upon Marxists to prove their assertion that contemporary urbanism is a product of capitalist development. Indeed, there is evidence that some communist societies struggle with urban problems strikingly similar to those of capitalist societies (Sawyers 1978). Bensman states: "General problems of urbanization, industrialism, population density, and the struggles for the control over scarce resources by organized elites, classes, regional groups, and rural and urban dwellers exist in all societies whether capitalist or socialist, developed or undeveloped, colonial or neo-colonial" (Hill 1984).

This review of the essential differences between Marxists and regulated market system proponents serves to explain some of the profound differences of opinion and approaches that inform the national housing and employment policy debate. Most policy experts, however, accept the need to fashion workable solutions within the context of our regulated market economy. As a result, it is appropriate to take a brief look at the theory of decisionmaking in the American policymaking process because, here too, there are considerable differences of opinion and approach.

THE AMERICAN POLICYMAKING PROCESS

The study of government in this country has a long and contentious history that has emerged from the intense debate surrounding representative theories of government. This debate involves attempts to assess the relative importance of conceptual notions concerning the rationality of man, the influence of bureaucracy, and the importance of interest groups, among others. This contentiousness continues to the present day and appears ready to outlast all of us. Briefly, the debate has been dominated by the pluralists, who see a somewhat open policymaking process, and the elitists, who see a very constrained policymaking process (Pateman 1970; Ricci 1971; Schultze 1985; Lindblom 1980).

Pluralists such as Merriam, Truman, and Schumpeter base their position on the need of public officials to periodically respond to the voters if they wish to keep their positions. Pluralists agree that influence is not equally dispersed in our society but maintain that concerned citizens can often have an effect on policy. They see policymaking as being influenced by the extreme diversity of interests that exist in a democratic society, a diversity that forces public officials to engage in politics if they wish to see anything accomplished. Thus policymaking is seen as emerging from a complex process of bargaining, persuasion, rewards, threats, as well as the exercise of leadership authority; bureaucrats, business managers, interest groups, elected and appointed officials, are seen as heavily involved in this process while most citizens are not (Ricci 1971; Lindblom 1980; Dahl 1961).

The policymaking process as envisioned by the pluralists is anything but rational. Rather, it is the product of countless incremental adjustments and compromises that are made in response to a particular issue or problem. Arriving at these adjustments and compromises is a difficult task often involving countless meetings with a myriad of individuals and groups all representing different interest. As a result, policymaking is seen as an intensely political process that often defies the best efforts of policy analysts to explain it much less develop predictive models for similar situations (Lindblom 1980).

On the other hand, elitist theorists such as E. E. Schattschneider, Mancur Olsen, William Domhoff, Floyd Hunter, and Henry Kariel see our society as being dominated by a business elite that effectively controls the policy agenda so that it remains responsive to the needs of private enterprise. This control extends to the political system and is so complete as to enable them to settle some issues out of the public spotlight and leave the inconsequential issues for public contention. This power emanates from the control of employment opportunities by the private business sector. Elitist theorists contend that relatively small groups of business-oriented individuals exert this control at both the local and national levels. Proponents of both theories stress the need to test their theories in real world situations. By and large, such tests focus on the exercise of power at the local level and avoid applications to broad issues like the persistence of slums and income disparities (Ricci 1971; Hunter 1953; Domhoff 1967; Bottomore 1966; Presthus 1974; Mills 1956; Dye 1983).

Much of the foregoing debate involves political scientists and sociologists. A separate but parallel school of thought can be found among students of public policy and administration. By and large, this school of thought focuses on a broader and more conceptual level of debate as it labors to defend the pluralist vision. According to its main proponents, the public policy process can be seen as following one of three basic models. The first is the centralized policymaking approach adhered to by countries with strong, often Marxist-oriented central governments. In such cases, the main claim made in favor of this method is that it affords a rational and comprehensive perspective on the policy process. Such a method assumes that the policymaker possesses a high degree of control over the policymaking process, access to complete information, techniques for choosing between competing courses of action, and a hierarchy of values by which to judge outcomes (Lindblom 1980).

Criticisms of this approach center on the fact that the requirements for the model are unattainable. Critics question the ability of any one policymaking source to operationalize a value hierarchy which could win public acceptance. In addition, Lindblom and others argue that it is simply not possible to absorb and relate the myriad conflicting informational inputs necessary to devise a rational policy.

Going beyond a critical analysis of centralized policymaking, Lindblom (1970) has developed a major conceptual alternative known variously as partisan mutual adjustment or disjointed incrementalism. This theory has policy being made by small scale marginal adjustments to current policy. Change is gradual since policy formulation is based on a "testing the waters" approach rather than centrally conceived goals. Thus, Lindblom argues that the proper policymaking process in a democracy is a product of the final compromise of many competing interests in society, a paradigm in keeping with the prevailing pluralistic view of American society.

Critics of this approach to decisionmaking point out that its formulation is based on the participation of partisans or affected parties and that this would ensure that the interests of the most powerful would prevail (Domhoff 1967; Rein and Marris 1968; Lowi 1969). Moreover, disjointed incrementalism, which relies on a series of marginal policy adjustments, abrogates any responsibility for charting new policy initiatives; marginal policy adjustments may lead to significant change but it is more likely that they would not. Rein, in particular, criticizes disjointed incrementalism since its stepped decisionmaking process might allow for a series of small scale rational decisions and yet lead to an irrational final outcome. More recently, Lindblom has admitted that large corporations do exert a disproportionate degree of influence, thereby lessening responsiveness to weaker interests (Lindblom 1977). Still, some policy analysts still feel that disjointed incrementalism provides a good description of some aspects of the policymaking process in this country (Lindblom 1980; Ricci 1971).

Unhappiness with the incrementalist paradigm has led to a number of derivative theories; one of the best known is authored by Etzioni. In it he tries to combine the salient aspects of the rational-comprehensive and the disjointed incremental approaches by positing what he calls "mixed scanning." A mixed scanning policymaking process would be composed of a mix of "fundamental" decisions and incremental decisions. These "fundamental" decisions would represent a limited form of rationalism in that these decisions are made with respect to policy goals but without the depth of detail and specification required by strict rationalism. A rotational principle is also built in so that all policy sectors would eventually come in for a fundamental review (Faludi 1973).

Mixed scanning represents a compromise that appears to answer some of the criticisms leveled at both existing decisionmaking paradigms. What it does not do is explain how to operationalize the fundamental review portion of the concept in a country having a governmental system characterized by elite-dominated decentralized decisionmaking. The prospects for such an approach are explored further in Chapter 11 (Lowi 1969).

To elitist theorists such a mixed scanning approach is utopian; it relies for its success on the very corporate interests that stand in the way of real societal change. As a consequence, any reforms resulting from "fundamental" decisions in such a system would be minimal at best. They may well be right, as evidenced by our continued toleration of the fact that a small but significant proportion of our citizens live in abject poverty and homelessness. Yet, history is replete with examples of the resiliency and adaptability of free market societies which, in other contexts, have been able to solve such problems. Postwar Britain and Scandinavia, among others, have evolved into highly organized welfare states with mixed economies that stress the advantages of combining the best features of centrally planned societies with those based on free markets (Eversley 1973; Crossman 1952; Titmuss 1963; Cole 1946; de Schweinitz 1943).

Students of American policymaking are still in search of a definitive paradigm that incorporates all of the various aspects discussed above. In order to prove their respective cases, proponents of a particular approach conduct elaborate tests of their theories based on the examination of actual decisions as well as the investigation of those reputed to exercise power in actual situations. Needless to say, there is continued debate over how best to establish a definitive measure of power in real life situations or whether or not the development of such a test is even possible (Ricci 1971).

IMPLICATIONS FOR POLICYMAKING AND ANALYSIS

Both elitists and pluralists agree that there are significant barriers to the promulgation of simple policy reform in American society. These blockages are due to a host of factors inherent in both the broader policymaking process as well as specific elements such as the limited competencies of system operators, inadequate resources, conflicting criteria, and the like. The complexities built into the process have been described by Lindblom:

Instead of reaching solutions that can be judged by standards of rationality, policy making reaches settlements, reconciliations, adjustments, and agreements that one can evaluate only inconclusively by such standards as fairness, acceptability, openness to reconsideration and responsiveness to a variety of interests. Sufficiently flexible, sufficiently open, and sufficiently given to endless reconsideration of policies, it encourages an eternal hopefulness even among the disadvantaged. Few people, consequently, try civil disorder or rebellion (Lindblom 1980, 122–23).

Lindblom is quick to point out that the blockages are not all systemic:

Many people do not understand that their fellow citizens are a principal obstacle to their achieving an influence on policy. In recent years many proponents of educational reform, new foreign policies, liberation movements, and other causes on the frontiers of public policy came to a stop, not simply because elites stand in their way but because millions of their equally empowered fellow citizens also do. To move them is a massive and improbable undertaking (Lindblom 1980, 124).

DISCUSSION

To return to a question posed at the beginning of this chapter, significant and effective policies are seldom enacted due to the confluence of interests arrayed against such reform. Those policies that are enacted into law are often ineffective due to the fact that they are the compromised product of the incredibly complex policymaking process with which all policymakers must deal (Popper 1981). A few policies such as Social Security stand apart and can be characterized as successful due to their relative simplicity and clarity (Lowi 1969). However, it should be remembered that Social Security was a product of the focused energies marshaled by a strong leader in the context of a business crisis. It also had the advantage of being a universal entitlement as distinct from potential programs for the poor and homeless.

The Marxists may well be right; liberal free market democracies may not be capable of adequately providing for their poor and needy due to the inherent social and economic contradictions of the free market and the extension of these contradictions into the policymaking process. Yet there are examples elsewhere of well regulated market societies such as Sweden that have ensured a more even distribution of wealth while preserving democratic institutions and private property interests. Why has it been so difficult for us to do the same? Why have our social and economic policies resulted in the continuing toleration of significant poverty and homelessness? The following section will look closely at recent trends in urban policy. It will examine the possibility that the urban policy process is incapable of resolving difficult or contentious issues when such a resolution stands to benefit some groups more than others. This examination will focus on two of the major postwar urban programs: urban categorical grants and special revenue sharing. It will conclude with an assessment of the potential future utilization of national urban policy planning in this country.

Part II
THE URBAN POLICY CONTEXT

3

The Urban Policy Process

The making of urban policy is a tortuous affair that is little understood. Much of the confusion can be traced to the shifting balance of power between the central and state and local governments in our federal system, a system complicated by the ambiguous status of cities within this framework. As a result, national urban policy tends to evolve by means of a complex struggle between myriad competing interests at the local and national levels. As discussed in Chapter 2, this struggle takes place in an essentially pro-business, pro-free market context. At its best, it produces praiseworthy compromises usually couched in vague policy goal statements; at its worst, it produces chaotic and discontinuous urban policies and programs that lead to tragedies such as the homelessness we are now experiencing. Increasingly, the result is often unsatisfactory to many citizens and promises to be more so in the future as business interests continue to exert their influence. This chapter will attempt to untangle some of the major features of what passes for national urban policy planning in this country and begin to focus on the often dysfunctional nature of this process.

THE NATIONAL URBAN POLICY PROCESS

In attempting to discern the thrust of national urban policy, it would seem sensible to begin by reviewing past pronouncements and programs developed by the respective national political parties. However, it is often noted that the national political parties are not particularly effective in deriving specific approaches to social and economic problems, much less ensuring that party members will support a particular policy approach. All this notwithstanding, the political parties are as good a place as any to start since they at least periodically take positions on national urban policy issues (Price 1984; Caputo 1985).

Political Parties

Most Americans would be able to articulate broad differences between the two main political parties. In particular, the Democrats are often viewed as being in favor of large, costly federal poverty and welfare programs designed to stimulate public employment and alleviate poverty. The Republicans, on the other hand, are seen as being in favor of local approaches allied with a reliance on market-oriented solutions to poverty. Specifically, they favor reduced taxation and regulation policies that will increase private investment, thereby creating more private sector jobs conducive to fostering individual independence. They see this as preferable to the risk of increased welfare dependency, a factor they see as inherent in all governmental programs be they low cost housing, public sector jobs, or welfare payments (Keefe 1988; Price 1984).

These basic categorizations are correct up to a point, but they obscure a real commonality between both parties; namely, both eschew truly national approaches to the alleviation of social and economic distress. Indeed, with the exception of the Social Security program, few truly national social programs exist. Instead, both parties favor essentially local voluntary approaches. The difference, for the most part, between the parties is that the Republicans favor devolving the whole process of urban policy planning and implementation to the state and local levels. The Democrats, on the other hand, favor a strong federal presence and involvement in the policy process. However, this federal role is usually limited to outlining specific programmatic categories and procedures under which state and local governments can apply for funds. Localities usually are free to participate in these programs on a voluntary basis and, if they do so, to control the day-to-day operation of the program. In short, both political parties favor the devolution of a large share of the decisionmaking power to the local level. Since program participation is voluntary, the effect of a particular national policy initiative is often skewed since those localities most in need of program benefits often refuse to participate. At other times, the poor in generally affluent areas are overlooked. The most dysfunctional outcome is when poorly drafted programs allow suburban areas to spend money on nonessential projects benefiting their middle-class population (Stone, Whelen, and Murin 1986; Reagan and Sanzone 1981).

In the postwar era, both parties have been involved in developing the two main approaches to this locally biased urban policy. These are the categorical grant programs associated with the Democrats and the block grant and revenue sharing approaches associated with the Republicans. Both these approaches are versions of the federal grant in aid approach to urban policy (Reagan and Sanzone 1981).

Grant in Aid Programs

Grant in aid programs provide federal revenues to local governments for specific purposes such as urban renewal. These programs usually entail some supervision or review by the federal government. Generally, there are two main types of grant in aid programs: block grants and categorical grants. Block grants are given for broadly defined purposes such as low cost housing, while categorical grants are given for specific purposes such as energy audits for housing. Federal controls are much more extensive with categorical grants than with block grants. For instance, the federal government might require that the local level provide a matching share of the total grant; often localities have to submit detailed plans for federal approval. Block grants do not require a match nor do they require detailed plans. As a result, they are considered much more flexible. The local jurisdiction sets its own goals, develops appropriate programs, and allocates the budget accordingly (Reagan and Sanzone 1981).

This flexibility is popular as it stands in contrast to the strong perception of federal categorical grants as the source of complex and expensive mandates and regulations. Specifically, all federal programs impose generally applicable requirements on all grants in furtherance of national social and economic policies. These regulations include nondiscrimination provisions on the basis of race, physical handicap, age, and sex. Also common are environmental regulations involving the local submission of environmental impact statements. In some instances, localities must comply with these regulations under threat of civil or criminal penalties. For instance, job discrimination at the state and local level on the basis of sex, race, religion, or natural origin is expressly prohibited. Localities found to have been in noncompliance in the past may be required to establish an affirmative action program. In most cases, the federal government does not require a particular action be taken, rather it simply withholds money in order to get the desired response (Reagan and Sanzone 1981; Stone, Whelen, and Murin 1986).

Urban Categorical Grant Programs

Federal responsibility for the needs of the poor and needy in our cities was institutionalized in the New Deal programs of the 1930s. The United States Conference of Mayors was established in 1932 due to the severe fiscal crisis in the cities and became a major lobbying organization for big cities. The strong federal–local relationship was a result of the efforts of this urban lobby in Washington. This lobby was able to establish a direct federal–city linkage, often bypassing state governments. This linkage, which involved direct federal administration of local programs for the unemployed, was eventually dropped but was reinstituted in the postwar period much to the dismay of governors and other state officials. This lobby consisted of the USCM and the National League of Cities which represented the interests of smaller cities with less than 50,000 population. It is interesting to note that in the preelection year of 1988 only two candidates for president responded to the invitation by this lobby to meet with its members and state his position with regard to the nation's urban areas. The decline in influence of our urban areas is indeed profound (Dommel 1974).

The Kennedy and Johnson administrations greatly expanded the categorical grant programs available to cities in the 1960s. In a related move, they also established the Department of Housing and Urban Development (HUD) in 1965. This department was to oversee categorical grants for the cities in such areas as urban renewal and housing. An especially significant development was that once again categorical grants involved direct federal–city linkages, cutting out the state level. Some programs under the Office of Economic Opportunity involved a direct federal–community organization link, cutting out even the city mayor's office. The 1960s saw the addition of a redistributive element into this federal–city relationship, a factor most evident in the so-called "War on Poverty" and the Model Cities programs. These programs were aimed at giving the poor some political clout to counterbalance the established business interests that controlled local governments. Indeed, twenty-three programs were established between 1960 and 1962 in which the states had no role, allowing city officials to consider themselves equal partners in the federal system. This development was bitterly resented by state officials cognizant of the fact that cities were legally creatures of the state. Mayor Lindsay of New York took this new approach to an extreme in his call for the creation of "National Cities" which would make the largest cities legally independent of state governments and formalize a special relationship between these cities and the federal government (Dommel 1974).

Significant criticisms of the categorical grant programs have been made. One of the major criticisms has been the rising cost of the programs. In 1974, some $45 billion was spent on the programs, constituting fully 21.3% of state and local revenues (Dommel 1974, 19). Critics cited fragmented federal and local administration and duplication of effort. Horror stories cited several federal agencies that funded essentially identical projects in the same jurisdiction. The 1960s saw a proliferation in the number of categorical grant programs: 160 in 1962 grew to 349 in 1966. As a result, mayors could not effectively monitor these programs. As these programs proliferated, grantsmanship became vogue since receipt of funds depended on the sophistication of the application and less on comparative need. Indeed, many obviously needy localities lost out in this competition (Reagan and Sanzone 1981).

Another major criticism of the categorical grant approach was that it often led localities to spend money in ways unrelated to local needs simply because there were federal funds available for a specific purpose. At the same time, pressing local priorities often could not be funded as they did not fit into an existing categorical grant program (Stone, Whelen, and Murin 1986).

For some politicians perhaps the most telling criticism was that the categorical grant programs favored the poor in urban localities at the expense of the suburban majority and the program empowered cities at the expense of the suburban and rurally-oriented state governments (Dommel 1974).

Those who felt themselves adversely affected by these combined forces coalesced into an effective opposition to the continued utilization of the categorical grant approach. As a result of the success of this opposition, categorical grants were phased out in favor of block grants. Thus, categorical grants were emphasized from the New Deal years through the 1960s, while more recently the emphasis has shifted to block grants.

It must be emphasized that the categorical grant approach often did not lead to clear or effective social policy. It was essentially a piecemeal approach with widely varying impacts across the nation. At its worst it could take on a life of its own divorced from the control of any elected officials and policymakers. Moynihan's retelling of the infighting that resulted in the "maximum feasible participation" clause of the "War on Poverty" is a classic example of a categorical grant program running amok. It is also true that these experimental programs often did not pursue more traditional physical development approaches such as increased public housing (Moynihan 1969; Reagan and Sanzone 1981).

This said, it is important to remember that categorical grant programs did effectively reduce poverty to its lowest postwar level. While they may have been based on a scattershot approach, they were to be seen in retrospect as a high point in American social policy development and, in particular, a high point in the influence of urban areas on the development of such policy (Stone, Whelen, and Murin 1986).

Revenue Sharing and Block Grants

A sea change in intergovernmental relations began with the Nixon administration and its revenue sharing initiative of 1972. "Creative federalism" was the term coined to describe the major changes enshrined in the 1972 Fiscal Assistance Act and the 1974 Housing and Community Development Act. These two acts had as their joint purpose the substitution of state and local government responsibility in place of the federal level with regard to many categorical urban physical and socioeconomic grant programs. Public and other low cost housing programs for the poor that might have prevented much of the homelessness we see today were among the programs that the federal level shed.

The revenue sharing program was established in order to implement a new approach to urban problems. Specifically, it allowed the federal government to return tax revenues to the state and local levels in order to allow these jurisdictions, with limited federal oversight, to decide which programs to spend it on. This effort was justified as increasing the power of localities to solve their own problems with the application of local expertise and insight instead of relying on a distant federal bureaucracy to do it for them. It also effectively got the federal government out of the business of providing national urban programs, such as public housing, to which many in the Nixon administration were philosophically opposed. If a locality wanted such programs, revenue sharing would be its source of funding (Reagan and Sanzone 1981; Dommel 1974).

General revenue sharing became law in 1972 when the Fiscal Assistance Act was passed. Originally intended as a program that would pass on federal budgetary surpluses to cities, the Republicans changed the thrust of the program to include all local communities. The reason for this change had more to do with the Republican strength in the suburbs and states than with any purported increase in programmatic efficiency; there were thirty-one Republican governors when Nixon, a Republican, was elected.

How well did the program operate? While it had very few strings attached for local governments, there was an expectation that they would fund the projects that had been financed by categorical grants. This was not the case however. Apparently mistrustful of the permanence of the program, local officials were loath to institute services which they might later have to maintain using local funds. Instead, they opted for a series of one-shot projects. Thus, instead of funding innovative social service or health programs, most local areas spent their money on street and road repairs and public safety; many used it to cut taxes or avoid a tax increase. Much of the money went to fund new capital improvements (Stone, Whelen, and Murin 1986; Reagan and Sanzone 1981; R. A. Smith and Cozad 1976).

Critics of revenue sharing stressed that local officials forgot about the needs of the poor and minorities the moment there was an easing of the federal pressure built into many categorical grant programs designed for these groups. Even those cities that sought to spend their funds on the poor found that they had less to spend than formerly under the categorical grant approach. There was less money for the poor since it was being distributed to all communities rather than just those whose need was greatest (Dommel 1974).

Revenue sharing fulfilled the worst fears held by advocates for the poor. Rather than spending on needed services, affluent suburban communities spent their money to build golf courses and horseback riding trails. Burlington, Vermont, for instance, spent $300,000 on uniforms for the municipal band and $160,000 for an ice rink and bathhouse. Some localities were irresponsible in their spending. In one community, revenue sharing funds were spent on a coliseum after voters had twice rejected it in local referendums (Stone, Whelen, and Murin 1986).

For central cities the problematic aspects of the program were compounded because not only did the suburbs get a share of the funds, they got a disproportionate share. This was due to the 1972 funding formula which discriminated against urban areas. Under this formula, cities did receive more funds per capita than suburban areas, but they received less than the suburbs when need was taken into account. A particular concern was that highly populated urban areas did not receive revenue sharing funds reflective of the revenue effort they provided. In addition, the civil rights protections that were built into revenue sharing often were not enforced. There were many examples of discriminatory funding practices under this program. Finally, there were charges of a serious undercount of the population in urban areas, charges that many thought were quite valid (Dommell 1974; Reagan and Sanzone 1981).

Many analysts of revenue sharing thought that the operation of the program called into question the popular American truism that "the closer to the people, the more responsive and responsible government will be" (Stone, Whelen, and Murin 1986). Indeed, it appears that the revenue sharing program was short on meaningful citizen participation. In Philadelphia, for instance, citizen participation consisted of citizens recording their input in a room empty of city officials or any authority. They were told that officials would listen to the tape at a later date.

As the federal level retreated from responsibility for the urban poor there was a heightened debate about the role of the revenue sharing program and its use by the strengthened localities. Advocates for the poor were concerned that the states would not show the concern for the urban poor that the federal level showed before. Indeed, they were fearful that the states, while more professionally administered than in the past, were still dominated by business interests that would direct funds into other areas (Reagan and Sanzone 1981). As central cities declined in population, and therefore in electoral strength, would the states safeguard their growing proportion of poor households?

Some analysts have expressed concern over whether the states were capable of assuming the federal mantle in this regard. Stone has written:

What about the special tie between federal officials and community groups? We can speculate that at best there will be an uncertain and hazardous future for the many community action and non-profit agencies which have served as quasi-public entities at the local level. These organizations dispense social services largely with federal dollars. In considering their future it is wise to remember that the federal government became involved in many of these policy areas because the states weren't doing much for the needy (Stone, Whelen, and Murin 1986, 67; Burt and Pittman 1986).

It was not only urban liberals who expressed concern about the impact of revenue sharing. Fiscal conservatives expressed fears about the no strings aspect of the program; to them, prudent fiscal management requires that the level of government that raised the money should be held accountable for how it was spent (Dommel 1974; Caputo and Cole 1976).

In 1976, revenue sharing was reauthorized and some limited modifications were made in light of these criticisms. Whatever the practical effect of these changes, general revenue sharing had become quite popular with local urban officials at least in the absence of anything to take its place. This popularity led them to resist attempts by the Reagan administration to eliminate the program (Meyers 1986). The administration eventually prevailed and general revenue sharing was eliminated by the Reagan administration in 1986 as part of the ongoing effort to shift all social programs to the states and localities. At that time, the program constituted about 5 or 6% of the typical city's income. This shortfall had to be made up with increased taxes or service reductions.

Special Revenue Sharing

The type of revenue sharing discussed above was known as general revenue sharing. There is a related program of special revenue sharing which consists of block grants established under the Community Development Block Grant program (CDBG). This program was established by the Housing and Community Development Act of 1974 to replace older urban categorical grants. Similar to general revenue sharing, these block grants give localities greater budget flexibility. Specifically, local matching requirements were eliminated so that local priorities are not skewed by having to play the grants game (L. H. Stone 1986). While general revenue sharing funds could be used to assist the poor and homeless, special revenue sharing has more direct application to the problem of homelessness since it can be used to fund low cost housing. Specifically, HUD regulations on CDBGs permit cities to conduct housing programs that have one of two objectives:

1. Activities are authorized that focus financial and other benefits on the low and moderate income residents as defined by HUD.
2. Programs are authorized that are aimed at the prevention or elimination of slums or blight.

The first category includes activities such as the provision of grants to low and moderate income persons for housing rehabilitation, rehabilitation financing, and rehabilitation services such as counseling, loan processing, and work write-ups. The second category includes the acquisition, disposition, clearance, code enforcement, and related activities. Under the CDBG program, a portion of these activities must benefit low and moderate income persons (Nenno and Brophy 1982; Reagan and Sanzone 1981).

This framework is supposed to allow local governments maximum flexibility to tailor programs to meet their local needs. The degree of federal regulation has varied considerably depending on the philosophy of the federal administration in power; the Nixon, Ford, and particularly the Reagan administrations exercised minimal controls while the Carter administration was more activist. The impact of this activism was very limited however. For instance, in keeping with Carter's national urban agenda, HUD was directed to adopt an anti-sprawl pro-urban policy stance. In one publicly reported instance, HUD threatened to withhold approval for an infrastructure grant needed for a major suburban development on the grounds that it contravened this policy. After much negotiation, HUD was forced to relent, leaving the clear impression that this approach would not produce a meaningful policy impact. Similarly, a study of the CDBG program by the Brookings Institution found that the program did not "significantly contribute to the legislative objective of encouraging 'spatial deconcentration' of housing for lower income persons." Thus, it is fair to say that regardless of varying enthusiasm for regulation, the CDBG program gives the federal government little direct control over local policies. Reagan and Sanzone have noted:

The objectives in the authorizing legislation are not specific enough. The best one can "hold on to" are a long laundry list of expectations and activities that qualify for funding. However, fragmented activities, no matter how noble, do not add up to a comprehensive community development strategy (Reagan and Sanzone 1981).

Given the flexibility built into the CDBG program, has there been a resultant improvement in the type and scale of programs designed to assist the poor and needy? Nenno reports that often cities simply have carried on doing what they had done under the old categorical grant approach. Local officials have been free to innovate but often do not recognize their freedom or are too constrained by local circumstances to act on it (Nenno and Brophy 1983).

This is not to say that innovations have not occurred. Indeed there is a whole raft of innovative public/private low income housing partnerships that have been developed on the local level. These have arisen as the only effective way to stretch the declining funds available for low cost urban housing. Thus, complicated financial arrangements of a complex mix of federal, state, and local public funds, as well as private loans and foundation grants, increasingly categorize the budget for these projects. This is not the place to catalog these experiments in local self-help. What is important to note is that they are very dependent on an aggressive organizational force that is adept at deal-making and creative financing—skills that hark back to the premium placed on grantsmanship under the earlier categorical grant approach. True too is the fact that these creative approaches have not been able to stem the tide of urban neighborhood decline any more than earlier programs. Indeed, there is evidence to suggest that they are often as cumbersome as the centrally controlled categorical grants they replaced (Reagan and Sanzone 1981; Nenno and Brophy 1983; Ahlbrandt and Brophy 1975).

Special revenue sharing has also been attacked as being anti-urban in its overall impact. Specifically, it has been attacked as being unfair in its allocation of funds both to and within cities. Additionally, it has been criticized for failing to promote citizen participation and broader social objectives such as the dispersal of low cost housing. The history of special revenue sharing is much like that of general revenue sharing: the favoring of suburban areas and new cities at the expense of older declining cities. Specifically, the initial funding formula took into account population, overcrowded housing, and poverty, which received a double weighting. While at first glance this formula appeared to recognize the needs of our older cities, it resulted in additional revenues for the burgeoning Sunbelt cities with growing populations and less for the Frostbelt cities. As a result of strong criticism of this inequity, in 1977 the formula was amended to include consideration of physical deterioration, aged housing stock, and population losses. This succeeded in creating a more evenly balanced funding pattern (Reagan and Sanzone 1981; Dommel 1974; Meyers 1986).

The way funds are apportioned within cities has also generated a great deal of controversy. Specifically, there is no guarantee that community development block grant funds will be spent on programs designed to alleviate poverty or create low cost housing. Initially the legislation merely required that the locality give "maximum feasible priority" to activities that benefit low or moderate income families and that prevent or help eliminate slums or blight. Subsequent guidelines required that localities spend 75%, recently amended to only 51%, in low and moderate income areas. Nonetheless, a city could easily spend its funds on a major central city capital project while ignoring the needs of the outlying low and moderate income neighborhoods. Indeed, local community advocates contend that just such a bias exists in many urban areas. Analysts also detect another danger, wherein the city spreads its limited funding over a myriad of community groups with little lasting impact or spill-over investment (Stone, Whelen, and Murin 1986; Reagan and Sanzone 1981). The response to this concern has been the tendency to target funding in so-called marginal areas in order to maximize the positive economic impact of the program. However, representatives of those low income areas that get left out are quick to label this approach a variant of triage. The Reagan administration went so far as to propose new rules that would eliminate any requirement to assist the poor although this effort was unsuccessful (Meyers 1986).

Citizen participation has also been problematic under this program since localities are only required to hold a public hearing. The fulsome provision of assistance to those who wished to become involved in the local planning process that existed in the 1960s has been eliminated. As a result, revenue sharing, which was trumpeted as bringing decisionmaking closer to the people, has failed to live up to its promise. Yet there is not much overt opposition to the program and some groups are quite supportive of it. In a longitudinal study of the revenue sharing program, Caputo and Cole

(1974, 1976) give evidence of the fact that the program was extremely popular among local officials in suburban areas. Less pleased were urban officials who felt cheated since they were initially told that revenue sharing would be in addition to the then existing categorical grant programs. Instead, they have seen the diminution of all funding programs for urban areas and an increased level of urban fiscal stress. Thus, revenue sharing has changed the focus of concern about social programs for the poor, but it has not gotten us any closer to developing a meaningful urban policy (Meyers 1986, Reagan and Sanzone 1981).

Special revenue sharing does operate under some federal oversight control. The Housing and Community Development Act of 1974 made the preparation of a local Housing Assistance Plan (HAP) a precondition for receiving community development assistance. The aim was to encourage the involvement of local governments in the low income housing assistance process. Under this plan, the community is to document its housing needs and the condition of its housing stock, develop a goal for assisted housing units, and identify locations for proposed assisted housing. The results of this oversight have been uneven at best. HUD reported that "In some cities the HAP is used to develop a coordinated local housing strategy whose implementation is actively pursued. . . . In other cities it is a mechanical exercise that sets goals that cannot be achieved" (Nenno and Brophy 1983). In any case, the localities are not required to follow prescribed HUD procedures in developing and implementing eligible programs.

The Two Approaches Compared

Both the categorical grant approach and revenue sharing are the policy mechanisms that originate from a liberal policy perspective in that they "seek to ameliorate an unpleasant situation" (Minogue 1963), specifically the disparity between rich and poor. The problem with both approaches is that they rely on local discretionary mechanisms to allocate the funds. These local mechanisms produce a disjointed and often unjust application. This is because the application of this remedy is discretionary. This remains a constant whether the local mechanism is based on a categorical grant to a central city or a particular interest group in that city. It is also true if it is a block grant to a local governing agency. The reason for the inability of all of these dispensing agents to achieve equity is their inability to achieve equality of program application across lines of governmental authority. This inability is due to the aforementioned fragmentation of local governments throughout the United States. This fragmentation, coupled with the respect for the prevailing free market ethos, home rule, and the constitutional separation of powers, has led to a social system that relies too heavily on the voluntary compliance on the part of local governments keen to do the bidding of powerful economic interests. Local autonomy is often very healthy, but it becomes dysfunctional when the policy in question deals with basic fundamental human rights such as adequate shelter and income (Meyers 1986).

Lowi has critiqued the local or decentralized bias in the American policy process. In his view, decentralization is an abdication since it merely pitches the issue under discussion into a decisionmaking framework that is incapable of arriving at a clear policy. Local decisionmaking enhances the number of actors that can get access to the decisionmaking process. Many of these actors are really interest groups that seek to advance their own agendas. Even if they are not directly affected by the outcome of the issue at hand, they may exert influence so as to build up support for their efforts to affect the outcome of other issues (Lowi 1969).

Much of the support for decentralization has come from advocates of increased citizen participation in policymaking. The literature on citizen participation is both broad and deep (Davidoff 1967; Burke 1968; Spiegel 1968; Columbia Law Review 1966; Hallman 1970; Cunningham 1972; Needleman and Needleman 1974). Yet there is no fundamental agreement on the efficacy of citizen participation in local affairs. It is a popular issue when viewed in the general sense. As Sherry Arnstein has said, "It is like motherhood, and apple pie, no one is against it in principle because it is good for you" (Yin 1972). While many would agree with this broad statement, there is little else authorities agree upon when it comes to citizen participation. There is no agreement as to what constitutes meaningful participation. The role of elites and powerful interests in the process leads many to think that true citizen participation is a chimera. Many argue that such interests organize all the meaningful decisions out of public view leaving the public alone to decide the unimportant issues. Others feel that citizen participation is good for a host of reasons related to the exercise of citizenship responsibilities. They claim, too, that when it occurs, there can be discernible deflection of policy decisions away from the interests of the dominant interests such as big business (Hart 1972).

Yet few would argue that the history of citizen participation has been smooth. Many agree with Moynihan who claims that many of the problems inherent in the "War on Poverty" can be traced to its requirement for the "maximum feasible participation" of the poor. The costs in time and money of fulfilling this requirement were significant. Worse was the sense that public policy was being driven by the whims and accidents of a volatile and often irrational grass roots community dynamic (Moynihan 1969). Tom Wolfe savagely satirized this process in an essay entitled "Radical Chic and Mau Mauing the Flack Catchers." The piece captured the essentially antidemocratic bias inherent in what was a decentralized decisionmaking process: the group that organized the loudest and "baddest" display of pressure on government bureaucrats got the cash for their program. What Wolfe did not discuss was the meaninglessness of the whole program with regard to the structural problems facing the participants (Wolfe 1970).

What is true at the local level is increasingly true at the regional and national levels. Participation in American politics is increasingly dominated by special interests that operate in a highly organized fashion to affect public policy. This phenomenon has been commented upon with great regularity by many authorities (Lowi 1969). To some extent, this tendency has helped to increase the participation of people who had heretofore been excluded from the political process. It has also widened the breadth of issues that are being actively considered by both national and local political parties. Specifically, the increased participation of blacks and other minorities in American politics is viewed as a positive feature of postwar political decentralization. Similarly positive are the policy deliberations resulting in limitations on powerful industrial interests in such fields as the environment, nuclear energy, and toxic waste. So pervasive is the impact of this process of citizen participation that Nixon, a Republican president, oversaw the passage of a host of bills such as the Environmental Protection Act and the Clean Water Act that placed restrictions on industry (Schlesinger 1986).

Overall, however, creative federalism had the effect of reducing the federal role and responsibility for important urban programs and shifting it over to the states and localities (Pagano and Moore 1985). Michael Reagan and John Sanzone (1981) refer to this as "buck passing by the national government." They underline this point by quoting Derthic who has written that the national legislature uses the grant system to commit itself to serving very broad national purposes (such as "more adequate" welfare) without assuming the burden of making all the political choices it would have to make in a unitary system (how much welfare, for whom?). The difficult choices are left to other governments.

While this lack of backbone on the part of the federal government is understandable in terms of political risk management, it is deplorable when the policies affect the very poor and homeless. It is also hard to avoid concluding that the postwar efforts to shift responsibility for poverty programs from one level of authority to another is intended to give the appearance of reformist activity when none is intended.

What this activity does is to play into a preexisting bias in favor of so-called home rule in local government. Briefly, home rule refers to the localized decisionmaking power for a whole host of services and regulatory functions long enjoyed by towns and cities in the United States. This power is controversial chiefly because of the regional economic disparities that exist in the United States; some localities and regions are very wealthy while others are not. Revenue sharing and other governmental financial programs do rely on formulas that take such disparities into account, but, be that as it may, there remain sharp differences in the wealth of different local areas and, therefore, their ability to help the poor in their midst. Revenue sharing has sharpened these differences and has exacerbated the problems inherent in planning for the less fortunate in our society. These individuals tend to be concentrated in our older and poorer cities, precisely those areas less financially able to devise and carry out effective programs to ameliorate the situation. Today, the bulk of our population lives in suburban enclaves safely buffered from the vicissitudes of urban reality and therefore is seldom called on to participate in a communal search for solutions (Pyle 1985; Herbers 1986; Jackson 1985; Meyers 1986). Previously, when the federal level was controlled by the Democrats, it could be counted on to champion the cause of the poor (Dellums 1986).

Since the federal retreat from involvement in urban programs, the search for solutions has been left to the localities, each viewing but a part of what is a national problem. It is an unfair assignment to expect these localities to individually solve severe social problems such as homelessness when they are not given the resources to do so. What is more important, even if they had the resources to solve their own problems there is no guarantee that other localities will see fit to do likewise. The end result will be a continued imbalance between stingy and caring jurisdictions resulting in the dumping of clients at the doorstep of the latter and restarting the problem cycle anew (Burt and Pittman 1986; Meyers 1986). The fact remains that we are only now realizing the results of the experiment in creative federalism started over ten years ago; federal encouragement for a new virulent strain of individualism and localism threatens to warp our traditional American values based on compassion for those less fortunate than ourselves (Etzioni 1983; Harrington 1984; Lekachman 1982; Schorr 1986).

To be sure, there are other factors that have helped tip the balance in favor of increased power and authority for localities in recent years. The

Reagan administration's veneration of deregulation and unfettered free market individualism served this purpose admirably. Less helpful to this mission was his administration's savage cutting of housing, block grant programs, and other federally funded social programs. Indeed, this has put the localities in a terrible bind in that they cannot carry out the programs for which they had so recently been given responsibility. Thus it can be said that the Reagan administration continued the initial work of the Nixon administration with a vengeance; it provided continued emphasis on local responsibility for social programs but less and less federal monetary assistance with which to carry them out (Aronson and Hilley 1986; Meyers 1986).

The situation has reached crisis proportions in many of our older urban areas. The valiant efforts of the heterogeneous group of state and local officials, volunteers, and nonprofit social agencies that have been trying to service the poor and homeless are simply not enough. Increasingly, it is being recognized that something must be done to address this situation (Harrington 1984; Etzioni 1983; Schorr 1986; Meyers 1986).

The problem is that we have lost the traditional balance between federal and local authority that prevailed since the Roosevelt administration's New Deal agenda. The Nixon initiative has tipped the scales in favor of the local level to a dysfunctional degree. What is needed now is a recognition of this imbalance and the development of policies aimed at reasserting a stronger role for the federal level in protecting the basic social and economic privileges of our poorest citizens.

Yet concern is raised that all these issues cloud the policy process since there is no mechanism to resolve competing claims by the avid proponents of each issue. In short, what issue has prominence? Where should domestic urban policy concentrate its efforts? Today there is a strong feeling that the pressure of interest groups is the decisive factor. Hence under Reagan, we had to endure eight years of his administration's efforts to restrict abortions, reintroduce school prayer in public schools, expand the application of so-called public choice options which largely benefit the middle and upper classes, and grant tax breaks for the parents of private school children. What was not done is equally important. The Reagan administration did not work hard to prosecute violations of the fair housing law; it did not pursue efforts to desegregate public schools; and it did not continue to subsidize public programs due to the relative weakness of groups favoring such policies (Schorr 1986; Center on Budget and Policy Priorities 1986).

There are many ways to explain these policy thrusts. Many simply lay the blame at Reagan's feet claiming that he was a strong leader who was able to influence the national policy agenda as few recent presidents have been able to do (Logan 1983; Friedlen 1983; Yago 1983). Some suggest that many of these programs were unpopular with local public officials (Peterson, Lewis, and Caro 1986). Others claim that the results are due to our governmental structure which puts severe limits on the authority of the central government. While this limitation may have been less important when we were a young growing country, this basic limitation of American government will increasingly be seen as a flaw. It will be seen as a flaw since it constitutes a basic impediment to the derivation and implementation of clear national policies. We do not have a national urban policy; instead, we have a series of disjointed incremental programmatic decisions dependent to a large extent on the degree of encouragement provided by the federal administration to the proponents of a particular agenda. In this context the overwhelming strength of national and local business interests must be reckoned with. To be sure, broadly constituted presidential commissions have from time to time pontificated on particular aspects of urban policy and issued goals but these had no legal basis and made little political impact. By and large, they are all soon forgotten by policymakers since we lack a workable mechanism for implementing plans of any type in this country. In this vein, it is instructive to look at the fate of recent efforts to develop a national urban policy (Lindblom 1977).

THE PRESIDENT'S NATIONAL URBAN POLICY REPORT OF 1980

The first national urban policy statement was issued by the Carter administration in 1980. Following the path blazed by the earlier President's Committee on Urban Housing (1968) and the National Commission on Urban Problems (1968), this comprehensive policy statement contained a list of positive pro-urban policies that would encourage urban revitalization as well as open up housing opportunities for low and moderate income households throughout metropolitan regions. The report touched all the required liberal reformist bases; indeed, there was specific reference to the administration's support for additional low and moderate income housing and suburban fair share housing policies. What was lacking in the Carter urban initiative was any new policy mechanisms to ensure that compliance with specific goals was achieved. Some of the new programmatic initiatives that were established and funded represented new revenues or retargeted revenues for hard-pressed cities. Nonetheless, they remained firmly couched in the categorical grant based approach adhered to by earlier presidential commissions and which had not led to notable success. Nowhere in the policy statement was there any recognition of the need to fashion new tools and approaches to policy implementation (President's National Urban Policy Report 1980; President's Committee on Urban Housing 1968; National Commission on Urban Problems 1968).

A similar approach was taken by the Committee on National Urban Policy in its 1983 report. This report outlined a policy statement that stressed the need to return the country to a competitive footing in the world economy. The means to this end would be a reliance on the free market and the free movement of labor resources within this market. Although there was much support for retraining schemes for displaced workers, the emphasis was on an anti-urban *laissez faire* approach remarkably similar to that of the Reagan administration (Hanson 1983).

DISCUSSION

One reason for this policy drift is that we do not have strong political parties that develop clear policy agendas on which all their candidates base their campaigns. Rather, the tendency is for both major parties to constantly seek to appeal to a broad spectrum of interests in the hope of fashioning a sufficiently broad public following. The very breadth of interests that must be spanned works against the possibility of such a party deriving clear and precise policy statements. One example of this search for broad consensus was the pairing of a liberal presidential candidate with a conservative vice presidential candidate by the Democrats in the 1988 election. Increasingly, middle-of-the-road conservative politics has typified postwar electoral contests at the national level (Keefe 1988; Price 1984). It is not surprising that clear policies seldom emerge from such an environment.

In the past there was relatively more distinction between the parties than at present. The old Roosevelt Democratic coalition was forged in response to a clear threat occasioned by the Great Depression. This coalition was made up of the poor and working classes that were found both in the large urban areas in the north as well as the rural south. This coalition was based on the party's clear willingness to intervene in the free market so as to mitigate its worst effects (McJimsey 1987). The Republicans, in contrast, were seen as the party of big business with a minimal interest in urban community development programs (Meyers 1986).

Today increased prosperity, coupled with new settlement patterns, has shattered the Democratic coalition. The core of support for the party has been reduced to the now smaller old Northern and Midwestern cities and the poor. There is much talk of the Republicans becoming the new national majority party supported by their burgeoning suburban political base. This talk is bolstered by the fact that Reagan won two terms in office by attracting many Democratic voters and there is evidence that Democratic voters, especially in the south, are increasingly willing to vote for Republican candidates (Herbers 1986; K. P. Phillips 1969).

The strong local, anti-urban bias in American policymaking has hindered the promulgation of a comprehensive urban policy capable of responding to the needs of our poorest citizens (Meyers 1986; Logan 1983; Friedlen 1983; Pyle 1985). The extent to which this hindrance affects the specific area of urban housing policy is discussed in the following chapters.

4

Urban Housing Policy

The picture that emerged from the preceding chapter was one of widespread antipathy to national level urban policy planning even in the face of mounting need for such an effort. A similar antipathy has greeted calls for developing a strong national housing policy. Yet it is wrong to say, as some do, that a national housing policy does not exist. In fact, our housing policy is quite clear; for housing all Americans we rely on the private market system. The main argument of this chapter is that while this system does an admirable job for the majority of our citizens, it is unable to produce or maintain adequate amounts of good quality low income housing for those on limited incomes (Glazer 1973). Also at issue in this chapter are the implications of the long-term disagreements between proponents of various low cost housing approaches.

It is important to review the history of the development of this national housing policy in order to understand the roots of the present housing crisis. Such a review serves to highlight the dysfunction in current national housing policy in general and in the low cost housing policy in particular. The dysfunction in low cost housing policy is directly responsible for the expansion of homelessness which we are now witnessing. Of particular importance is our attitude toward government-subsidized housing since such housing appears to offer an obvious approach to meeting the needs of the homeless. A central concern expressed here is that even the new, more expansive funding for low cost housing that is likely to emerge from Congress will be based on existing housing policies and will therefore run the risk of producing low cost housing of the wrong kind and in the wrong places. As a result, many such units are at risk of becoming quickly overstressed and abandoned, thereby risking continued political and public support for governmental housing assistance.

FEDERAL HOUSING GOALS

Federal housing goals have been developed over time and now are composed of a fulsome list of policies aimed at more than simply maintaining a sufficient stock of private housing. Initially our housing goal was stated succinctly: "a decent home and healthy surroundings for every American family" (President's Committee on Urban Housing 1968). Over time, this simple goal statement has been considerably embellished. Today, our housing goals can be summarized as follows:

1. to reduce the amount of physically inadequate housing;
2. to reduce crowding;
3. to reduce the financial burden of housing;
4. to promote economic and racial integration;
5. to promote homeownership;
6. to promote neighborhood revitalization and preservation and community development;
7. to increase the supply of housing for particular groups such as the elderly and the poor; and
8. to increase and stabilize residential construction through fiscal measures (Aaron 1981, 70).

OVERVIEW OF THE HOUSING DELIVERY SYSTEM

Housing has always been one of the basic necessities of life. Most nations find it difficult to produce housing in sufficient quantities of the right type, size, and in the proper location. The United States has been relatively fortunate in this regard. Its private market housing delivery system is unmatched, producing some 35.2 million units of housing since 1960. Its homeownership rate is also the highest; some 64% of Americans own their own homes. The quality of all types of housing has improved continuously so that by 1977, only 7.5% of all households lived in units in need of rehabilitation (President's Commission on Housing 1982; Hughes and Sternlieb 1987). Average house size is increasing; the median house size was 800 square feet just after World War II, today it is about 1,600 square feet (President's Commission on Housing 1982).

A recent analysis of housing market trends foresees continued improvement in housing quality and affordability for the majority of working Americans even as population growth rates and household size continue to decline. Indeed, the aging of the "baby boom" generation and the expected downsizing of its housing needs may produce additional housing opportunities for first time home buyers in the near future. So long as the economy is robust and households can afford to maintain their units, the choices open to prospective home buyers will be enhanced. This is a sizable accomplishment if one recognizes the housing delivery system needs to house some 1.3 million new households per year. The strength of the housing production system can be gleaned from both the historical increase in housing starts and the growth in the supply of housing units between 1970 and 1983 which exceeded the growth in population, as well as the growth in households (Hughes and Sternlieb 1987, 188). Given a stable economy, the prognosis is for homeownership to increase to 67% and the rental market to continue to shrink as it loses the more affluent to homeownership (Hughes and Sternlieb 1987).

Today, there is considerable agreement that even in the face of good overall housing output and generally good levels of affordability, there is a housing problem of considerable proportions among those of low income. Where there is disagreement is over how to ameliorate this problem. Many authorities such as Porter (1976) point to aggregate housing output as proof that America's housing industry is capable of providing a sufficient amount of housing for all income groups. Porter and others who defend the current approach to housing provision would admit that problems do exist in certain geographically discrete housing sub-markets, in particular, the bottom end of the housing market. He would hold that the solution to such problems would be to fine tune the existing housing delivery system to encourage the renewal or rehabilitation of housing in such areas.

A major factor in maintaining housing demand is the affordability of housing. Looking at several measures of ownership affordability, Hughes and Sternlieb (1987) note that while always subject to forces in the economy, the housing market for new homes has become less accessible to the middle and lower income groups. This burden is greater for single headed households, a situation that has prevailed for some time. When housing costs for all owner-occupiers are considered, it is clear that costs have risen over time though not to prohibitive levels (Hughes and Sternlieb 1987).

Affordability is also influenced by the availability of housing. Accordingly, it is important to note what sectors of the housing market have sustained losses. The study by Hughes and Sternlieb showed that removals from the housing inventory were concentrated in the rental sector and that minority renters were the most affected by such removals. Most crucial was the fact that the removals were concentrated in the low cost end of the cost spectrum. New rental units were constructed but were more costly.

This process reflects the functioning of the so-called "filtering process" with the low cost units being replaced as unfit or substandard. While this is a salutary process for the housing stock as a whole, it is a crisis for those low income households who are faced with fewer affordable options. The result is a decline in low cost rental housing that has a disproportional effect on the minority poor (Hughes and Sternlieb 1987).

LOW COST HOUSING SHORTFALL

Most criticism of federal housing policy is based on the growing shortfall in available housing for low income households. These critics feel this shortfall is due to the failure of the private market to deliver sufficient low cost units and the failure of the federal government to step into this breach by providing sufficient publicly supported units. They point out that the housing industry failed to meet the housing target set in the 1968 Housing Act: a target of 26 million units by 1978. Only two-thirds of that number were built and the greatest shortfall was in the failure to reach the goal of 6 million assisted housing units for low and moderate income families. Less than half of these, 2.7 million, were built. Today, some 4% or 3.5 million assisted units exist out of a total of 80 million units. Long term reliance on the free market has produced a system unable to meet government-set aggregate goals nor to handle problems in local areas where market distortions produce particularly severe shortages of low cost housing. Critics of current housing policies feel that this situation is not temporary or due to cyclical economic forces affecting the housing industry but rather it is due to the self-interested privatistic decisionmaking process upon which the housing delivery system is based. They argue only an aggressive interventionist approach led by the federal government can ensure a more equitable and functional allocation of housing resources (Hartman 1983; Clay 1987; Dolbeare 1985, 1987; Downs 1983; National Housing Task Force 1988).

HISTORY OF HOUSING POLICY

Housing production in the United States was strictly an activity of the private sector until the Great Depression. Up until that time, the government restricted itself to the adoption of local zoning and building codes and other safety measures. There were a few scattered examples of government-sponsored housing for war industry workers developed during World War I but after the war, they were returned to the private market.

Interestingly, some of these developments were extremely successful (Boyer 1986, 144; Glazer 1973).

The exigencies of the Depression changed the prevailing free market approach. It prompted Congress to support in peacetime what it heretofore only accepted in time of war: governmental involvement in the housing market. Congress responded to the rising incidence of homelessness and housing deprivation and, most centrally, the need to stimulate employment by passing several pieces of legislation that were to permanently alter the free market housing production system. Specifically, the Federal Home Loan Bank system was created in 1932; the Public Works Administration was created under the National Recovery Act of 1933 and authorized the first federally funded low income housing. In addition, the National Housing Act of 1934 created the Federal Housing Administration (FHA) to guarantee mortgages at more favorable terms than privately available (Boyer 1986; Nenno and Brophy 1983; M. Stone 1973; Abrams 1946).

Public Housing

The United States Housing Act of 1937 established a permanent federally funded public housing program. It must be stressed that with only a few exceptions, in all of these "federal" programs, the initiation and financing were federal but the responsibility for the administration and implementation was local and program participation was on a voluntary basis. Construction output for public housing reached its highest level in the late 1960s and declined thereafter as the following figures show: 78,000 units in 1950, 89,000 units in 1951, and in 1967–70 70,000, 109,000, and 101,000 were started (Nenno and Brophy 1983; Glazer 1973).

A number of observers have pointed out the complexity of the administrative arrangements between the local housing authority, the local government, and the federal government. The local housing authority is nominally independent of the municipality but both the municipality and the federal government can affect its operations. A local housing authority controls the development, construction, and management of the project that it owns. Today some 1.25 million units of public housing exist that house some 3 million low income individuals or 1.5% of the population. They are widely dispersed in terms of the number of local authorities that control them (2,900) and strongly concentrated in terms of geographic location in urban areas; 29 cities with populations of more than 400,000 have more than 31% of all public housing units. Most public housing large enough for families is concentrated in large urban areas while small cities and towns tend to have only smaller units catering to the elderly (Hartman 1975; M. Stone 1973).

It is important to understand the degree of local control inherent in the public housing program. Public housing is controlled by the local housing authority (LHA). The LHA decides what the local housing need is, where housing should be built, who will live in it, how to manage it when it is completed, and all other matters regarding housing for low income families in the community (Roske 1983). The federal government (HUD) provides general oversight in terms of the selection of the site, design of the housing units, and the amount of parking and play space.

Today, public housing is highly segregated; over 70% of all households in public housing are nonwhite. In Atlanta and Chicago over 95% of all non-elderly households in public housing are black. This segregation has been perpetuated by policy decisions made by the LHA. For instance, public housing projects were located in accordance with prevailing neighborhood patterns; projects for blacks were placed in black neighborhoods and projects for whites were placed in white neighborhoods. Supporting this approach, tenant assignments were made so as to maintain the racial characteristics of the project. This policy has been declared illegal by the courts but prevails to this day in many urban areas (Hartman 1975; L. Friedman 1973; Polikoff 1978).

Public housing was established to house those who were not adequately served by the private housing market; nonetheless it serves only a fraction of those who would fit this definition. Many are excluded due to the shortage of units; three year long waiting periods are typical in most cities. Others are excluded due to their inability to meet exacting program guidelines. In fact, these guidelines exclude the majority of the nation's poor (Hartman 1975, 127).

Dissatisfactions with Public Housing

Public housing is very unpopular in this country. It evokes images of overregulation, stigmatization, isolation, racial animosity, and rampant social problems. These negative images are so pervasive that a high percentage of eligible families refuse to consider living in public housing. Most of these attitudes can be traced to public awareness of the problems associated with the more recent large urban public housing projects such as the notorious Pruitt Igoe project in Saint Louis. In Pruitt Igoe, the problems occasioned by poor site planning and interior design resulted in a physical design in which social order was hard to maintain. In addition, inadequate management and an imbalanced tenant mix resulted in such a high degree of crime and other social pathologies that the project was demolished. Many other cities can provide similar case studies of how not to develop and manage public housing (Neuman 1972; Roske 1983; Rainwater 1973; Bellush and Hausknecht 1973).

Negative attitudes toward public housing are shared by many of the tenants. Their complaints stress the poor condition of the units and public areas, the arbitrary and unnecessary rules, poor quality of management and staff, and the generally demeaning treatment of tenants. HUD has responded to many of these complaints and now requires housing authorities to accord tenants the rights they would have in private housing. In addition, there has been a move toward tenant management schemes that have been successful in taming projects previously plagued with social and physical problems (Roske 1983; National Housing Task Force 1988; Friedman 1973).

Public housing has become synonymous with large high-rise high density "projects" that are rife with crime and other social problems (Bellush and Hausknecht 1973). This characterization is unfortunate and indeed inaccurate. The first public housing units were built at a low density of one to three stories. It was only in the 1950s and 1960s when high land costs—due to the refusal of suburban jurisdictions to accept public housing—led planners to propose large comprehensive urban public housing developments. The lack of success of these developments has led to a recent stress on low density scattered site public housing (Hartman 1975). Unfortunately, in terms of popular support, the damage has been done and a major effort to highlight the quiet success of many public housing developments may need to be undertaken.

It is also true that not all large comprehensive public housing developments become the locus of social pathologies. As mentioned above, some of the most notable examples of public housing were constructed during World War I for workers in the defense industries. It was the exigencies of war time that allowed public housing proponents to gain political support at the federal level. The result was a series of planned residential communities much like the New Towns then being developed in Europe. Although successful, these communities were quickly sold after the war. Moreover, the planners of these communities were criticized by Congress for having developed communities that were "too good"; the fear was that if the public saw what good public housing could be like, they would demand a major program to the detriment of the private housing industry. There are many observers who feel that our longstanding national antipathy to public housing has adversely affected all the assisted housing programs; this antipathy has led to the design of "least cost" public housing programs, shorn of all amenities, that are subconsciously designed to fail and thereby prove the superiority of private housing (Scott 1971; Boyer 1986).

Another Approach: New Towns

Evidence of successful public housing can be found in many other countries. Britain, France, Germany, and the Scandinavian countries have been particularly successful in developing public New Town programs that are largely based on the provision of public housing.

The United States is alone among industrialized countries in not having a New Towns or new communities program. Such programs are considered the centerpiece of postwar housing policy in most European countries. They are particularly successful in providing low cost housing to former blue-collar inner city residents in a dynamic suburban economy, something American housing policy fails to do. A few private New Towns have been developed, but these cater largely to the middle and upper classes (Fishman 1977; Scott 1971; Eichler and Kaplan 1967, 1973).

Congress did attempt to develop a government-sponsored new communities program in the mid-1960s. The program proceeded in typical American fashion: federal involvement was limited to the offer of financial incentives to private developers who met general program guidelines. A major problem was that the guidelines were quite vague. There was no basic definition of what constituted a new community as in the European approach. Accordingly, many preexisting suburban development projects were recycled in order to qualify for government funds. The project was based on the participation of private developers who received low cost financing and grants for infrastructure improvements and local amenities from the government. These developers were supposed to include low cost housing as part of the overall community plan. In reality, the developers consistently postponed the development of the low cost housing arguing that they had to develop a critical mass of market-based middle-class housing first. But the lack of a clear policy focus was to be the program's undoing. Spiraling costs and lack of public support led to the program's demise in 1982 (Hartman 1975; Eichler and Kaplan 1973).

Urban Renewal

The urban renewal program originated in the Housing Act of 1949 and was aimed at alleviating slum conditions in American cities. This program was based on the designation of blighted neighborhoods which would then be condemned, acquired, and cleared under eminent domain proceedings. The vacant land would then be marketed to the private sector and new housing constructed. If necessary, a subsidy could be applied to the land to bring down the per acre cost.

The program had a tumultuous history, chiefly due to the fact that it often resulted in the loss of entire neighborhoods of low cost housing and the concomitant expansion of office and commercial land uses. There were many critical studies of this program that centered on its pernicious effect on the stock of low cost housing and the neighborhoods that they made up (M. Anderson 1964). In response to this criticism, housing rehabilitation was made eligible for urban renewal funding in 1954. This reform resulted in the salutary saving of older, often historic housing stock near the central business district but did not ensure that such units remained low cost housing. This was because the process of land assembly and housing rehabilitation forced the original inhabitants out in almost every case. After the rehabilitation was complete, those who could be found and were willing to return were seldom able to pay the new higher rents charged.

The public antipathy to urban renewal programs became so widespread that cities found it increasingly difficult to obtain city council support for an urban renewal designation in any area because community groups were ready and waiting to do battle. Relocation plans for the original residents also came in for considerable criticism since inhabitants were scattered to diverse areas and often forced to accept inferior yet more costly housing than what they left behind. Thus again, the poor lost out on the benefits of a program that was supposed to meet their needs (Nenno and Brophy 1982; Roske 1983; J. Q. Wilson 1966).

Housing Subsidies: The 235–236 Program

The 1960s saw a renewed concern for the poor, particularly in our urban areas. This concern was fueled by the urban protests of this era as well as the increasing polarity between the affluent white suburbs and the poor minority-dominated city. As part of the 1968 Housing Act, the federal government funded the 235 and 236 subsidy programs which were designed to stimulate the rehabilitation of older urban properties and support their sale to low and moderate income households. Once again, the federal government relied on the private housing industry to carry out the program. The program was based on private contractors rehabilitating older single family housing units. Local realtors would assist prospective buyers in obtaining below market rate mortgage loans from participating private lenders who were insured by the government against default (Schafer and Field 1973). Eligibility limits were set about 35% higher than for public housing. This program soon became the largest subsidized housing program, accounting for some 400,000 units from its inception through 1974 (Nenno and Brophy 1982).

This program ran into severe difficulties which, as many observers noted, were due to the lack of safeguards over private sector performance. Several problem areas arose with respect to the quality of the initial rehabilitations. Government inspectors were often paid off by private contractors so that the poor quality work went unreported. These flaws came to light when the low income householder discovered major problems with the house that could not be repaired under the program. As many of these first time homeowners under this program had little extra capital savings, they had no recourse but to attempt to carry out the repairs themselves. Many low income families were not able to do so and as a result of having an unmarketable house, they went into default on their mortgage (Hartman 1975; Schafer and Field 1973).

Additional problems arose with regard to the financing of this program. Specifically, private lenders were overly quick to give mortgages to high risk households. These lenders were lax due to the fact that they knew that the mortgages were guaranteed by the government. Consequently, credit reports and employment records were sometimes given only a cursory look. The result was that too many households with insufficient income were mortgaged which led to a high default rate. As information about these problems became public, a political furor arose concerning the alleged kickbacks and the poor administration of the program. Investigations were undertaken and some local officials were jailed. The program itself was severely cut back and eventually ended (Hartman 1975; Schafer and Field 1973).

The legacy of this program was that by the late 1960s and early 1970s the federal government became the nation's largest urban slumlord as the defaults mounted. In most instances, the federal government simply sold the units in "as is" condition to housing speculators, many of whom held on to them in the hope of future appreciation. In many less affluent areas, the result was to encourage a disinvestment process that led to a considerable amount of abandoned and deteriorated housing (Hartman 1975).

The profusion of different housing programs was to prove increasingly confusing for laymen and officials alike. From 1954 until 1974, the basic housing assistance mechanism for lower income families not in public housing changed or was substantially altered at least ten times. As a result, there was little opportunity for housing officials to gain skills in operating the various programs or for the federal level to establish and administer a well-conceived oversight function. All this led to some major programmatic mistakes, scandals, and ultimately to increased questioning of the value of federal involvement in low cost housing production. As a result of this questioning, there was increased interest in a new approach: housing allowances (Nenno and Brophy 1982).

A New Approach: Housing Allowances, Section 8

After seeing the problems in existing federal housing programs, many housing reformers in the early 1970s tended to oppose continued supply-side subsidies and instead favored giving the low income consumer more money to spend directly on housing by means of a housing allowance (Schafer and Field 1973; Solomon 1973; Welfeld 1973). Due to the confluence of forces ranged against continued federal support for the production of low cost housing, in 1973 the Nixon administration placed a moratorium on all new federal housing assistance. In 1974, this moratorium was lifted with the creation of the Section 8 housing assistance program as a part of the 1974 Housing and Community Development Act. This act was a watershed in that it signaled the retreat of the federal level from involvement in housing assistance programs and the passing of increasing responsibility for this function to the state and local levels (Nenno and Brophy 1982).

The Section 8 existing housing program is a new mechanism for federal housing assistance since, unlike earlier mechanisms, the program provides no funds for the construction of housing. Rather, the program relies on the private sector to produce the housing units for which housing developers have to secure their own financing through private sources. What Section 8 does is to pay the difference between the monthly cost of renting these private units and what a low income family can afford to pay. Low income households are expected to pay 25% of their income on rent. The federal payment would be the difference between this amount and the total housing cost calculated at a fair market rent in the area. Housing allowances are to support housing demand so that sufficient low cost units are made available (Nenno and Brophy 1982; Roske 1983).

A major problem with this program is its dependence on the free housing market. While this market is successful in housing the middle classes and affluent, it does not provide a sufficient amount and variety of standard housing for the poor. In particular, the quality of these units has been problematic; studies give evidence of a high proportion of substandard and poor quality units created under such programs. In suburban areas with a low vacancy rate, it is highly unlikely that adequate low cost housing could be secured since the Section 8 program benefits are not a sufficient enticement for housing developers. In addition, patterns of discrimination based on race, lifestyle, family size, number of children, welfare status, and age have been magnified. Thus, while housing allowances have been touted as giving the poor mobility when selecting a housing unit, many cannot actually find any suitable housing (Netzer 1973; Bradbury and Downs 1981; President's Commission on Housing 1982, 26).

Another problem with this program has been the increasing cost of meeting the total annual assistance payments; in 1981, the federal obligation for assisted housing programs stood at more than $220 billion. The Reagan administration responded to this spiraling commitment by cutting the budget for this program in fiscal 1982 and 1983. The administration proposed replacing the public housing and Section 8 programs with a modified form of Section 8 or housing voucher that would help families occupy existing housing. There have been several housing voucher pilot programs in several cities (Nenno and Brophy 1982; Bradbury and Downs 1981).

Housing Allowances—Discussion

For many years, there has been a spirited debate between housing specialists regarding the most cost-effective way to assist the poor to improve their housing. Some maintain that housing programs per se are the wrong way to go about it as they are too costly to administer compared to existing and proposed welfare or jobs programs. Thus, many experts advocate a functionally specific minimum income plan or housing allowance coupled with job training or a public jobs program as the way to solve housing problems. This approach is based on the idea that with sufficient resources pushing up demand, private housing will be created (Aaron 1981, 85; Solomon 1973; Welfeld 1973).

Another faction prefers to approach the problem by means of subsidized low cost housing. The basic debate here has centered on the efficacy of a demand approach which puts money into the hands of low income households that they can spend on housing versus a supply approach which sees the need to build additional low cost units. Needless to say, there are many variations of both approaches and a good deal of overlap which has made analysis of the costs and benefits of each approach difficult. An expensive ten year experimental program in housing allowances was conducted. A noteworthy aspect of this experiment was the fact that the allowances could be utilized in any jurisdiction, thereby affording a high degree of mobility to the poor. As happened with the well known experiment with a minimum income plan, the artificiality of the experiment, such as its limited duration, set up unique dynamics that would not be present in a true national permanent program (Bradbury and Downs 1981; Welfeld 1973; Solomon 1973).

In any case, housing allowances did not live up to their promise. Specifically, they were expensive to administer, and as many as half of all eligible households did not participate in the program (Bradbury and Downs 1981, 383). In particular, those living in the poorest quality housing did not participate. Allowances also did not achieve significant economic or racial integration (Rossi 1981, 172). Finally, allowances failed to upgrade existing housing units as landlords failed to perceive a financial incentive as the increased rents were predicated on costly improvements (Bradbury and Downs 1981, 402).

One of the clear advantages of the housing allowance approach was the reduction of costs by about one half compared to a construction subsidy approach (Bradbury and Downs 1981). It was not clear, however, whether or not the full costs of providing low cost housing were included in these cost calculations. Specifically, it was not clear whether this analysis included the cost of market housing that is paid by the government via tax and investment programs that make such housing an attractive investment. An allowances program is predicated on the maintenance of a sufficient supply of market rate housing and continued government support programs that need to be considered part of the cost. In addition, construction-based programs have been considered as costly due to the considerable increase in construction costs. Allowance-based programs have not had similar per unit increases due to the relative stability of rents over time (Allen, Fitts, and Glatt 1981, 31). This stability has led to the decline in available units and as a result represents an artificial short-term saving. Rents would have to rise considerably in order for supply to increase, thereby wiping out a large portion of the cost advantage of allowances. While the results of the evaluation were not conclusive, they did provide some justification for housing allowances which became the Reagan administration's sole low cost housing initiative.

Evaluations of current Section 8 existing housing, which is similar to the housing allowance program, continue to show mixed results. The program has allowed consumers some additional mobility to improve their housing quality and has allowed them to occupy housing largely free of the stigma of public housing projects. The program works best for the elderly and small households. Major problems concern the inability of very poor large families to secure housing in the private market. When such families are of a minority group, they experience particular problems (Roske 1983, 274). A longstanding goal of this program is desegregation. By allowing participants to select their own units of housing, they are freed from the concentrating effect of housing projects. In an analysis of the Section 8 program and its effect on furthering desegregation, HUD found that it had a marginal effect in most cases. Participants who moved tended to move to areas that were only somewhat less segregated than their prior neighborhoods. Indeed, participants who felt their new areas were less segregated were balanced by those who said their new areas were more segregated (Stucker 1986, 257).

A real problem with allowances is that there is not the kind of coalition of support that exists for construction related subsidies: the well-organized housing industry and a host of related jobbers, mortgage bankers, realtors, etc. Subsidies for low cost housing construction have the advantage of a quick and visible passthrough to these industries. Perhaps as a result, the federal government has been slow to make Section 8 certificates available; some 9.7 million households are eligible for the Section 8 program but only some 800,000 households are currently assisted (Stucker 1986, 259).

Budgetary Aspects

There was governmental concern about the rising costs of the various low cost housing programs before Reagan took office. The concern was based on the fact that all such housing programs depend on establishing a multi-year funding stream. This necessitates the setting aside of budget allocations that may be outstripped by additional program costs in future years. In 1979, the Congressional Budget Office released a study that compared the per unit costs of public housing, Section 8 existing housing, and Section 8 new housing/rehabilitation programs. This study concluded that both Section 8 existing housing and public housing were considerably less expensive than the Section 8 new/rehabilitated housing program. This report, in part, fueled Reagan's policy of favoring housing allowances for existing housing (Congressional Budget Office 1979). Indeed, in 1980, 81% of all of HUD's expenditures for new units were for new or rehabilitated units under programs that tied the subsidy to the unit. In 1987, only 23% of such expenditures were for such units and the rest went for housing vouchers or Section 8 existing housing certificates (Dolbeare 1987, 8).

The report did admit that part of the cost differential between public housing and Section 8 existing housing was the low rent levels charged public housing tenants. The report then explored several scenarios that would have the effect of reducing program costs. All proposed limiting access of the poor or increasing their rental costs for this housing (Congressional Budget Office 1979). A significant expansion of the public housing program was one scenario not considered in the report. Such an expansion would improve the mix of public housing tenants and would help reduce per unit costs. This would entail a long term federal commitment to support low cost housing—something lacking in current approaches.

Low Cost Housing and the Tax Code

A major thrust of American housing policy is to encourage the investment of private funds in low cost rental housing. This is done by means of the tax code and provisions that allow for the rapid depreciation of costs as well as "recapture" provisions at the time of sale which also serve to increase investors' income by reducing their taxes. A major criticism of these provisions are their regressive aspects; they afford upper income investors significant tax relief. In addition, the low cost housing that they develop need not remain low cost beyond a given period. Critics contend that direct government assistance is both less costly in the long run and more equitable. In any case, under the 1986 Tax Reform Act, most of the incentives for investors in low income housing have been eliminated or cut back (Hartman 1975, 151; Clay 1987).

THE CURRENT SHORTFALL IN LOW COST HOUSING

All of the above programs functioned to provide a considerable number of low cost housing units. Yet many Americans live in substandard housing or continue to pay too much of their disposable income for adequate housing. This is in part due to the fact that existing subsidized units are beyond the means of a significant number of low income households. In addition, there are not enough of these units to meet current needs. While many blame the Reagan administration for the low cost housing crisis, Dolbeare (1987) suggests that the problem transcends the policies of the Reagan administration:

The root cause of most housing problems in this country is the large and growing gap between the cost of decent housing as provided by the private sector and the income which is available to pay for it. The housing policies of the Reagan administration exacerbated this problem, but they did not cause it. The underlying problem is so severe that we would have a growing housing crisis even if not one penny had been cut from the low income housing budgets since the Reagan administration took office.

Dolbeare (1987) points out that while the number of subsidized housing units doubled during the decade between 1975 and 1985—from about two million units to about four million units—this did not compensate for the impact of inflation which led to the virtual disappearance of unsubsidized affordable low income housing units.

Looking first at the situation in 1981, there were some 7.0 million units or 9.3% of the housing stock deemed seriously and/or significantly deficient. A significant proportion of those living in such units were paying too high a proportion of their available income for housing. Some 7.2 million owners and renters or 11.4% of all households paid more than half of their income for housing. Some 2.2 million owners, 85% of whom had incomes below $10,000 per year, paid more than 50% of their income for housing; half of those in substandard or overcrowded housing had incomes below $7,000 and almost 90% had incomes below $20,000.

Bleak as this situation appears, low income owners in general are better off than renters since a significant proportion have considerable equity in their homes which they own free and clear and need only pay for maintenance, taxes, utilities, and insurance costs.

Low income renters are in a much worse position since fully 63% of all substandard or overcrowded housing in 1980 was rental housing. Indeed, some three-fifths of all renters living in substandard housing had incomes below $7,000. As if this were not bad enough, they were also overcharged; in particular, 62% of the 2.7 million renter households with annual incomes below $3,000 in 1980 spent more than 60% of their income on rent. Of those who made between $3,000 and $7,000 a year, 30% spent over 60% of their income on rent. Only a small proportion of low income renters lived in housing they could afford; 86% of renter households with incomes below $3,000 paid more than 25% of their income for rent, as did 81% of those with incomes between $3,000 and $7,000 per year (Dolbeare 1987). Those with higher incomes paid proportionately less for housing. Some 90% of households with an annual income of over $25,000 paid less than 25% of their income for rent.

There is a simple reason why so many low income households spend too much of their income on rent: units that they can afford are not available on the private market. A low income household making $5,000 per year has only $104 monthly available for housing and utilities. At $7,000 per year the household can afford $146 per month, and at $10,000 it can afford $208. This amount is not sufficient to garner adequate housing on the free housing market. Looking at median rents as a percentage of median income, it is clear that low income single renters are being forced to pay an increasing proportion of their low incomes on rent, leaving less for other necessities. For single females it has now reached 45% and this is an average figure for all such renters thus obscuring those who must pay more than 45% (Hughes and Sternlieb 1987, 201).

With this limited amount of income for rent, it is not surprising that housing supply is restricted. Indeed, among those households with incomes below $5,000, there are only half as many affordable units and not all those units are available to them since many will be occupied by higher income households paying less than 25% of their income (Dolbeare 1987).

It should be pointed out that using the percentage of income approach to gauging housing affordability can be very misleading. Such standards obscure the real differences in maintenance cost for a household of one or two persons with that of a large family with children. A better concept of affordability would be one that was based on the assumption that housing costs should not be so high as to deny the household access to the basic necessities of life—the so-called "market basket" of needs. In 1985, approximately 9.9 million of the nation's 88.5 million households could not afford to pay anything for housing and still live on this modest budget. This market basket approach illustrates that many households cannot pay 25 or 30% of their income for rent even if such low cost housing were available (Dolbeare 1987).

The National League of Cities has estimated the number of households receiving housing assistance for four levels of need: poverty level, below 125% of poverty level, below 50% of median, and below 80% of median. Whichever measure is used, it is clear that only a small proportion of low income households receive federal housing assistance (Dolbeare 1985). The rest cope by utilizing the private rental sector, a sector that is poised to shrink dramatically.

THE COSTS OF SUBSIDIZED HOUSING

One of the major factors hindering the implementation of an adequate assisted housing program is cost. The cost of existing assisted housing commitments is felt to be too high. It is for this reason that the Reagan administration cut back on housing assistance and suggested that local governmental, private, and nonprofit sectors do more to provide such housing assistance (Struyk, Mayer, and Tuccillo 1983).

In 1984, some 4 million households were receiving direct federal housing rental assistance at a cost of $9.9 billion. In addition, there were some three-quarters of a million rural and small town households receiving assistance through the Farmers Home Administration. Because this agency operates its programs on a revolving loan basis, it is not possible to obtain comparable cost figures but they do not involve direct federal subsidy payments from the federal government (Dolbeare 1987). Today, programs for low income homeowners are limited to a loan and grant program and an interest subsidy program. The Farmers Home Administration has a low income repair loan and grant program.

HOUSING SUBSIDIES FOR THE MIDDLE CLASS

It is important to take a close look at all existing housing assistance programs. The experience resembles that of Alice in Wonderland—things simply are not what they appear to be: one person's assistance program is another's tax deduction. This would not be so bad if there were a proportional treatment based on income or even if there were a rough equality of treatment, but the opposite prevails. The low income housing programs cost the federal government a fraction of what it pays (in lost tax revenue) for maintaining the private middle-class housing "program." The extent of the bias against the low income households is profound.

Those who favor government provision of low cost housing are quick to point out that it is the poor who are forced to deal with the free housing market as they search for affordable rental accommodation while the middle-class homeowners need only contend with a heavily subsidized market. This subsidy is hidden in the form of federal income tax deductions on mortgage interest on first and second homes. This tax deduction results in a housing subsidy for the middle classes that is five times as large as all federal housing assistance programs.

Most Americans would reject the notion of these deductions as being synonymous with a housing assistance or subsidy program. To some extent this has to do with the fact that the subsidy is packaged in the form of tax relief to homeowners rather than a direct housing grant. But it is also true that one's position often colors one's vision; the middle classes have a vested interest in denying that their tax benefits amount to a federal housing subsidy. Yet there appears to be an increasing willingness by the federal government to recognize this reality. The Congressional Budget Act of 1974 requires a listing of "tax expenditures" in the budget. Tax expenditures are defined as "revenue losses attributable to provisions of the federal tax laws which allow a special exclusion exemption or deduction from gross income or which provide a special credit, a preferential rate of tax, or a deferral of liability." Notes Dolbeare: "Their operation . . . is comparable to outlay programs, such as milk supports and *rent subsidies* that also provide a subsidy to particular activities. For this reason the expression tax subsidies and tax expenditures are often used synonymously" (Dolbeare 1983). As a result of this shifting attitude, the mortgage interest deductions were subject to a good deal of scrutiny in the drafting of the 1986 Tax Reform Act. Although deductions for first and second homes were left intact, there was a growing recognition on the part of congressional lawmakers that these deductions will need to be restricted further (Hartman 1975).

These tax expenditures are considerable; in 1984, the cost of housing-related tax expenditures was estimated by the Congressional Joint Committee on Taxation at $43,775 trillion. There is no current information about the number of individuals receiving these benefits. Of this total by far the largest share is for mortgage interest. Some 90% of all tax expenditures are accounted for by the mortgage interest tax deduction by owners of first and second homes and the deferral or exemption from capital gains on home sales (Dolbeare 1985).

It is also useful to compare total expenditures for homeownership with that of a low cost housing program. Homeowner housing tax expenditures are rising at a much faster rate than the cost of all low cost federal housing assistance as can be seen in Figure 4.1. This fact is not due to a policy decision so much as the inflation in real estate values, mortgage interest rates, and the number of mortgaged homes which has increased the value

Figure 4.1

Homeowner Deductions and Assisted Housing Payments

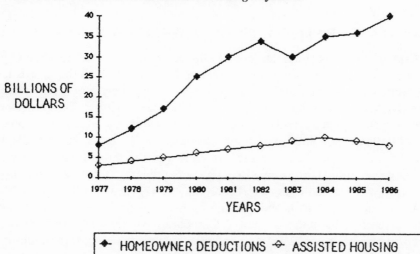

Source: Dolbeare 1985, 35.

of the homeowner deductions. The tax code encourages such borrowing. Indeed, there are periods when real interest rates were negative after accounting for inflation and tax deductions. Not surprisingly, upper income people receive a disproportional share of total housing expenditures counting both direct and tax code based sources. Those making over $30,000 received nearly 68% of the total benefits. In addition, the proportion of those receiving benefits rises by income. Some four-fifths of those making over $50,000 receive housing subsidies while just one fifth of those making under $10,000 receive such subsidies. The average monthly amount also rises by income with those making over $50,000 receiving some $155 per month while those making below $10,000 receive only $22 per month (Dolbeare 1985).

Dolbeare (1983) has pointed out that the mortgage deduction for homeowners was codified in 1913 when the national income tax was first established and income was defined so as to exclude all interest payments. Initially with low homeownership and no long-term mortgages, the impact of this provision was slight. She suggests therefore, that there was and is no policy basis to this deduction. While this was certainly true at the outset, her contention ignores the postwar federal encouragement of homeownership that stressed the deductibility of mortgage interest. The continued protection accorded this tax provision in the 1986 Tax Reform Act is due to the fact that it is seen as a spur to housing demand and a necessary part of a "private" housing market system which is seen as a crucial component of the overall economy.

THE ACCELERATING LOSS OF LOW COST HOUSING

Due to the combined effects of the tax code and federal housing programs, there is a massive imbalance in housing benefits that needs to be addressed. Worrisome as this imbalance is, there are even more immediate problems that flow from this imbalance. Specifically, a number of analysts predicted a real decline in the number of available low income rental units in the 1980s and an increase in need. Today, it appears clear that this shortage is a real one and has led to much of the homelessness we are experiencing. Unfortunately, there are reasons to believe that this situation will worsen in the short run (Clay 1987; Downs 1983).

The major problem is that private rental housing is becoming a less attractive investment in his country. Compared to other means of securing a return on investment capital, it appears that rental housing, particularly low cost private rental housing, is becoming increasingly unattractive. This is due to the interplay between government tax and development policies, and the housing market. Simply put, as a result of squeezed profits on the one hand and rent controls and other government restrictions on the other, the supply of rental housing is dwindling (Dolbeare 1983; Clay 1987; Downs 1983).

Several sources suggest that the shortage of rental housing will be severe. One study, for the Neighborhood Reinvestment Corporation, puts the gap between the total low cost housing supply (subsidized and unsubsidized) and households needing such housing at 7.8 million by the year 2003. This is because between 1983 and 2003 the low cost housing stock is projected to fall from 12.9 million units to 9.4 million units—a loss of 27%. In this same period, those needing such housing is expected to increase from 11.9 million to 17.2 million—an increase of 44% (Clay 1987).

A significant portion of this lost housing may be traceable to expiring federal contracts and use restrictions on 1.9 million federally subsidized private low income rental units. Estimates are that 900,000 units could be conventionally refinanced and leave the low cost housing stock by 1995. Other reasons for the loss of low cost housing are the Reagan administration's policy of demolishing or selling some public housing or transferring it to nongovernmental control where it may eventually revert to market rate housing (Clay 1987; President's Commission on Housing 1982).

The Tax Reform Act of 1986 has reduced the incentives for private low cost housing investment by reducing the tax benefits of such investments. In addition, rents have not increased sufficiently so as to enable landlords to recover additional costs. Rents have been stable largely due to the loss of higher income renters to homeownership. The increased prevalence of local rent control ordinances has also had a stabilizing impact on rents. As a result, the pool of renters has become predominantly lower income, occasioning a lessened interest in such housing from investors. Continued production and rehabilitation of low cost rental units must therefore come from local government or nonprofit sources.

However, losses to the stock of low cost housing have accrued quite apart from any possible future impacts from expiring use restrictions and subsidies and this loss has been profound. In 1970, there was an excess of low cost units over low income households. By 1980, the situation had reversed and there was a severe shortage of low cost units as compared with needy households. The picture for those making below $10,000 is not quite as bad as for the very low income household, yet here too the gap is wide and growing. While low income households declined, available low cost units declined much faster. The gap in 1983 was 1.5 million:

11.9 million such households and 10.4 million units renting for $250 per month or less (Dolbeare 1987, 5). Millions of such units have been lost, swamping the modest expansion of subsidized low cost units. Needless to say, these aggregate figures obscure the fact that the situation is much worse in some areas than in others. Nor does it address questions of unit size, quality, or availability.

The result is that the government must decide whether it wants to reintroduce sufficient financial incentives to attract private investment back into rental housing and accept the regressive aspect to such an approach, or whether to step in and provide public housing as was done in Great Britain in the postwar era. Many housing advocates again favor policies aimed at producing permanent public or nonprofit-sponsored low cost housing and have become leery of reliance on the private sector since this approach results in expensive short-term programs. In any case, increased federal involvement and expenditure will be required to meet the growing shortage of low cost housing.

THE REAGAN HOUSING POLICY

Federal housing policy under Reagan is not difficult to discern; indeed it is an elaboration of the privatized ethic that has always characterized our housing policy. It is based on support of the free market in housing and the shifting of federal low cost housing commitments to the states and localities. These general themes were sounded in President Reagan's 1981 housing commission report which stated: ". . . the genius of the market economy, freed of the distortions forced by government housing policies and regulations that swung erratically from loving to hostile, can provide for housing far better than the federal programs" (President's Commission on Housing 1982, xvii). In attempting to locate a quotation from the president that characterized his concern for housing, the best the Commission could do was the following: "I believe that our citizens should have a real *opportunity* to live in decent, affordable housing. I pledge to foster good housing for all Americans *through sound economic policies*" (emphasis added) (President's Commission on Housing 1982, xv). Clearly, Reagan does not favor housing programs that provide direct housing assistance and prefers to leave housing to the free housing market which provides low cost housing via the filtering process.

While the needs of low income households were acknowledged, a housing voucher approach was considered preferable to the construction of public housing or a subsidy approach. The Commission's operating principles best sum up the administration's approach; these principles held that national policy must:

—achieve fiscal responsibility and monetary responsibility in the economy;

—encourage free and deregulated housing markets;

—rely on the private sector;

—promote an enlightened federalism with minimal governmental intervention;

—recognize a continuing role of government to address the housing needs of the poor;

—direct programs towards people rather than towards structures; and

—assure maximum freedom of housing choice (President's Commission on Housing 1982, xviii).

In its discussion on low cost housing, the Commission stated that

the primary national need is not for massive production of new apartments for the poor, but for income supplements that will enable low-income families to live in available, decent housing at a cost they can afford. The purpose of federal housing programs should be to help people, not build projects (President's Commission on Housing 1982, xxii).

Interestingly, the President's Commission recognized the limitations of the housing allowance approach:

[S]uch a program may not be sufficient in places where there is a serious shortage of adequate rental units . . . and . . . allowances are less likely to help people now living in seriously substandard housing. Landlords simply do not find the payments great enough to justify major rehabilitation, and the residents of such units are more likely to drop out of the program than undertake the mess and expense of moving (President's Commission on Housing 1982, xxiii).

The limits of federal responsibility for housing the poor were also clearly stated: "Housing payments are not meant to be an entitlement program; the nation cannot afford yet another system of entitlements expanding endlessly out of effective control" (President's Commission on Housing 1982, xxiii).

A notable proposal of the Commission concerned the suggested federal retreat from responsibility for public housing. The Commission outlined a series of options that expressed this new approach; among these were to sell the project or convert it to homeownership, to deprogram the project by selling or demolishing it, or to free up its rents.

The Commission was concerned about the decreasing attractiveness of private investment in rental housing. The Commission felt that the best way to stimulate the production of private rental housing was to extend and expand tax incentives for low cost housing producers and to fight rent control ordinances vigorously.

The Commission was strongly against all land use regulations that might exert an upward pressure on prices or individual access to low housing opportunities. Accordingly, they argued against both environmental zoning and growth controls as well as all exclusionary or large lot zoning.

Their general approach was one of deregulation and private housing market incentives. Indeed, this report, unlike its two better known predecessors, did not set a target for housing production but preferred to leave output in the hands of the local private housing market.

PAST AND CURRENT SPENDING PATTERNS

Recent spending for low cost housing can be characterized very simply: it was cut in every year of the Reagan administration and the last budget request was no exception despite the well-publicized plight of the homeless. Table 4.1 shows the units provided and the declining pattern of federal spending. To put these costs in perspective, they constitute 1% of the federal budget. As a point of comparison, all federal low cost housing costs to date do not exceed the amount of housing-related tax expenditures afforded to homeowners for 1985 and 1986 (Dolbeare 1987, 7).

The Reagan administration followed through on these policy themes by

Table 4.1
Units Provided and Federal Spending for Housing, 1980–88

Year	Units (thousands)			Federal Spending (billions)		
	HUD	FMHA	All	BA[1]	Outlays	Tax Exps
1980	251	110	363	$26.7	$ 4.5	$26.5
1981	217	104	321	30.2	5.7	33.3
1982	36	95	131	17.7	6.7	36.6
1983	-5	82	77	8.7	7.8	35.4
1984	75	77	152	9.9	8.8	37.9
1985	89	73	162	10.8	10.0	40.6
1986	83	54	137	9.7	10.0	48.5
1987	69	86	155	7.3	9.5	42.6
1988	82	20	102	3.8	10.1	39.8

[1]By allocation.
Source: Dolbeare 1987, 7.

continuing to propose cuts in housing programs with the exception of housing vouchers which will receive a modest increase of 108,000 units. Public housing operating subsidies would be cut from $1.5 billion (FY 88) to $1.45 billion in FY 89 while funds for modernization would be cut from $1.7 billion (FY 88) to $1 billion in FY 89. The budget also proposes a cut in the rental rehabilitation program from $200 million in FY 88 to $150 million in FY 89. The administration plans to seek legislation to deny such funding to communities with rent controls. The administration requested no funding for Housing Development Grants (HODAG), Urban Development Action Grants (UDAG), Section 312 Rehabilitation Loans, Section 235 Homeowner Assistance, Section 8 Moderate Rehabilitation, and Section 8 Existing Certificates. Finally, the Community Development Block Grant Program under which localities may fund low cost housing has been reduced from $2.88 billion (FY 88) to $2.6 billion (FY 89) (United States Conference of Mayors 1988).

Discussion

The debate between those who favor an allowances approach and those who favor a construction subsidy approach will continue unabated since there is a mix of policy benefits that flow from each approach. In addition, national and local political realities skew this bundle of costs and benefits so that it becomes impossible to suggest that any one approach is clearly best in all instances. As a result, many analysts argue in favor of mixed approaches that allow housing officials to tailor their programs to a given situation while accentuating particular housing policy goals. Thus, what is needed is greater federal funding for public housing, as well as additional housing allowances (National Housing Task Force 1988).

CURRENT HOUSING POLICY INITIATIVES

One of the more recent reports on national housing policy has been produced by the National Housing Task Force and is entitled "A Decent Place to Live" (1988). In this report, the lack of adequate affordable housing is examined by members of a panel drawn from business, banking, home builders, community service, and state and local government. A motivating force behind the development of this report was the increased incidence of homelessness. The report takes as its operating premise that in terms of offering affordable housing, "we have not only fallen short, but we are losing ground." The panel calls for a true national program based on the efforts of all parties in the housing production process: the private and nonprofit sectors as well as all levels of government, especially the federal level which the panel faults for not doing enough in recent years. The report suggests that a Housing Opportunity Program be established. This program is designed to foster and stimulate state and local initiatives to develop and renovate and conserve low cost housing. The suggested first year federal appropriation would be $3 billion with a target of some 150,000 to 200,000 affordable housing units. Federal funds would have to be matched to some degree by the states. The program places maximum stress on local approaches to creating affordable housing. The federal level is seen more as a silent financial partner. The suggested program is to be completed by the year 2000 (National Housing Task Force 1988). Some aspects of this program may emerge from the current deliberations on future housing policy that are being held by Senators Cranston and D'Amato of the Senate Banking, Housing, and Urban Affairs Committee (1988).

While this program is clearly a step in the right direction, there may be some major problems in its overall conception. Specifically, there is little mention of where to provide low cost housing opportunities and what is mentioned is unclear. At one point, the report calls for providing such housing "where the need is greatest" which can be interpreted to mean in the old inner cities. This clearly implies a "fix up the ghetto" approach. While later there is a discussion of the need to strengthen the reinforcement of fair housing laws so as to ensure that "[r]ental assistance can be used to enable families to remain in improving neighborhoods and to assist them in finding housing outside areas of low income concentration." In addition, the report called for "the removal of land use barriers" (National Housing Task Force 1988, 54). In terms of remedy, it suggests that "state action be taken" and, failing that, that federal funds be awarded directly to nonprofit or local developers who will provide such housing (National Housing Task Force 1988, 54).

This approach, if adopted, constitutes a new concept for low cost housing delivery. Unfortunately, it is dependent on a host of local actors who may be working at cross purposes. The problem here is that the report is advocating another decentralized nongovernmental approach to what should be a governmental responsibility. The potential for dysfunction appears immense. One must recall Lowi's admonition to keep programs simple. This policy approach is anything but simple (Lowi 1969).

SUMMARY

Low cost housing production has evolved from an initial free market orientation to a much more complex mix of private and government involvement. Government involvement started with the direct production of public housing at the federal level which evolved into construction subsidy programs. Apart from the promulgation of fairly broad programmatic guidelines, these programs were never highly centralized; instead, they were subject to maximum local control. More recently, policy has evolved further into an even more decentralized approach stressing the subsidy of households in the private market. Unfortunately, this approach to housing policy has not worked for the poor in our society. M. Stone (1973) argues that the whole financial apparatus that controls the lending of mortgages for owner-occupied housing constitutes a major locus of capitalist power and authority capable of deflecting housing policy away from the needs of the poor. Looking at the data on affordability, it is clear that there is a housing crisis for the poor. What is less clear is how this crisis should be met.

Current approaches stress simply increasing federal funding for the system as it exists (Committee on Banking, Housing and Urban Affairs 1987). Housing advocates support increased spending but only in conjunction with a new national fair share public housing program that would ensure the existence of adequate low cost housing (O'Connor and Shaffer 1988). This program would operate in conjunction with the prevailing private housing industry as well as nonprofit housing sponsors. The public housing program would stand as a basic statement of the government's intention to be the houser of last resort and that this housing would be permanent rather than tied to time-limited subsidies. Such a program, if coupled with a national jobs program, could supply options for geographic and economic mobility for those who have been bottled up in urban ghettos. This should not be interpreted as a suggestion that advocates of such a housing policy would seek to disperse the urban poor, but that opportunities for mobility should be enhanced so that free choice can be exercised. In a country where a "jobs to the people" strategy has been rejected, the poor will need to be able to locate in those areas where jobs exist. A central component of this approach could well be a pro-active fair share national public housing program.

There are many possible approaches to establishing such an inclusionary housing policy. The next chapter will examine one suggested policy which calls for local attempts to expand the supply of affordable housing.

Part III

POLICY INITIATIVES
TO PRODUCE
LOW COST HOUSING

5

Low Cost Housing Initiatives

Homelessness has gripped most of our older urban areas and is straining the cities' capacity to respond effectively. The problems of sheltering and feeding the homeless mount daily. Writers of articles in various local papers have begun to blame local officials for creating the problem citing their largess in providing services; rebuttals to the charges printed in letters to the editor take on a defensive tone. Clearly, the strain is beginning to show.

Overcrowding and poor service standards are routinely reported in various city run shelters and other temporary accommodations for the homeless. It is the making of a local tragedy, one that is repeated in numerous urban and rural locations throughout the nation. Before we can analyze the web of policy decisions that produced this growing problem, it is necessary to take a close look at the efforts that have been made at the local level to forestall homelessness. One of the major thrusts over the last few years has been local efforts to encourage the production of low cost, affordable housing.

AFFORDABLE HOUSING

An adequate housing policy is one that functions well for all income groups in the society. It has been suggested that the American housing production process has been remarkably successful both in the total numbers and in the range of housing types produced. Increased floor space per individual and increased amenities are hallmarks of the current free market system (Hughes and Sternlieb 1987). Yet within this overall context we also see the specter of dysfunction in the form of outright homelessness. The problems of housing affordability did not arise with the advent of widespread homelessness. This issue was under intense discussion throughout the 1970s as home prices and mortgage rates rose precipitously, putting homeownership beyond the reach of many working Americans. Local housing officials and the American home builders lobby were gravely concerned about this development. Numerous local and national forums and conventions were called in order to grapple with this issue. These efforts resulted in an array of local measures designed to reduce the cost of new housing.

Simultaneously, community organizations representing the interests of low income homeowners and renters became concerned about the negative effects of increased borrowing costs, displacement, and housing abandonment among other issues. They, too, saw the housing situation worsen for their constituency. As a result, they also developed an array of local measures for low income communities to protect and maintain the stock of low cost housing. Thus, it is worthwhile to examine the issue of affordable housing in order to see why this effort has not helped forestall the rise of homelessness in the 1980s.

Affordable housing has achieved popularity among local housing officials as a shorthand expression encompassing those local policies and programs involving regulatory changes that can reduce the cost of new and renovated housing. Local low cost housing policy centers on finding the means to protect and expand existing stocks of low cost accommodation. Both local policy initiatives are aimed at increasing the availability of low and moderate cost housing. The first part of this chapter will review low cost/affordable housing policies developed at the local level. An assessment of the effectiveness of these policies concludes the chapter.

There are a number of vehicles for reducing the cost of delivered housing and protecting existing low cost housing stocks. They can be grouped under four categories:

1. *Innovative forms of tenure:* limited equity cooperatives, housing associations, shared housing, accessory apartments, reverse/shared equity mortgages, urban land trusts, squatting, land banking, homesteading, owner-built housing;

2. *Modified housing development regulations and techniques:* liberalized building codes, liberalized zoning regulations, density bonuses, negotiated investment strategies, replacement housing laws, code enforcement, industrialized housing;

3. *Local housing market restrictions:* tax circuit breakers, anti-speculator laws, condo conversion regulations, rent control, housing advocacy;

4. *Financial supports:* nonprofit housing corporations, public/private partnerships, governmental financial programs, private financial programs, Community Reinvestment efforts, local mortgage plans, local tax abatement, neighborhood preservation programs.

INNOVATIVE FORMS OF TENURE

Limited Equity Cooperative Housing

Cooperative housing has never been a major force in the American housing market. This is a function of the success of the private market in meeting the needs of the majority of the middle-class home buyers most of whom prefer single family accommodation. Cooperatives are best suited for multiple occupant operations. In this context, limited equity cooperatives have the potential for delivering low cost housing since they can be operated on a nonprofit basis. In limited equity cooperatives, buyers purchase a share in the cooperative which entitles them to live in a unit. Mortgage interest and other expenses are deductible as in a homeownership situation. Shareholders become voting members of the cooperative which oversees the operation and maintenance of the building. Rents are set so as to cover the construction/purchase cost, maintenance, and financing costs. This ensures that rents are kept lower than prevailing rents in for-profit buildings. Rents rise only when it is necessary to recapture increased expenses for the operation of the building. Share appreciation is usually limited by prior agreement and made part of the contract occupants sign at the time of share purchase. Many cooperatives, particularly those found in the upscale New York City market, are stock cooperatives where the market determines the share price. In Europe, limited equity cooperatives are more frequently utilized as a means of ensuring the continued presence of low and moderate cost accommodation in appreciating housing markets. The use of co-ops to house the homeless has been tried in New York City on a very limited basis. Clearly, this is a form of housing tenure that needs greater exposure (Hartman, Keating, and LeGates 1982; McFadden 1988).

Reverse Equity Housing

Reverse equity housing is a new form of housing tenure that adds flexibility to the housing delivery system. Initially it was a European concept that grew out of attempts by affluent households to buy into tight housing markets. Reverse equity housing is based on the continued occupation of a house by its original owner after it is sold. Moreover, the buyers agree to pay the seller a monthly figure that draws down the final sales price of the house. In short, the seller is able to live off the equity that the home has built up over the years. Clearly, such arrangements are limited to the elderly who are more likely to have a sizable equity share in their property. Nonetheless, these arrangements result in a lowering of housing costs for the elderly who are often living on diminished incomes. If the property in question is large enough, the new buyer may occupy a portion of it. Since many transactions may involve the buyer's willingness to postpone full occupation of the property for an indeterminate length of time, this approach is of severely limited application in most housing markets. A related problem concerns the restrictions placed on joint occupation of single family homes in many jurisdictions. The original owners must also exercise care to safeguard their rights in such instances as when the new owners default on their mortgage payments. Variations of this approach, such as shared equity mortgages and graduated payment mortgages, have also been suggested but have limited application as investments to most traditional sources of housing funds (Hartman, Keating, and LeGates 1982).

Accessory Apartments

Accessory apartments are those separate housing units that are added to older single family housing units. This is often done to allow older relatives to reside with their children. It also provides added rental income which allows the owner to cover operating and maintenance expenses on a larger home.

Accessory apartments are self-contained although at times they share an entrance with the primary residence. Such units often constitute the only low cost accommodation that can be created in already built-up suburban single family districts. The fact that they are units within an existing single family home acts to keep rents low in contrast to purpose-built housing. The main problem with accessory apartments is that many are created in defiance of local zoning codes which prohibit them in single family districts. Those that are created illegally can be of dubious quality and can adversely affect prevailing market values. Advocates of this form of housing suggest their inclusion in the relevant housing codes so that they can be regulated. A crucial regulation would be one requiring the modified building to be owner-occupied. This and related regulations would ensure that high quality units are created that conform to the local building, fire, and safety codes and thereby add value to the property and the district. A sensitive program can ensure that suburban areas can accommodate a greater diversity of households with differing housing needs and thereby add to the stock of affordable housing (Harkins 1987).

Shared Housing

Shared housing represents a novel approach to lowering the cost of housing for those individuals willing to share ownership of their dwelling with others. It differs from other housing forms in that there is some sharing of facilities such as the kitchen or perhaps the living room. This approach has been successfully utilized in California and other areas. It represents a means of increasing the rate of occupation of large homes after most of the primary family members have left to form their own households. It is often aimed at senior citizens who might benefit from the companionship and mutual support that shared housing offers. Since there is a shared equity situation between unrelated individuals, there is little likelihood that conventional loans could be available for such a purchase. Those homeowners with sufficient equity in an existing property could simply purchase their share for cash yet there would still be the problem of finding a buyer for an individual share. Thus, some shared housing programs involve the purchase of a share in the cooperative that owns the house as in a multiple unit cooperative. Low income individuals would have to work with a governmental housing finance agency in order to secure financing. New Jersey is currently planning such an effort on an experimental basis. Mortgage interest and other fees are deductible as in a homeownership situation. The major obstacle preventing widespread application of this approach is the lack of confidence of the traditional housing finance system in the market demand for shared housing. The resistance of local zoning authorities to the notion of a single family house being shared by unrelated individuals is also considerable (Friedman 1983).

Community Land Trusts

Community land trusts represent a dynamic new approach to ensuring that low cost housing, once it is developed, remains low cost for future generations—a factor lacking in all other forms of low cost housing including public housing. They are quite similar to limited equity cooperatives in many respects. Essentially, community land trust housing allows the homeowners to partake of the tax benefits of homeownership, but it restricts their ability to profit from the appreciation of the property over time.

Low cost owner-occupied housing that is located in an appreciating area often appreciates to the point where it is out of reach of low income purchasers. Where there is an initial subsidy that allows the first owner to purchase the property, its ultimate effect is to increase the profit margin of this individual when the property is sold at prevailing rates.

Land trusts represent a novel approach to controlling the profit made on private market housing. Prospective home buyers purchase a housing unit but not the land upon which it sits. The land is owned in common by the land trust which leases it to the homeowner. In most instances, through deed restrictions, the home buyer must agree to sell his home back to the land trust for his initial investment and an agreed upon increment to cover inflation. The trust will then resell the property to another low income family. Since the trust owns the land, it has a legal interest in the property which can be maintained. The concept allows for considerable flexibility since it can be adapted to single family, shared, and cooperative multiple family housing situations. While this approach appears promising for maintaining low income housing in existing neighborhoods which face the prospect of significant local housing market appreciation, it is limited by the need to negotiate complex individual agreements with each prospective home buyer. Another problem is the hesitancy of traditional lenders to support initial land purchases by the trust, although there is some evidence that this attitude is changing. Community land trusts appear to be a promising vehicle for communities that wish to ensure the future availability of low cost housing. Pilot programs have begun in Camden, New Jersey, and in Cincinnati, Ohio (Hartman, Keating, and LeGates 1982).

Housing Associations

Housing associations operate low cost housing in many of our older urban areas. Their long history reaches back to the social work movement that accompanied the rise of the great industrial cities. Many of these programs included housing counseling with "friendly visitors" assisting the poor by inculcating homemaking skills and values. Many, such as the Octavia Hill Housing Association in Philadelphia, continue to serve the poor to this day. Essentially these associations operate by buying low cost accommodations and renting to the poor at low rents based on their income. If some of this housing appreciates, they respond to the housing market by renting such units that become vacant at prevailing rents to newcomers who thereby subsidize the poor tenants and additional property acquisitions. Housing associations are successful in their mission but have had a limited impact due to the high operating costs of such a program. They are dependent on the charitable instincts of community-minded individuals who support and operate these programs. In Philadelphia, housing associations control fewer than 1,000 units (A. Davis 1967; Keyes 1973).

Squatting

Urban squatting creates the most basic low cost housing. Such housing is not the result of a program in any official sense; rather, it consists of the occupation, rehabilitation, and, in some cases, eventual acquisition of property that has been abandoned for a long period of time. Most of these units are found in the poorest of inner city areas. It is a very controversial form of tenure as it may consist of the occupation of what is still legally another person's house. In fact, most squatting takes place in tax fore-closed property that is owned by governmental agencies (Kearns 1980).

Squatting can take several forms. Most squatting is disorganized and occurs when homeless individuals simply seek out and occupy an abandoned dwelling. Many urban localities have a sizable stock of abandoned units scattered throughout their jurisdiction that are often utilized by squatters. There is no way to get an accurate count of the number of such individuals. Organized squatting has occurred as a form of protest over government housing programs that fail to rehabilitate abandoned units. Many of the older cities have experienced such protests. In some cases, these protests have resulted in squatter programs sponsored by local community organizations dedicated to the long-term rehabilitation of such properties. Costs can be kept low by a cooperative method of purchasing building materials and the sharing of labor resources. In some cases, there is a highly organized effort to screen applicants for the program, secure training and support personnel, and to oversee the long-term administration of the program. Some organizations claim considerable success with this approach. In most cases, the total number of properties involved is very small. Surveys of two American cities show about 100 properties occupied as part of organized squatting programs. Interestingly, a majority of the households in the organized programs are female-headed (M. H. Lang 1985b). There have been no longitudinal surveys conducted to determine the long-term success of this form of housing. Such surveys would allow an assessment of the potential of this concept for producing low cost accommodation for the very poor.

Squatting is a powerful element in the housing production process in many countries. Such squatting consists of the rapid construction of shacks on the urban periphery by the occupants. While peripheral squatting is concentrated in the Third World, in Europe there are many examples of urban squatting (Bailey 1973; Waites and Wolmar 1980). Some European local governments work cooperatively with urban squatter organizations, routinely making vacant units available to them. In the United States, local governments have exhibited considerable hostility toward the concept of squatting. In a few instances, they have agreed to convey a limited number of abandoned housing units to squatter programs only after extensive local protests. As a result, the potential of this vehicle for rehabilitating housing in poor areas has yet to be tested in this country.

Many authorities feel that squatting should be seen only as a social movement or protest phenomenon designed to force government to provide decent housing for its citizens. While it may also serve the function of providing emergency short-term shelter, these authorities consider it regressive to accord squatting a place in any housing production system (Ward 1982).

Land Banking

Land banking is practiced extensively in Europe as a means of controlling the private land use development process so as to maximize the public benefit. The effect of land banking is to make the municipality a developer of sorts since open land is purchased by the municipality and held for long-term appreciation. Some of the land will later be sold at a profit to private developers. A sizable portion is leased to local farmers for agricultural purposes, ensuring a green belt in proximity to the urbanizing areas. Some land may be held indefinitely as open space or environmental areas. Since the municipality owns the land, it can ensure that the development process includes provision of housing for low and moderate income households either by making this a requirement when the land is sold or, more directly, by constructing public housing. Since the land was purchased at predevelopment prices, land banking avoids the frequently encountered problem of escalating land costs that often make suburban public housing prohibitively expensive. Land banking offers a means of ensuring the orderly and balanced development of land that the private market alone cannot deliver, particularly in the context of the weak planning controls that prevail in this country. For example, in Fairfax County, Virginia, a land banking program was specifically established to secure land for low and moderate income housing. While there are many examples of its application here in the United States, there are also many barriers to its speedy utilization as a vehicle for developing affordable housing. Most of these barriers concern raising the sizable up front costs associated with such a program and the lack of government authority to preempt private market sales in some instances. In Europe, the central or regional government provides the bulk of the monetary support (Strong 1979).

Owner-Built Housing

The self-help movement of the 1970s spawned a great deal of interest in the concept of owner-built housing. The impetus came from a series of books by J. F. C. Turner. He points out the high unit output potential of the self-built house so ubiquitous in Third World cities. These houses are built often overnight by squatters who are usually rural migrants. They are constructed of scrap wood, metal sheets, and whatever materials are at hand. Their virtues are the rapid production of minimal shelter at very low cost. Additions and modifications can be added as householder income rises. The advantages of this form of deregulated housing production process have occasioned much positive comment in the literature and several derivative experimental housing developments sponsored by the United States Agency for International Development.

On the other hand, critics point out that the self-build approach serves to relieve the government of its responsibility to provide basic services to the population. Turner has run into additional difficulties when he suggested the adaptation of these approaches to industrialized western societies. For instance, government regulations regarding minimum housing standards make self-built housing illegal in most parts of this country; building by licensed professionals is required by law in almost all urbanized areas. In addition, most people do not possess the skills needed to construct "up to code" housing. As a result, most authorities predict that a radical deregulation of the home building process for owner-occupants would lead to a decline in housing standards and the production of too few units to justify the inherent safety risk. At the same time, Turner is correct in suggesting that the organized self-help approach can be best utilized in the rehabilitation of existing housing so as to keep down overall costs. Indeed, the closest example of the Third World-style owner-built housing in the United States can be found in the limited instances of urban squatting and housing rehabilitation (Turner 1976; Turner and Fichter 1977; Ward 1982; Burns 1987).

Homesteading

Not so long ago, urban homesteading was heralded as the savior of older cities. By giving poor people title to empty boarded up properties, homesteading would provide a means for salvaging the vast number of these properties that dot the urban landscape. This program was first started in Baltimore and soon spread to most other older urban areas by the mid-1970s. The program was also heralded as a way to allow the poor to achieve homeownership while helping the city financially when property tax payments again could be collected. It appeared to be the true zero sum game in which everybody would win.

Homesteading involves the transfer of title of tax delinquent and foreclosed properties to an appropriate housing agency. The agency would then select from a list of applicants, usually by a lottery system. The applicant then takes possession by means of a minimal payment, often as little as one dollar. The new owner has to agree to fix the property up to housing code standards within a set period of time. There is also a stipulation that the owner would occupy the property for a set number of years before selling it.

However, the program has achieved only spotty results. It is still perceived as having been successful in Baltimore, but not in most other areas where administrative problems led to low output. Homesteading has been most successful when it allowed the middle classes access to cheap properties in areas experiencing the early stages of urban revitalization such as those near to the central business district. Problems with the program can be summarized as being due to the character of urban housing submarkets. Specifically, the fact that those homes available for homesteading are scattered throughout the city's poorer areas makes it difficult to match properties with interested and capable homesteaders. It also increases the difficulty of providing needed technical assistance and counseling services. The tremendous variance in the physical condition of these homes and the lack of skills on the part of many poor applicants make the reality of homestead-style homeownership less appealing than the initial concept had implied. The costs of rehabilitating an abandoned building, coupled with the difficulties of putting together both a financial and a rehabilitation plan, were sufficient to disqualify most truly poor individuals. More important, homesteading has not filled the need of homeowners to be able to trade up to better housing in the future, one of the most important functions of free market housing. Specifically, money spent in rehabilitating an abandoned home in a poor inner city neighborhood cannot be easily recouped by selling the property because its price would be depressed by its location in an area of prevailing housing decay.

Thus, homesteading works only for those who intend to reside permanently in the area. Overall, while there have been success stories, their impact has been dwarfed by the mounting number of units abandoned each year. Homesteading has also been criticized as constituting a governmental bargain basement low income housing policy that places too much responsibility on the shoulders of the occupants (Ward 1982).

MODIFIED HOUSING REGULATIONS AND TECHNIQUES

Code Enforcement

This is a traditional housing preservation technique utilized in many low income areas. The approach is based on a targeted housing inspection program aimed at bringing nonconforming buildings up to code. Fire, safety, and general housing improvement issues are included. A crucial component to an effective program is a companion loan and grant program to assist low income homeowners in financing improvements. Without such support, code enforcement can lead to further housing abandonment since many owners will simply opt out if they cannot afford the cost of rehabilitation. Such programs often achieve spotty results due to the hesitancy of lower income households to take on a loan commitment. The grant portion of the program is usually quite small and aimed only at outside cosmetic improvements rather than substantial rehabilitation (Hartman, Keating, and LeGates 1982; Levi 1973; Teitz and Rosenthal 1973).

Density Bonuses; Transfer of Development Rights; Negotiated Investment Strategies

The negotiated investment approach to developing low cost housing has been successfully pursued in Boston, New York, and other strong housing and commercial development markets. The approach is based on local planning and housing officials negotiating with private developers who wish to develop offices or other commercial ventures. Local zoning regulations often constrain the maximum utilization of a particular site, leading the developer to apply for a zoning variance to exceed the height and bulk limitations currently on the site. At this point, local housing officials may approach the developers with the suggestion that they consider adding a low cost housing component to their plan in return for a more flexible ruling on their application to exceed the zoning limitations. Such bargaining has led to the production of significant amounts of low cost housing in the tight housing markets in some central cities. The case-by-case bargaining relationship means that results depend on the skill of the negotiators and the demand for the site—which is a function of the availability of alternative development sites. As a result, this approach can have only limited application in weak markets.

Transfer of development rights (TDR) is a more regulated variant of the negotiated investment approach. It is an approach often utilized to protect a low density area from redevelopment at a higher density. TDR entails the purchase of the difference in value between the existing low density use and the allowable density under the existing zoning code. This difference in development density can then be applied by the purchaser to another property in order to increase the density of the project. A low and moderate income housing component can be included in a TDR program by further increasing allowable densities in return for the production of low cost housing. Again, this approach has been most successful in cities with a strong housing/commercial demand. It has been much less successful in suburban areas due to low demand for development rights and the inability of local authorities to ensure a ready market for sellers of development rights.

Liberalized Housing and Building Regulations

Local measures for lowering the cost of housing are limited. It is a basic fact of the housing delivery system that fixed costs ensure that even basic housing is not true low cost housing. Land acquisition, financing costs, zoning and building code requirements, etc., all tend to increase total costs. However, some savings can be achieved by increasing the flexibility of local building regulations. One approach has been to update local building and safety codes with an eye toward effecting cost savings. The most obvious approach is to allow for the development of multiple unit buildings, town houses, and cluster developments. The cost savings inherent in these designs found considerable favor in the 1970s in many suburban jurisdictions. Nonetheless, the finished product remained clearly in the middle income range. Further cost savings have been obtained by zoning modifications that allowed smaller lots and reduced developer-provided amenities such as sidewalks. In some instances, building codes have been relaxed so as to allow more prefabricated materials such as zero clearance fireplaces and chimneys, plastic water and sewer lines, prefabricated trusses, etc. (New Jersey Department of Community Affairs 1982).

Industrialized Housing

For many years, industrialized housing techniques were touted as the way to reduce the cost of housing by applying modern factory floor methods to the housing production process that was, and still is, a piece-meal production process. Beginning with HUD's Operation Breakthrough in the 1960s, there have been periodic attempts to capitalize on the cost savings potential of this approach. The idea was to adapt automated production processes to the building trades. Factory-built modular units could be delivered to prepared sites and quickly brought on line, thereby saving labor costs that could be passed on to the consumer. Regrettably, the building trades have proved resistant to this new approach as have many consumers who initially shunned modular homes. Many localities also discouraged such housing with restrictive zoning and building codes. Today, there is increased pressure on localities to allow such housing in their jurisdictions. Public acceptance of today's improved modular housing, which is often indistinguishable from regular housing, has also grown (New Jersey Department of Community Affairs 1982).

A considerable problem has been that the anticipated cost savings, while significant, have not been sufficient to make such housing affordable to the poor. Costs of modular homes are frequently in the $38,000 to $50,000 range in the Northeast (Harkins 1987). The median cost of mobile homes reached $28,700 in the western part of the country in 1985 (Hughes and Sternlieb 1987). Modular housing developments are still the exception in most areas of the country.

Industrialized housing techniques have resulted in the gradual utilization of prefabricated components in the traditional homebuilding process. Thus today, prefabricated items such as trusses, wall panels, prehung door assemblies, fireplaces, and chimney units are frequently utilized. Their use only dampens the inflationary pressure on prices rather than producing a real decline. A recent twist to industrialized housing has been developed in response to the needs of the homeless. In the South, many homeless live under highway bridges. Local architecture students, calling themselves the Mad Housers, designed a plywood shelter that can be produced for about $150. It is large enough to accommodate one person and his or her belongings. It is designed to fold up so it is portable to a degree; clearly, this may be America's ultimate low cost housing. This design has been presented and utilized as a serious approach to providing temporary housing for the homeless and is testimony of the extent of deprivation facing the homeless today (Hager 1988).

HOUSING MARKET RESTRICTIONS

Some housing advocates have proposed the passage of local legislation designed to halt the destruction of limited low cost housing stock due to speculation, urban revitalization, and redevelopment projects. Often these measures are not viewed favorably by local officials who wish to encourage the revitalization of their older districts. While such local market restrictions may place a competitive disadvantage on revitalizing urban economies, such regulations may be necessary in the absence of a clear pro-active local low cost housing program.

Other restrictive measures are designed to protect the low cost housing stock from more brutal forms of destruction such as demolition and arson. If carefully applied, these measures need not forestall urban revitalization but merely mitigate against its harmful effects on low and moderate income groups. The suggested measures are varied and creative: rent control ordinances; tax increases on profits from speculation; fines for owners of vacant units in high demand areas; a cap on property tax increases for long-term low and moderate income residents; a move from property to land-based taxation; redevelopment restrictions and/or replacement requirements in areas with a shortage of low cost, especially SRO, units; a right to relocation benefits; an extension of notification periods of condominium conversion; and a tenant's right to first refusal law. With the exception of rent control, few communities have enacted such laws. Rent control, in particular, is very contentious since one of its side effects can be to decrease the supply of private low cost housing. This is not the place for an in-depth analysis of each measure. What is important is that there exists a series of local policy measures which, if sensitively applied, can protect the supply of low cost housing (Hartman, Keating, and LeGates 1982).

In reality most of these measures have not been enacted in our cities. In the few instances when they have been passed, so many amendments have been added by the pro-development lobby that the measures are rendered ineffective and/or overly cumbersome to administer. As a result, as revitalization proceeds, displacement proceeds apace. It has been estimated that some 2.5 million Americans are displaced annually and some 500,000 low rent units are lost (Clay 1987; Hartman, Keating, and LeGates 1982).

Housing Advocacy

New Jersey has taken an activist stance by establishing a state level office of Housing Advocacy in early 1988 within its Department of

Community Affairs. This office was established so as to provide prospective low cost housing sponsors with step-by-step guidance in meeting the host of regulatory, programmatic, and financial requirements inherent in the development process. Its aim is to lessen the impact of this regulatory burden on new small-scale low cost housing developers. In this way, they hope to encourage the development of a pool of qualified low cost housing sponsors and boost the output of such housing. Sponsors may be municipalities, housing authorities, nonprofit, or private developers (New Jersey Department of Community Affairs 1988a).

FINANCIAL SUPPORTS

Nonprofit Housing

Nonprofit Housing Development Corporations (HDC) are a central component of any low cost housing strategy. The typical nonprofit housing development corporation is a small community-based organization with a capacity to develop 20 to 100 units of housing per year. They offer the ability to rehabilitate old units and construct new units at cost. They can couple such housing with available government subsidies so as to bring the final price or rent within reach of low and moderate income households. These HDCs have been quite successful in a variety of projects. Today, some 2,000 such organizations exist and are widely perceived as representing one of the true success stories of low cost housing. A recent study by the National Congress for Community Economic Development estimated that in 1986 and 1987, some 46,000 low income housing units were produced by community-based development organizations. In this same period, the study estimates the federal government produced about 19,000 low income housing units (Lehman 1989). At the same time, it should be stressed that they represent a limited approach to a major problem. Specifically, these corporations are usually not able to develop sufficient units to counter the loss of low cost housing due to continued abandonment, decline, and other market factors. Another problem is that housing development corporations can deliver affordable housing but these units require steep subsidies if they are to be affordable by the truly poor. As a result, they are currently limited by the degree to which a locality is able to provide such subsidies. In addition, there are many imposing development hurdles that stymie even experienced organizations. Total output can be very low and slow to come on line. For instance, in New York City five low cost projects for the homeless were awarded in April 1985 and only three were completed by June of 1988 (Oser 1988; Housing and Community Research Groups 1973; Keyes 1973).

Public and Private Partnerships

In the late 1970s and into the 1980s, public and private partnerships were touted as a way to produce low cost housing. The notion involves the matching of private developers with a capital stake in the project with local government financing at favorable rates. The private sector involvement is encouraged by favorable federal tax policies for investors in historic properties or for developments that house low and moderate income households for a set number of years. The partnership allows the local government to insist that a portion of the development be set aside for low and moderate income households. Many innovative ideas have been successfully utilized to keep down the costs associated with low cost housing rehabilitation and development and there has been an expansion of such development projects in our urban areas (Nenno and Brophy 1983). By 1988, the total output of such projects has totaled some 650,000 units nationwide.

A key component of this approach is strong organizational support that allows the program to move beyond dealing with ad hoc projects and move on to encompass the revitalization of entire residential neighborhoods. This organization must include members of local financial institutions, community leaders, local residents, and public officials. Today, there are several umbrella organizations that have developed programmatic approaches in a number of low income urban areas. The most notable are the Neighborhood Reinvestment Task Force and the Local Initiatives Support Corporation. These organizations represent a national coalition of foundations, large banks, financial institutions, and governmental agencies that work with their local counterparts to stabilize marginal low and low moderate income areas (Ahlbrandt and Brophy 1975). Some local efforts have produced notable results: the Savannah Landmarks Rehabilitation Project was successful in rehabilitating a significant number of historic properties without displacing all the original low income residents. Overall, there is a mixed record of success with this approach. While there are many examples of successful efforts in some areas, other areas have failed to respond positively (Boyea 1982).

Strict Enforcement of Community Reinvestment Laws

Locating market rate financing is one of the most severe problems facing communities that wish to preserve their stock of low cost housing.

As they age and decline, many low income areas find themselves unable to attract private financing from local banks that do business in their area. Much has been written on the injustice of these institutions accepting the deposits of customers to whom they refuse to lend money for mortgages or renovations. Such a policy often guarantees the economic decline of the area (Tomer 1980; Taggert and K. W. Smith 1981). As a result, there has been significant political pressure on the federal government to take action. In 1975, Congress passed the Home Mortgage Disclosure Act which made bank lending patterns public information. Soon after, they passed the Community Reinvestment Act (1977) which required lending institutions to demonstrate that they were lending money in the areas where they were located and received deposits. Those institutions that did not do so could have their charters revoked and expansion plans vetoed. There are many instances of low income community groups using these laws to force lending institutions to make loan commitments in their communities. When successful, such capital infusions can support the retention of significant numbers of low cost housing units. The success of such efforts is highly dependent on local organizational acumen.

Local Mortgage Plans

One of the more notable local approaches to supporting low cost housing is the Philadelphia Mortgage Plan. This program entails a flexible approach to underwriting a mortgage in low income areas of the city. As such, it is a local response to bankers, who have claimed that certain neighborhoods did not meet current underwriting standards, and to charges by local housing advocates that some lenders had "redlined" certain poor areas of the city which were then denied mortgage loans or rehabilitation loans. The plan is a risksharing agreement by a consortium of local banks to offer market rate loans on properties that, by virtue of their location or the financial background of the mortgage applicant, constitute an enhanced risk to the lender. Specifically, the plan allows consideration of properties located in areas of significant housing abandonment, it places no lower limit on the size of the loan, and it takes a flexible approach when determining the applicant's income and credit history. This plan has met a real need since, ironically, many low cost housing units cannot be purchased due to their low price. This is because many lenders do not want to make loans below $50,000 because their overhead remains static and their fees are based on a percentage of the loan amount. By removing these obstacles, the plan is able to target a segment of the low income home buying public that is not served by current private institutions. Yet the element of enhanced risk is real as this plan has a current default rate of 20% which is significantly higher than the prevailing rate. Nonetheless, due to its success, this plan has been emulated in a number of cities nationwide (M. H. Lang 1985a; Young 1978).

State Housing Finance Corporations

State housing finance corporations often offer a government-supported version of a banker's mortgage plan. The chief distinction between the plans is that the state plan makes loans available statewide and, since they raise their funds through bond sales, they can offer below-market rates. It shares the flexible approach to underwriting that characterizes the private plans. Many of these programs offer "set asides" for urban areas and even particular neighborhoods. This allows local officials to effectively market the area to prospective buyers. One of the real problems these programs have encountered is that many low income people have poor job records, outstanding debts, or poor credit histories that prevent them from qualifying for these mortgages. Thus, funds allocated for low income areas often are not utilized (M. H. Lang 1985a; Saltman 1982).

Local Tax Abatement

One way localities have been able to assist in the production of affordable housing is to agree to waive or lower real estate taxes for a period of time in a given housing development. Such a policy can assist moderate income households in making their monthly housing payments. Taxes added at a later date would be less burdensome since it can be anticipated that available income would have risen. The effect of such a policy on low income households would be negligible (Saltman 1982).

Neighborhood Preservation Programs

Many states' departments of community development offer programs in housing preservation. They are targeted at specific low and moderate income areas that can benefit from below-market loans and outright grants to enable owners to fix and rehabilitate their property. The concept is based on the policy of stabilizing so-called marginal areas: those areas that exhibit the initial signs of blight and deterioration but do not have all the multiple problems typical of the worst neighborhoods. This program functions as a low cost housing maintenance program as it is aimed at forestalling the decline and abandonment of the area that might otherwise take place. The policy relies on encouraging homeowners to invest in their properties by offering a financial incentive to do so. Nonetheless, it is often difficult to convince low income homeowners to take on additional debt. As a result, such programs often achieve an uneven application. As was noted in the discussion about code enforcement programs, there is a natural tendency for residents to accept the small fix-up grants and avoid the loan component of the program. It is difficult to determine the impact of these programs since no comparative longitudinal studies have been conducted (Boyea 1982).

Balanced Housing Program; Public/Private Partnerships

As a result of a strong statewide initiative to encourage the construction of low and moderate income housing, the New Jersey legislature passed the Fair Housing Act of 1985 (New Jersey Public Law 1985, Ch. 222) which established the Balanced Housing Program. This program is carried out by the Council on Affordable Housing which has the responsibility for determining housing regions and setting low and moderate housing obligations in each municipality based on regional needs. The act also allocated funds from a new statewide realty transfer tax for the subsidization of low and moderate income housing construction costs. It should be noted that municipalities can elect to shed a portion of their responsibility for siting such housing by entering into a Regional Contribution Agreement with another municipality willing to accept the units. A Housing Demonstration Program was also established to fund innovative approaches to creating low and moderate income housing (Council on Affordable Housing 1986).

In order to stimulate the involvement of new and existing nonprofit low cost housing providers, New Jersey has recently established the Office of Housing Advocacy within the Department of Community Affairs. In addition, this office will work with public/private partnerships to identify sources of subsidized housing loans (New Jersey Department of Community Affairs 1988b). Other programs, such as the municipal loan program of the new Casino Redevelopment Authority, hold the promise of possible funding for low income housing. The output of this program has yet to be determined and it must be stressed that low cost housing is but one of the many possible candidates for the authority's funding (Casino Redevelopment Authority Annual Report 1986). It is too soon to know the effect of these various efforts but the array of forces antagonistic to the construction of significant amounts of low cost housing remain strong. The likely winner in this contest is detailed in Chapter 6.

SUMMARY

Local approaches to affordable housing have been effective in lowering the cost of housing in many instances. The problem is that much of the cost savings has been absorbed by inflation resulting in a marginal effect on total housing costs. Affordable housing policies have resulted in only a limited program of local measures designed to minimize housing cost increases so as to keep housing costs within range of the suburban middle class and their upwardly mobile offspring. By and large, these measures have not proved effective in reaching the low income inner city households (Keyes 1973; Boyea 1982; Housing and Community Research Groups 1973; Mallach 1988).

Some local efforts have proven themselves able to produce significant amounts of affordable housing. Public/private ventures are notable in this regard. However, in most instances, these exemplary programs remain just that: examples of how things might be done. All too often total units delivered remain too low to constitute an effective response to the problem. Atlas and Dreier (1988) of the National Housing Institute have aptly summarized the situation: "The success of the community-based housing movement of the 1980s has been impressive. But their success [sic] has only dramatized the fact that local and state government in cooperation with area funders, cannot provide the resources needed to turn the community-based housing movement into a major supplier of affordable housing."

The failure is due to the magnitude of the task that confronts these separate local housing efforts which often result in a fragmented approach to low cost housing delivery. Each entity is required to be able to absorb and apply significant amounts of expertise. For instance, public/private ventures require a flexible and knowledgeable approach to local housing finance, planning, and administration. A knowledge of funding sources and mechanisms is crucial as is the ability to engage in community planning in the locality. Staff have to relate knowledgeably with a host of actors in the housing delivery process: land owners, developers, builders, mortgage bankers, management agents, as well as government program administrators. It is not surprising that it is often difficult to mount and maintain such efforts (Boyea 1982; Oser 1988; Atlas and Dreier 1988; Housing and Community Research Groups 1973).

Another major problem is the severe shortage of funding for such projects, a shortage which may be partially alleviated with the passage of the Community Housing Partnership Act. This act proposes that the federal government provide matching funds in a three-to-one ratio to locally based nonprofit housing groups. Federal funds would match those from local government, businesses, foundations, and religious groups, etc. (Atlas and Dreier 1988).

Those measures that were intended to protect the available stock of low cost housing have also been of limited effectiveness. This is due to the array of interests that can be marshaled against legislative proposals aimed at protecting such housing. For instance, for several years Philadelphia legislators have tried unsuccessfully to pass a real estate tax circuit breaker that would lessen tax increases for long-term residents in newly gentrifying areas. Local real estate and development interests and the mayor have prevented its passage to date.

Marxists would quickly point out that all of the measures suggested here are based on the acceptance of the free market in housing and its companion financial system. Such measures represent token efforts to get development interests to pay so-called "blood money" in return for the right to go on making profits. Moreover, many of these measures have the effect of placing a portion of the responsibility for housing production on the shoulders of the needy themselves. It has been said, "What developers like to do least is to renovate cheap housing; building cheap houses runs a close second" (Economist 1988, 13). Nonetheless, the poor results obtained by such measures are due to the array of powerful interests that are antagonistic to both the ends and means implied in these approaches. The interests of profit and class dictate the outcome.

There is another way to explain the poor results obtained by these measures. A market interventionist interpretation would stress that these measures, while well meaning, suffer from a common flaw: all are local approaches to what is a national problem. Accordingly, the search for significant local solutions is a fool's errand since only national level intervention by the federal government, in combination with existing local approaches, can truly address the problem and counterbalance those forces antagonistic to the production of significant low cost housing (Atlas and Dreier 1988; Winerip 1988a).

In truth, while exemplary programs exist, successful local approaches to low cost housing delivery have had limited overall impact, an argument made in more detail in Chapter 8. This is not to say that these local efforts are unnecessary; to the contrary, they are a vital component of the overall housing delivery system. Yet is must be recognized that if we truly wish to ameliorate the dearth of affordable housing for the low income groups in our society, a comprehensive national level approach needs to be developed in tandem with local and regional efforts. Such a comprehensive program must address the problems of funding and location (Clay

1987; Downs 1983; Dolbeare 1987; Atlas and Dreier 1988). The next chapter provides a case study of the difficulties confronting such a program in one state which tried to grapple with its responsibility to provide a regional approach for low cost housing.

6

Fair Share/ Balanced Housing Initiatives

One of the most important aspects of local and regional housing policy concerns the lack of low and moderate income housing in the developing suburbs and nonmetropolitan areas (Lichter 1986; Stearns and Logan 1986). Understanding the socioeconomic effects of persistent segregated housing patterns is necessary if we are to find a solution to the crisis of homelessness. It makes little sense to provide improved housing and shelter in our cities if we are not prepared to make meaningful efforts to integrate the poor into the mainstream of society by assisting in the development of viable balanced suburban communities (Summers 1976; Dear and Wolch 1987). Today, we are a highly segregated society; the poor live in urban and rural enclaves devoid of meaningful economic opportunity and set apart from the rest of society. It is not surprising that such a milieu has led to a significant growth in dysfunctional behaviors. Many sociologists believe the recent loss of low skilled job opportunities is a prime explanatory factor for destructive social behaviors such as crime and drug abuse that flourish in these areas. Such behavior patterns put these communities under great strain. Most low cost housing programs are place-oriented and seek to reestablish and refurbish the ghetto. Those programs are doomed to failure since many of the rehoused will soon be homeless again due to the lack of an economically viable and supportive local community. Such an approach constitutes a design for failure perpetrated by the government on its own people since these housing programs will then be branded as wasteful, much as occurred with earlier low cost housing programs (W. J. Wilson 1987; Ellwood 1987; Danielson 1976; Downs 1973; Haar and Iatrides 1974; Lake 1981; Harrison 1984).

Ironically, conservative critics of ghetto enrichment social welfare policies avoid supporting balanced community development policies that would work. Instead, they advocate job training and other policies that assume a freedom of mobility that does not exist in our society (Collins 1983). They refuse to acknowledge the barriers that exist for some groups of people. One of the largest barriers is the lack of low cost housing in developing suburban areas of the country—areas that increasingly contain the greatest number of new job opportunities for less skilled workers (Gilder 1981).

There have been many attempts to increase the mobility of the lower income groups in our society so that they might be able to benefit from the social and economic opportunities present in diverse communities (Downs and Bradbury 1981; Milgram 1979; Burchell and Listoken 1983). This chapter will review the fair share concept—one salient approach that has been pursued in the hope that it would produce widespread community economic integration. This review will focus on the failure of New Jersey to find a mechanism to promulgate this policy after twelve years of significant effort. The failure of this local effort can be seen as evidence of the need for more assertive national level programs that seek innovative and long-term solutions to the low cost housing crisis. This is not an easy issue to bring to the fore. Many local law makers are aware of the impotence of local fair share efforts but cynically pursue them anyway. Their efforts are presented as evidence of their good intentions and allow them to postpone grappling with the issues of how and with whom to design a truly workable program for community and housing integration (Orfield 1983). Indeed, were a meaningful program developed, a whole array of city and suburban interest groups would attempt to block its enactment (Polikoff 1978). Many city politicians are also less than enthusiastic about fair share policies since they see them as having a negative impact on minority-based political strength. This emerging political strength has recently begun to result in the capture of local elective offices to a significant degree. In addition, many advocates for urban low income communities fear the loss of access to community services under a fair share policy. The strength of this combined opposition is enormous. Indeed, many long-term fair share advocates despair of ever seeing such a program enacted (Danielson 1976). Yet, it is possible that the failure of local efforts was something that had to be experienced before support for a meaningful federal level balanced communities program could be found.

FAIR SHARE

It has been over ten years since the New Jersey Supreme Court released its now famous Mount Laurel I decision which required suburban municipalities to amend their zoning ordinances to include provisions for low and moderate income housing (Southern Burlington County NAACP v. Township of Mount Laurel 1975). These past years have seen extensive litigation but very little low and moderate income housing has actually been built. After reviewing the facts behind the campaign for fair share low cost housing, the reasons for the seemingly neverending litigation become apparent. This chapter will review the New Jersey Supreme Court decisions flowing from its initial involvement in the fair share issue. Municipal responses to these initiatives will be discussed along with those of the housing development industry. A few of the housing developments in which low and moderate income housing has been or will be constructed will be examined, as well as the current efforts by municipalities to design workable housing plans. Finally, newly enacted state legislation will be reviewed.

Supreme Court Decisions

In 1975, the New Jersey Supreme Court was asked to rule on the constitutionality of so-called exclusionary zoning. Such zoning is commonly based on the communitywide imposition of large lot requirements for all housing developments and the exclusion of multi-family housing, townhouses, and mobile homes. The result of such an ordinance is to exclude from the community all those who cannot afford to pay for an expensive single family home on a large lot. Moreover, to the extent that exclusionary zoning prevailed in all or most of the region's developing suburbs, this constituted a severe constraint on the ability of the poor to migrate out of the depressed inner cities where they were concentrated. The State Supreme Court held, in its Mount Laurel I decision, that exclusionary zoning ordinances were unconstitutional because they contravened the general welfare clause of the Constitution. The Court went further than simply requiring municipalities to include provisions for low cost developments in their zoning code; it also articulated the so-called Mount Laurel doctrine. The core of the doctrine provides that a community should ". . . by its land use regulations, make realistically possible an appropriate variety and choice of housing. It cannot foreclose the opportunity and . . . must affirmatively afford the opportunity for low and moderate income housing" (Mallach 1988).

Thus, communities were held to have a responsibility to provide low cost housing for a fair share portion of the total low income population in the region as well as their own residents. There were many questions regarding the interpretation and implementation of this decision. While some communities responded by redrafting their zoning ordinances, most waited for further indications of what the Court expected to accomplish (Mallach 1988). Further litigation followed two years later when the New Jersey Supreme Court decided Oakwood v. Madison (371 A.2d 1192 (1977)). In this case, the Supreme Court tried to stay out of making complex determinations of what constituted a community's fair share. Instead, the Court said it would look at the "substance" of a zoning ordinance and determine whether it reflected "bona fide efforts" to remove exclusionary barriers (Hyson 1984).

The ensuing years saw some efforts at rezoning by some municipalities that set aside some areas for townhouses and reduced lot size requirements in others. However, no low cost units were actually built in these areas save for a number of developments open only to senior citizens. This was partly due to lack of affirmative marketing on the part of the municipality and the lack of developer interest since developers did not perceive these opportunities as leading to a profitable development.

With little progress in providing low and moderate income housing, low cost housing proponents again brought suit against Mount Laurel resulting in the Supreme Court's 1983 Mount Laurel II decision (Southern Burlington County NAACP v. Township of Mount Laurel 1983). The Mount Laurel II decision has a number of key provisions:

Each municipality must provide a realistic opportunity for decent housing for its indigenous poor unless the poor make up a disproportionately large segment of the local population. If in a growth area as designated in the State Development Guide Plan (SDGP), the municipality must provide a realistic opportunity for a fair share of the region's present and prospective low* and moderate income housing to be constructed. Litigation will no longer be numberless. It is to include proof of the number of units needed to meet the fair share requirement. More than the removal of exclusionary barriers is required. Affirmative governmental devices should be used. Subsidies and inclusionary devices, such as incentive zoning and mandatory set asides, are suggested. "Builder's remedies" will be granted if a municipality's ordinances are not in compliance and if the builder's proposed project includes an appropriate portion of low and moderate income housing units (Hyson 1984).

---

*Low income families are defined as those families whose incomes do not exceed 50% of the median of the area. Moderate income families are those whose incomes are no less than 50% and no greater than 80% of the median of the area.

The preparation of a State Development Guide Plan (SDGP) in 1980 was seen as making this decision possible since the Court relied heavily on this plan in determining the presence and location of growth areas. In the Mount Laurel II decision, the Court recommended that the SDGP be revised no later than January 1, 1985, and every three years thereafter. New Jersey Governor Kean responded by abolishing the New Jersey Division of Planning, the division that produced the plan, thus removing the executive branch from this politically sensitive decisionmaking area. The SDGP was not revised until 1988 and only after its importance to this issue was severely limited by subsequent action by the state legislature detailed below (Blaesser 1984a).

Interpreting Mount Laurel II

A major effect of the Mount Laurel II decision was that it shifted the burden of proof for future litigation. Up to this point, the plaintiff had to prove that an ordinance was "unfair." The plaintiff now only has to establish a "prima facie case." The burden is then shifted to the defendant to put forth rebutting evidence. In addition, "assignment judges" were given the responsibility to review zoning ordinances in all New Jersey municipalities in order to see if they met the criteria set out in the Mount Laurel II decision (Blaesser 1984b).

Implementing Mount Laurel via the Builder's Remedy

The Supreme Court suggested that in order to ensure that low cost housing actually got built, they were prepared to accept the so-called builder's remedy. A builder's remedy allows a builder to base a municipal suit on the contention that the local zoning ordinance does not meet the Mount Laurel doctrine. If the Court agrees that the ordinance does not provide for the municipality's fair share and if the builder's proposed development does provide for a percentage of low and moderate income housing, the Court can grant approval for the "builder's remedy." Specifically, the builder gets relief from ordinance density requirements to build at a higher density so long as a proportion of low and moderate income units are constructed as well. The numbers that have been agreed upon by the Court in granting builder's remedy suits are that four regular price units are needed to offset and subsidize the cost of one low or moderate price unit (Mastro 1984).

For a considerable period, it appeared that the builder's remedy would be the principal means for implementing the construction of the allocated fair share regional distribution. However, as a result of escalating builder's remedy suits throughout the suburbs, the considerable impact of the builder's remedy on suburban growth rates became clear and provoked a strong public reaction (Lentini 1985).

Moorestown, New Jersey, was a good example of what can occur as a result of a builder's remedy. Currently, the township consists of approximately 5,000 dwelling units. More than 10,000 new market-rate dwelling units would have to be constructed to provide for Moorestown's allocation of 2,000-plus fair share units using this formula. The community was thus faced with accepting a significant amount of poor households and a level of growth that would have completely restructured the social order in the community. Two builder's remedy suits were filed against Moorestown. Public reaction was largely negative due in part to the desire to protect the small town character of Moorestown. As a result of political pressure by the residents, township officials refused to settle. Negotiations had reached the point where the allocation judge would have accepted a 35% fair share allocation and extended a grant of immunity from further suits for a given time period, but the residents and elected officials refused this offer (Mastro 1984).

The result of the Court's ruling in Mount Laurel II and its identification of the builder's remedy was to set in motion a complex series of legal and political maneuverings at the local level. These maneuvers served to take up an enormous amount of time and public expenditure for professional services which were aimed at stalling for time in order to see what level of compliance the Court could actually enforce. The cost of fair share litigation in one community (Bedminster) has exceeded $1,000,000 just in legal fees connected with one project. Needless to say, the developer had significant legal and professional costs as well (Eldred 1985).

MODULAR HOUSING

One seemingly obvious approach to providing low cost housing in the suburbs is to allow the construction of modular housing or mobile homes. There have been some examples of this approach in New Jersey but the results have not been as might be expected. Tricia Meadows is a mobile home development in Mount Laurel established as a result of a builder's remedy. The site has been approved for 456 units on 102 acres. The builder had been allowed to intervene as a plaintiff in the Mount Laurel II litigation. He agreed to secure Section 8 subsidies for 20% of the units. In granting the builder's remedy, the Court provided that if he did not get the subsidies, he still had to build 20% of the units for low and moderate incomes. Federal subsidies are currently unavailable. No low or moderate cost units are available in the first section of the development, apparently to allow a cash flow to be established (A. Davis 1984).

Tricia Meadows is not an inexpensive development. The cost of these double wide mobile units ranges from $38,000 to $50,000. The lots are all about 6,000 square feet, but a significant percentage do not have road frontage of their own. In addition to mortgage costs for the unit, there is a $200 per month lease cost for the lot. The units are not considered real estate improvements under current state law so there is no property tax on the unit. The units are anchored to a cement pad and skirted. The roads are private, and municipal services are not provided. The marketing information for Tricia Meadows states that it is designed for small families and for adults without children. A maximum of four residents per home is allowed. Lot leases will be renewed as long as residents abide by the terms of the lease and the rules and regulations of the development. If property is not maintained, the management will correct the problem and bill the resident for services. All indications are that the community is really designed for senior citizens. It appears that it will be difficult to offset the cost of low and moderate cost units in this type of development (A. Davis, 1984).

THE BUILDER'S REMEDY APPROACH IMPLEMENTED: A CASE STUDY

The Hills at Bedminster in Somerset County is one of several new developments constructed to date with its percentage of low and moderate cost units. This development is the result of a builder's remedy suit which was filed before the Mount Laurel II case, but decided about one month after. The original zoning ordinance had required three acre single family development. The builder wanted to break Bedminster's exclusionary zoning in order to build a townhouse development at about ten units per acre, but he did not want to build low and moderate cost units. He was forced into it in order to get approval for his project (Eldred 1985).

The Hills consists of 1,287 units, 260 of them low and moderate cost units. They range in size from 500 to 800 square feet. There are one, two, and three bedroom units. The price range for low income purchasers is from $27,000 to $34,200, and for moderate income purchasers it is from $48,900 to $57,000. It is an attractive development. The exterior of the low and moderate cost units is the same as the more expensive units (Eldred 1985).

However, there has been difficulty in finding people to qualify for the units. The Hills pays the down payment and the application fee, but many prospective purchasers have difficulty getting mortgage approval. The rather broad Mount Laurel income guidelines qualify two out of five New Jersey households. It includes a family of four earning as much as $35,000 per year in the more affluent parts of the state and a welfare mother receiving less than 20% of that amount. In New Jersey, this formula assures that a significant proportion of the sons and daughters of the suburban middle class will qualify. Actual purchasers have turned out to be these upwardly mobile sons and daughters of the stable suburban middle class (Mallach 1988; Schoenberg 1984). This profile is typical of most of the occupants of New Jersey's Mount Laurel units since most marketing efforts by local governments have been aimed at meeting the needs of this group. As a result, few inner city poor people have found the Mount Laurel decision to be the key that opened up the suburbs (Mallach 1988).

This unexpected purchasing group does demonstrate the general need for low and moderate cost housing. There has been a tremendous shift in the housing market since the Mount Laurel I decision 15 years ago. As a result, many more people have since been shut out of the homeownership market. The low and moderate cost units in the Hills project are meeting a need, but not the one the Court originally intended it to (Schoenberg 1984; Mallach 1988).

We see that in the years since the Mount Laurel II decision, litigation has continued unabated. This was not the Court's intention. At the beginning, the Court stated:

The obligation is to provide a realistic opportunity for housing, not litigation. We have learned from experience, however, that unless a strong judicial hand is used, Mount Laurel will not result in housing, but in paper, process, witnesses, trials and appeals. We intend by this decision to strengthen it, clarify it, and make it easier for public officials, including judges, to apply it (Hyson 1984).

Instead, we have had an endless stream of litigation and very little low and moderate income housing being constructed. By 1985, some 150 builder's remedy suits have been filed by developers or landowners in nearly 100 different municipalities (Mallach 1988). The next section discusses the various actions taken by municipal governments primarily in southern New Jersey in response to the builder's remedy litigation.

MUNICIPAL RESPONSE: LITIGATION

As a result of all this confusion and the builder's remedy suits filed against them, the municipalities have started to initiate litigation. On

March 28, 1985, twenty-three municipalities filed two separate petitions. One was by Cranford, which has 750 homes and a low–moderate fair share allocation of 816 units. At the agreed upon 4:1 ratio, 4,080 units would have to be constructed to meet this obligation. Five builder's remedy suits have been filed against Cranford. A separate petition was filed by twenty-two other municipalities which requested a moratorium on Mount Laurel lawsuits until state legislation is adopted which addresses zoning and subsidies. They also requested a rehearing of the Mount Laurel II decision. The New Jersey Supreme Court in a one page decision ruled against the request for a moratorium, citing "insufficient cause." A rehearing of Mount Laurel II was denied. The twenty-two towns have also agreed to file in U.S. District Court, contending that the Mount Laurel decision interferes with a citizen's constitutional rights and corporate municipal rights. The projected cost to the twenty-two municipalities would be about $10,000 to $15,000 each to hire a Manhattan law firm to file the suit (Sonnenberg 1984).

The result of the Mount Laurel I and II decisions has been to prompt a tremendous amount of local civic and governmental activity. Some of this activity is undeniably protectionist in nature but much is based on a true willingness to search for solutions. Yet it must be added that even in the latter case municipalities worry about doing "too much" and becoming a low cost housing mecca. As a result, social concern is always tempered with a judiciousness that inadvertently adds to the procedural delays that characterize this process.

STATE FAIR HOUSING LEGISLATION

The turmoil that resulted from the local political maneuvering around the fair share issue resulted in the mobilization of intense political pressure on the governor. This pressure came from parties on both sides of the issue: local officials who wanted some relief from builder's remedy suits and local fair share advocates who wanted a more effective mechanism for ensuring that low cost housing actually got built. The result of this confluence of forces was the passage of the New Jersey Fair Housing Act of July 2, 1985. This act provided a comprehensive planning and implementation process for the municipal constitutional obligation to provide fair share housing. The Act established the Council on Affordable Housing (COAH) and empowered it to define housing regions and estimate the present and prospective need for low and moderate income housing at the state and regional level. Additionally, the Council was mandated to set criteria and guidelines for municipalities to determine their own fair share,

to adjust that number where applicable, to phase in their housing obligations, and, if desired, to transfer some of that housing to a willing
municipality through negotiations (Mallach 1988; New Jersey Public Law
1985).

The Act provided a more flexible interpretation of municipal fair share
than had prevailed earlier:

Municipal adjustment of the present and prospective fair share based upon available
vacant and developable land, infrastructure considerations, or environmental or historic
preservation factors and adjustments shall be made whenever:

(a) The preservation of historically or important architecture and sites and their
    environs or environmentally sensitive lands may be jeopardized,

(b) the established pattern of development in the community would be drastically
    altered,

(c) adequate land for recreational, conservational, or agricultural and farmland
    preservation purposes would not be provided,

(d) adequate open space would not be provided,

(e) the pattern of development is contrary to the planning designation in the state
    development and redevelopment plan,

(f) vacant and developable land is not available to the municipality,

(g) adequate public facilities and infrastructure capacities are not available or
    would result in costs prohibitive to the public if provided (New Jersey
    Public Law 1985, 6)

The responsibility to provide realistic opportunities for low and moderate income housing remains with the individual municipalities. With this
responsibility comes the opportunity and the flexibility to develop a
housing element that addresses the low and moderate housing needs of
that municipality and considers the specific concerns of the community.
Each municipality needs to have this housing element and their fair share
plan approved by the Council on Affordable Housing. For example, a
community may choose to give a density bonus to developers in exchange
for construction of the required housing. Also, a municipality may decide
to rehabilitate substandard housing or convert vacant structures into
residential units, or it may elect to subsidize specific developments of low
and moderate income housing to minimize or eliminate the number of
permitted market value units (N.J. P.L. 1985). A municipality may choose
to meet up to 50% of its obligation through a Regional Contribution
Agreement (RCA) by paying a second municipality to build the housing
within its borders. This provision was seen by some as a tool for rebuilding
urban areas while others saw it as a weakening of the commitment to open
the suburbs to low and moderate income families (Mallach 1988).

Municipalities have the freedom to structure their responses to their Mount Laurel obligations as long as a realistic opportunity for the required low and moderate income housing, as indicated by the Council on Affordable Housing, is created. The form of those responses will vary from municipality to municipality depending on the nature of the need and the municipality's willingness to play an active role in the construction or rehabilitation of sound low and moderate income housing.

The obstacles to low and moderate income housing vary throughout the state. The cost of land, absence of federal subsidies, land improvement costs, high property taxes, and home insurance rates all make the delivery of affordable housing very difficult. Yet the Council thinks that affordable housing is possible with appropriate land use regulations or through other innovative techniques selected by a municipality. For example, a municipality may, in structuring its response to Mount Laurel, choose to donate land, rezone for greater densities, use community development block grant funds to improve land, design smaller yet sound housing units, incorporate modular technology and/or offer tax abatement to deliver affordable housing units.

Whatever innovative technique is employed, the delivery of low and moderate income housing units involves some form of subsidy. The Fair Housing Act has appropriated funds for the State Department of Community Affairs (DCA) and for the State Housing and Mortgage Finance Agency (HMFA) to be used in subsidizing low and moderate income housing. HMFA's "Affordable Housing Program" has $15 million available to interested municipalities. In addition, HMFA has reserved 25% of its bond proceeds for the permanent financing of low and moderate income units. DCA's "Neighborhood Preservation Balanced Housing Program" is primarily funded through the realty transfer tax.

The Fair Housing Act requires the DCA program to direct a substantial portion of its awards to state-designated urban aid cities and to provide funding to complete regional contribution agreements. Thus, the Balanced Housing Program also provides urban areas an opportunity to leverage resources to deliver affordable housing (N.J. P.L. 1985).

Admittedly, the subsidy provided by the Fair Housing Act is limited as are other monies available through HMFA and DCA and various surviving federal programs. Thus, to subsidize their response to Mount Laurel, some municipalities have levied fees on residential and nonresidential developments. Whether municipalities have the authority to impose such fees is unsettled at present. A bill to grant such power is pending in the state legislature.

The funding for state subsidies is at least a start. But, a long term, stable funding source is needed. A one or two year infusion of money is not going to subsidize any significant number of units. Many feel that New Jersey should not be acting alone in providing this funding. They argue that New York, Pennsylvania, and Delaware should have similar programs so that New Jersey does not become the repository of low and moderate income households in the Middle-Atlantic region of the country.

The results under the Fair Housing Act are difficult to assess at this early date but there are reasons to be concerned with some of the policy decisions made so far. For example, the COAH was prepared to allow the subsidy of moderate income housing units to count toward a suburban community's fair share obligation even though the subsidy would expire after six years and the rents would then be raised to market levels. The fact is that limited capital and the need to base most efforts in the private sector tend to lead to low outputs and temporary solutions (O'Connor and Shaffer 1988). In addition, the impact of these programs has been limited due to an 8% cap on equity for private developers, rent caps, and other restrictions that make participation in the program uneconomic for private developers (Wisnosky 1988). Interest in a program of tax credits for developers of low cost housing has been particularly disappointing since only $1.3 million of the state's $9.5 million allocation was used in 1987. Accordingly, in 1988, only $3.1 million was allocated for this program and less than $1 million has been projected for use in 1989 (Wisnosky 1988).

The Mount Laurel decisions have placed additional financial and regulatory burdens on municipal governments. Recognizing the limitation on existing funding, some energetic people have tried innovative ideas aimed at meeting the spirit of the Mount Laurel decisions.

A FAIR SHARE PROGRAM

There have been some committed individuals and groups that have poured a great deal of energy and resources into the fair share concept. One notable effort is the Fair Share Housing Development Inc. of Cherry Hill, New Jersey. This group is staffed by individuals who have been advocating the fair share approach from its earliest stages.

This effort has gone forward with a small staff of two full-time individuals and a host of volunteers. The full-time staff members actively promote fair share policy at the state level and were involved in securing the passage of the new Fair Housing Act. The development group has as its mission:

—the development, ownership and management of safe, decent and affordable "fair share" housing for low and moderate income persons in the State of New Jersey; and

—the implementation of a comprehensive human services program for the residents of the housing provided (O'Connor and Shaffer 1988).

This group sees its mission as combating the increased risk of homelessness due to the lack of low cost housing units, particularly in the suburbs. Currently, this group manages some 580 units of low cost housing in three counties which cater to the elderly, low income, or handicapped. It is currently involved in a project in Mount Laurel consisting of an additional 310 units of low and moderate income housing. This project is seen as particularly challenging due to the affluence of the surrounding community (O'Connor and Shaffer 1988).

The group provides housing in suburban as well as urban locations. A review of the history of this group provides evidence of the tremendous dedication in terms of time and energy that this form of housing delivery requires. It also demonstrates a rather limited output of units. After some ten years of activity, Fair Share Housing Development Inc. has produced or is in the planning stages for the following units:

Northgate II, in Camden City—urban locale:
308 highrise apartment units for the low income elderly
94 low rise units for low income families

North Camden, in Camden City—urban locale:
16 row house rehabilitation units for low income families

Cooper Plaza, in Camden City—urban locale:
64 units (44 market rate, 20 low and moderate mix

New Sharon Woods, Sewell, N.J.—suburban locale:
50 units for low income families
24 townhouses for moderate income families
4 duplexes for moderate income families

Mount Laurel, N.J.—suburban locale:
310 units (half low income, half moderate income) (O'Connor and Shaffer 1988)

This yields some 826 units, 330 of which are for low income families. Only 210 of these units are located in the suburbs. There are no units for single low income households. This low output is a result of the forces arrayed against the fair share approach in a state where it has been most vociferously supported by the highest courts. The fact remains that the packaging of such projects remains cumbersome and time consuming. Mr. P. J. O'Connor, the president of the group and the attorney who argued the original Mount Laurel case, has admitted to a sense of exhaustion on the part of those who are trying to implement the fair share approach. The only way to effectively accomplish it, he said, would be to change the land use development process at the national level by linking all federal funding for local governments to local fair share compliance (O'Connor and Shaffer 1988).

POLICY EVALUATION AND RECOMMENDATIONS

The enormity of the problem is finally being realized by all participants. Had the Court limited itself to exclusionary zoning issues, it could have been considered somewhat successful since much exclusionary zoning has disappeared as a result of the Mount Laurel rulings. Most communities now allow a much greater range of housing types at a greater range of densities; minimum house and unit square footage requirements have been eliminated and development improvement standards are being reduced if for no other reason than their high long-term maintenance costs to the municipality. In addition, the New Jersey Uniform Construction Code permits most of the new cost saving construction methods. As a result, new construction in the suburbs, under these conditions at least, provides more affordable units and permits some version of the trickle down effect.

Certainly, the problem of the real cost of actually building new low and moderate cost units cannot be underestimated. Many local communities have reached the point of accepting "some" units only if they could find a reasonable means. Under these circumstances, will low and moderate income housing be built? Probably some will be built, but the numbers will be far less than suggested by the Court in its prospective fair share allocations. At the federal level, there is no money for subsidies and none can be anticipated for at least the short term.

In New Jersey, the Council on Affordable Housing has been granted extensive autonomy and power, which is clearly required in this situation. However, splitting the administration of the affordable housing program between two existing agencies (DCA and HMFA) may hamper the effective administration of the program since these agencies were not created for the mission of providing low and moderate income housing. While some such housing will probably result under their administration (certainly they could do no worse than the courts), they have not been given the power and autonomy needed to deal with the problem. Leverage beyond the use of litigation for compliance is needed. For example, developing municipalities are usually "ratable hungry," actively seeking commercial and industrial development. The power to impose moratoriums on all commercial and industrial development in municipalities not in compliance could serve as a powerful tool for the Council.

The Mount Laurel decisions are a good example of the judicial activism that has flourished in New Jersey. A longer time period is needed to determine if these opinions will be regarded as a costly legal exercise caused by judicial intervention in areas beyond their range of control, or as the catalyst that increased the housing opportunities for the low and moderate income members of society. As of this writing, it can be noted that the number of attorneys and planners newly affluent as a result of this opinion probably exceeds the number of formerly urban low and moderate income families with new Mount Laurel housing in the suburbs. While there are no firm figures, it has been estimated that some 2,000 affordable housing units in fourteen communities have been built since 1975 and many more are in the development pipeline. The State Council on Affordable Housing would like to see 145,707 units by 1993 but many housing advocates doubt it has the authority to make recalcitrant localities comply (Hanley 1988; Mallach 1988). One authority on the New Jersey experience, Alan Mallach (1988) has written that

. . . the housing situation for the poor in New Jersey has gotten worse in the last five years, rather than better. The efforts triggered by the Mount Laurel decision to provide more affordable housing appear modest, even trivial, if compared to the massive economic pressures at work making housing more and more expensive, while shrinking the remaining affordable housing to the vanishing point.

Indeed, the failure of the New Jersey fair share approach can be seen in the transformation of the fair share principle from one of opening the suburbs to the inner city poor to one of assisting the upwardly mobile suburbanites. This transformation was accomplished with the approval of all the major actors in the process: the developers, politicians, and suburban residents. Mallach (1988) goes so far as to suggest that the State Council on Affordable Housing has participated in this transformation due to its indifference to the fact that the inner city poor are not being helped by their program.

They have made no effort to ensure that Mt. Laurel units are affordable to the deeply poor; have made only token efforts to generate the production of rental housing, or promote affirmative marketing of lower income units in urban areas; and have adopted rules that ensure that nearly all of the units being built will return to marketplace prices in six, ten, or at most, twenty years from today.

In addition, the Regional Contribution Agreements have also tended to benefit the "good" moderate income households who desire an urban locale, thereby stimulating the urban gentrification process (Mallach 1988).

The proof of these assertions can be seen from an analysis of the impact of fair share policies on low income households. Low income households are defined as those whose income is below 50% of the median income in their housing region while moderate income is defined as falling between 50 and 80% of this median. Based on the latest figures from COAH, the median income for a family of three living in housing region five (Camden, Gloucester, Burlington, and Mercer Counties) is $32,085. Thus, a moderate income for a family of three would be no more than $25,668 per year and a low income family would earn below $16,010 per year. Total need for low income units has been estimated at some 81,360 or two-thirds of the total fair share allocation. According to COAH guidelines, "At least half of all units devoted to low and moderate income households shall be affordable to low income." Clearly, there is a pressing need to deliver low cost units, and, due to the limited amount of resources that low income households have available for housing, a significant amount of this housing will have to be rental (Gregorio 1988).

However, looking at current figures, little truly low cost housing is in the pipeline. Specifically, municipalities that have a fair share obligation of 125 units or more must provide a rental component of 20% of the total number of low and moderate income units. Half of this number must be affordable to those of low income. Of the fifty-five municipalities to whom COAH has granted substantive certification, 11,461 fair share units have been allocated of which just 2,501 will be rental units and only half of these will be for low income households. Seen in relation to the need for low income units, the current rate of progress under the Fair Housing Act appears insufficient (Gregorio 1988).

Another problem is that the new Mount Laurel process has become dominated by developers, politicians, and others who have little interest in ensuring the promulgation of policies in the spirit of the initial Mount Laurel principles. Those who are concerned, namely the low income housing advocates, have been "frozen out" of the process since they are a perceived threat to the existing accommodation (Mallach 1988). Worse, one prominent low income housing activist has been subjected to an outright political attack for his continuing efforts to promote truly low cost suburban housing for the inner city poor (O'Connor and Shaffer 1988).

The Court still has a remaining option. The Court can award damages. There is no indication that it has considered doing so thus far. However, the threat of damages, particularly punitive damages, would probably get faster and more innovative compliance than any further Court decisions and legislative requirements. That the Court is reluctant to utilize this option is perfectly understandable given the ongoing furor over the decisions.

FEDERAL EFFORTS AT PROVIDING
FAIR SHARE HOUSING

The local level has been the venue for most of the recent attempts to implement a fair share policy but a significant federal fair share policy was also attempted. The major experiment with federal fair share policy occurred in 1969 as the Nixon administration prepared to respond to Congressional authorization to build significant amounts of low cost housing. In answer to the question of where all this housing would be located, an administration spokesperson said, "There is no reason why the suburbs cannot set aside areas for public and publicly supported housing" (Polikoff 1978, 32). This pronouncement was elevated to a policy statement in the "President's Second Annual Report on National Housing Goals" issued in 1970. The report stated, "There must be an end to the concentration of the poor in land short central cities, and the inaccessibility to the growth of employment opportunities in suburban areas." Nixon articulated this approach as fostering the development of "open communities" that provided jobs and housing for families of all income levels and racial characteristics.

It appears that the administration was initially sincere in its efforts to see this policy reach implementation. The policy was to be implemented by means of linking it to other federal program expenditures. Throughout the first half of 1970, there was a steady stream of supportive rhetoric, several strong expressions of presidential support and a specific legislative proposal to ensure the implementation of this policy. The legislative proposal sent to the House Subcommittee on Housing would have empowered the federal government to override local zoning ordinances that excluded subsidized low income housing projects. However, in the space of a few months, the administration retreated from its support for this policy and accepted a weakened version that relied on local governments for any dispersal.

The reasons for this about-face are detailed elsewhere in some detail. Suffice it to say that the issue of fair share was quickly turned into one of forced integration by suburban local officials. A firestorm of protest confronted George Romney, the Secretary of HUD, in a Chicago suburb when he attempted to explain his support for open communities. The political pressure was too much for him and the administration to bear. The retreat from the fair share policy was rapid and disorderly. From then on, the administration made it clear that it was not mandating that any suburban community accept low cost housing as a price for participating in federal programs. In a further concession, "fair housing" was defined by the administration as ensuring equal access for people of similar income levels regardless of race, but citizens had to select private housing within their means. The administration's new policy for locating low cost housing could be summarized as follows: "It would be helpful if you would accept some of the ghetto poor, but the law does not require you to do so and, as long as you avoid overt racial discrimination, preserving your local land use decisionmaking prerogatives is a more important value than racial and economic deconcentration" (Polikoff 1978, 47). With that, the retreat was complete.

It should be mentioned that Secretary Romney worked tirelessly for the principle of fair share based on regional cooperation of cities and suburbs. He forcefully promoted it as the only antidote to the pernicious segregating effect of the country's fragmented pattern of local government authority. Romney was not the first public official to raise this issue but his particularly close association with this controversial policy would in large measure lead to his eventual ouster from the Nixon administration. Romney was a liability, an advocate of forceful federal intervention at a time when the administration was happily anticipating the freedom promised by the soon to be unveiled new federalism. At the end, forced out of government, he was reduced to trying to promote his policy by means of an organized citizens' movement that produced no lasting impact.

ADDITIONAL FEDERAL FAIR SHARE INITIATIVES

Many authorities feel that national fair share policies can be found in the federal community development program requirements for housing assistance plans and the encouragement of states and localities to modify exclusionary suburban zoning (Mandelker et al. 1981, 20). While these policy thrusts are clearly present, their effectiveness remains quite minimal due to the host of bureaucratic and legal maneuvers open to localities that are loath to comply.

Federal Fair Housing Efforts

The thrust of fair housing legislation is similar to fair share in that it seeks to enhance access to all housing markets on behalf of those who have previously been excluded. However, fair housing legislation focuses on acts of discrimination against racial and ethnic minorities rather than economic minorities.

Title VIII of the Civil Rights Act of 1968, amended by the Housing and

Community Development Act of 1974, the "Fair Housing Law" enacted by Congress, declared "A national policy of providing fair housing throughout the United States." This law makes discrimination based on race, color, religion, sex, or national origin illegal in connection with the sale or rental of most housing and any vacant land offered for residential construction or use (U.S. H.U.D. 1984b). Certain acts are prohibited by the Fair Housing Law:

1. Refusing to sell or rent to, deal or negotiate with any person (Section 804(a)).
2. Discriminating in terms or conditions for buying or renting housing (Section 804(b)).
3. Discriminating by advertising that housing is available only to persons of a certain race, color, religion, sex, or national origin (Section 804(c)).
4. Denying that housing is available for inspection, sale, or rent when it really is available (Section 804(d)).
5. "Blockbusting"—For profit, persuading owners to sell or rent housing by telling them that minority groups are moving into the neighborhood (Section 804(e)).
6. Denying or making different terms or conditions for home loans by commercial lenders, such as banks, savings and loan associations and insurance companies (Section 805).
7. Denying to anyone the use of or participation in any real estate services, such as brokers' organizations, multiple listing services, or other facilities related to the selling or renting of housing (Section 806) (U.S. H.U.D. 1984).

Other efforts were undertaken by the federal government to expand housing choices. In 1972, the Affirmative Fair Housing Marketing (AFHM) Regulations were adopted by the Department of Housing and Urban Development (HUD). These regulations require all developers of federally assisted or insured housing to "market in a manner designed to attract 'those persons who traditionally would not have been expected to apply for housing,' primarily Blacks, Spanish-Americans, Orientals and American Indians" (U.S. H.U.D. 1975).

Relatively few studies of the effectiveness of the fair housing enforcement agencies have been conducted. However, in one recent study, Goering (1986b) claims that there has been a measurable improvement in their performance. While the empirical evidence points to some improvement, most authorities would agree with Goering's conclusion that:

Minority households continue to experience substantial levels of housing deprivation, segregation, and discrimination. Their housing conditions, though gradually improving in physical condition and the extent of crowding, are increasingly affected by the higher costs of renting and purchasing a home. Minorities in search of decent housing will have to pay more as well as risk experiencing either subtle or direct forms of discrimination, in order to find a home comparable to that of whites. All too often the act of discrimination will remain unfelt and undetected. Different or fewer apartments or homes are shown to minorities but not to whites (Goering 1986b, 209).

Up to this point, we have examined the progress of local and federal level efforts to develop low and moderate income housing in the suburbs. The rest of this chapter will examine some of the reasons that this approach has proven so costly and ineffective. The major reason advanced here is that attempts to develop suburban low income housing are antithetical to a number of strong American traditions, most centrally, the local home rule tradition.

THEORETICAL EXPLANATION
FOR SUBURBAN EXCLUSIVITY

It seems clear that local and federal fair share policies have failed to produce meaningful amounts of low cost housing even in a context of strong legal support and after years of dedicated efforts by local advocates. Simply put, the strength of the opposition has proved formidable. As a result, it is helpful to seek a theoretical explanation of this policy failure.

Much good research has been done on the persistence of suburban exclusivity in the United States (Downs 1973; Danielson 1976; Polikoff 1978; Momeni 1986). Perhaps the most persuasive explanation of this phenomenon can be found in an insightful work on community change written by Constance Perin. The attraction of the American vision of highly independent home rule communities can be gleaned from her book *Everything In Its Place*. In this book, she examines the social meaning behind America's highly segregated land use patterns which are typified by affluent white-dominated suburbs surrounding much less affluent black and minority-dominated inner cities. The basic thrust of her argument is that these patterns arose because they were consciously established at the local level by the "old timers" eager to set demarcated zones separating the various classes and groups in our society. The arena for this was the suburbs because the city was too large and already too heterogeneous to control. Thus, restrictive suburban zoning laws were passed to ensure that only those people with an income mirroring that which already prevailed could reside in their town. The zoning ordinance was the vehicle for this process. It was utilized to regulate and control land use for health and safety reasons. The "old timers" would resist any change or growth in their community, but when presented with the inevitability of growth, they would see that it was carefully controlled. Land use control was interpreted as meaning the encouragement of single family detached housing on large lots. Thus zoning was used to control the rate and type of change that a suburban community would undergo and most importantly, it would ensure that the newcomers were like the "old timers" to the maximum degree possible. Thus, efforts were aimed at excluding large apartments that might be affordable for city minorities. Only small studio or one bedroom apartments might be allowed so as to afford accommodation to the local elderly and single people. The degree of control exercised by these localities can be seen from a partial list of land uses excluded from single family zones. For instance, the possibility of unrelated individuals pooling resources to buy a large home was excluded, as was the possibility of making part of the home into a separate "granny flat" so as to enable an aged mother to reside with the homeowner (Perin 1977).

Perin stresses the local nature of this land use control process. She argues that it is a social mechanism that allows the community to define and control its destiny. But while zoning imparts a high degree of social control, it fails to allow for truly well planned communities. This is because zoning allows each development proposal to be decided on its merits without resort to precedent. There is no mechanism that allows the community to see the big picture of where these individual decisions are leading. While communities do prepare master plans, they have no legal force so they are routinely ignored. It is a chaotic situation that produces abominable communities: dreary subdivisions of identical houses serviced by garish strip shopping areas or massive malls. Ironically, it is often socially dysfunctional in the long run. As suburbanites age and seek smaller accommodations, they are often forced to leave their home community in search of apartments or townhouses.

Racism and ethnocentrism play a central role here. Perin cites the fact that strong zoning enabling legislation grew up concurrently with the political movement to restrict foreign immigration to the United States. This movement grew by playing on the prejudices of those fearful of coming into contact with people different from themselves.

Whether the causal factors were essentially economic as the Marxists hold, or a combination of both social and economic forces, as Perin claims, the operations of our suburban land use control mechanisms have resulted in an increase in the degree of segregation in our society. Another negative effect has been that this development pattern lured the best and the brightest in American society from those urban communities that were grappling with problems of unemployment, poverty, and homelessness. More importantly, it removed their tax dollars from city treasuries ensuring that cities would always stagger from one fiscal crisis to another and never be fully able to respond to the housing crisis or any crisis. The rapid loss of the white middle classes ensured that most city schools would become increasingly segregated which would in turn occasion more white flight and a stagnant housing market. This socioeconomic segregation ensures that the cities have been the locus of a significant proportion of our housing problems but are denied the funds with which to address them effectively.

THE REPUBLICAN ADMINISTRATION'S APPROACH TO HOME RULE

Exclusionary suburbs are not a new phenomenon (Downs 1973; Danielson 1976). What is new is the broadening political impact of these home rule communities. It should be stressed that local home rule in the broad sense of the term is a laudatory concept when applied in partnership with a strong federal government. What is problematic with the Republican administration's approach to home rule is that it accentuates the self-interested and ultimately exclusionary thread that is a necessary component of this concept. It does this by abdicating federal responsibility for those who need the help of governmental authority and who are not likely to receive it at the local suburban level. It has added the federal government to the list of those unwilling to lend assistance. Indeed, it has further empowered those very units of government most disinclined to do so. "Creative federalism" has allowed these negative aspects of home rule to become predominant where before they were held in check by the more inclusionary community-oriented components which received federal encouragement and support. The result is that today there is a lack of balance in the social fabric of our communities that was less prevalent forty years ago (Schorr 1986; Harrington 1984; W. J. Wilson 1987; Lekachman 1982; Dear and Wolch 1987). We are in danger of becoming a country characterized by a series of segregated communities that are increasingly self-interested and fearful. This is not a good or just or even safe way to build for the future.

INTERRELATIONSHIP OF FAIR SHARE HOUSING POLICY AND HOMELESSNESS

Fair share housing policy is directly relevant to the resolution of homelessness in our society since it provides a response to the increasing class segregation that prevails as a result of our community development process. So long as we allow the maintenance of segregated slum housing, there will be recurring cycles of homelessness, poverty, and poverty-based behavior. The long-term solution to homelessness is to be found in the full economic, social, and physical integration of the poor into American society (Hochschild 1984; Lukas 1985; Burt and Pittman 1986; Badcock 1984; Dear and Wolch 1987; Logan 1983). The fair share housing policy must be at the heart of any policy aimed at reducing homelessness.

Without a fair share component, homelessness will be tackled in a piecemeal place-oriented fashion that will not get at the root of the problem. That can be done only by broad social and economic programs at the national and state levels which will be discussed in the final section. Prior to that, the next section will review some of the difficulties associated with various programmatic efforts to directly assist the homeless.

Part IV

POLICY INITIATIVES
TO ASSIST
THE HOMELESS

7

Policies and Programs to Alleviate Homelessness

The rising numbers of homeless in our cities and towns have been chronicled in newspapers and television. As a result, homelessness is now perceived as an issue of importance at both the local level and national level. Since homelessness is a highly visible social problem that has existed for some time, the extent of any governmental response is central to any policy analysis. Accordingly, this chapter will assess the essentially local response that has greeted the rise in homelessness in this country. It will also analyze some of the policy issues that have confronted local leaders as they struggle to assist the homeless.

SHELTER PROVISION; POLICY ISSUES

Whatever the root causes of homelessness, by the early 1980s many communities were confronted with the need to respond to the plight of a growing number of individuals without shelter or any immediate way to secure it. In many instances, the initial local policy debate regarding the homeless centered on what responsibility, if any, a locality had for providing shelter for its own homeless as well as those from other localities and regions. Many localities approached the problem of homelessness by denying any responsibility for providing shelter. Having to cope with the problem, some shipped their homeless out of their jurisdiction, usually to nearby urban municipalities which were known to provide shelters. Many localities denied their homeless access to municipal welfare due to the fact that they did not have a fixed address. Recent court rulings in several states have made it clear that these interpretations are insufficient and that localities must provide emergency food, clothing, and shelter to the homeless in a speedy manner (Governor's Task Force on the Homeless 1985).

Homeless advocates in these states, having established the right of the homeless to temporary emergency municipal shelter services, are now turning to the question of how to best provide these services to the homeless on a long-term basis. As a result, there is a continuing professional debate concerning what kind of shelters should be established, their location, their range of staffing, etc. (New Jersey Department of Human Services 1986).

For example, a few municipalities have established their own shelters for the homeless while many more work with and support a network of church-related and other nonprofit service providers. These providers supply an array of services for the homeless. Services range from basic evening accommodation in a church basement provided by lay volunteers during the cold months, to 24-hour shelters staffed with professional social workers. One type of accommodation for the homeless that is provided by many municipal social service agencies and some churches is short-term lodging in local motels. This situation is seen as emergency housing to bridge the gap until permanent housing is secured. However, short term often ends up becoming long term. Moreover, due to lack of available space, municipalities often have to send their homeless outside the boundaries of their community in search of a motel that will take them. This increases the problems of servicing these families since they must return to their home community for schooling and other needs. The cost of "welfare taxis" that transport the offspring back and forth to school is prohibitively expensive. The trauma of such a dislocated life for youngsters is profound. The quality of these motels varies widely. Some provide a fairly good living environment while others are too chaotic and have all the drawbacks of the poorly-run SROs.

Specialized services at these shelters range from nonexistent to substantial. Therefore, some shelters are able to respond to individual social and economic needs of their guests and help them begin to work toward reentry into society while others are hard-pressed to provide basic services. The patchwork nature of this system is evident as is its inability to adequately respond to the fundamental causal factors of homelessness that threaten to overwhelm it (New Jersey Department of Community Affairs 1986; Mayer and Shuster 1985; Schutt 1987; Hope and Young 1986a).

A major problem with providing sheltering services concerns the extent to which a municipality and shelter providers can force people into a shelter even if it appears to be in their own best interests. An example would be someone sleeping over a steam vent in freezing weather. In some localities, authorities pick up anyone found outside if the temperature falls below a certain point. Many civil libertarians are cognizant of the fact that many of the homeless choose to avoid shelters because they find them dangerous places. Others are aware that some prefer sleeping outdoors, a facet of their lifestyle built up over the years and not voluntarily changed. Whether our society protects someone's right to place him or herself at risk of death is an issue further complicated by the realities surrounding the lifestyle of these often mentally troubled people. This issue is still being debated in our courts (Kozol 1988; Hope and Young 1986a; Schutt 1987; Baxter and Hopper 1981; Campi 1985).

The quality of care and the rules and regulations that accompany this care is also an important matter. Many shelters, particularly those that are religiously affiliated, require adherence to specific rules and regulations by those who occupy their shelters. Some of these rules are common sense safety regulations but other rules place unwelcome restrictions on the freedoms of the individual guests. Some shelters require the presence of guests at religious services for instance, while others require all personal belongings be turned in to a warden. Clearly, such restrictions may serve to keep appreciable numbers of the needy away, often forcing them out on the streets (Schutt 1987; Hope and Young 1986a; Kates 1985).

There are many obstacles to the sheltering of the homeless that exist on the local level. One of the most salient is the "not in my backyard" (NIMBY) syndrome so prevalent in communities. Trying to locate a shelter, particularly in a residential setting, is a very difficult and often impossible process in this country. Local community organizations join together to put intense political pressure on local officials. As a result, they concoct any and every expedient in order to block approval of the shelter (Haar and Iatrides 1974; Polikoff 1978; Schmitt 1987; Bourney 1986; Ritzdorf and Sharpe 1987).

Shelters, due to their public service orientation, need to be regulated. Often there are state health and fire safety regulations specifically drawn up for group homes, boarding homes, and the like. The regulations cover safety features such as sprinkler systems, number of bathrooms, fire escapes, size and type of exit doors, as well as a host of related considerations. Local building and safety codes usually must be satisfied as well. These govern the type of materials used in any renovation, as well as electricity and plumbing certifications. Zoning also controls the use to which a building can be put. Occupancy permits, specifying the maximum number of individuals allowed to reside at the facility, must be secured. A license must be obtained if food is to be prepared and served in the shelter (Governor's Task Force on the Homeless 1985).

All these requirements provide ample opportunity for obstruction and delay. For instance, communities often try to ensure that no shelter will be located in their community by prohibiting them in all zoning districts. Many states such as New Jersey have passed laws specifically prohibiting the complete zoning out of shelters and other multiple occupancy uses. Nonetheless, permits and approvals must be obtained before a local shelter can commence operation (Governor's Task Force on the Homeless 1985). The difficulty this often presents is discussed below.

Suburban Site Feasibility

It is important to note that there exist relatively few shelters in suburban areas. Those shelters that exist in the suburbs are connected to local churches and synagogues. As long as these shelters operate on property owned by the religious institution and in conformance with the local health code or any state regulations for public shelters, they cannot be prevented from operating by a municipality alleging a breach of local zoning regulations. Such shelters are often established in the church basement, the rectory, or the equivalent. In some cases, these small shelters operate on a rotating basis utilizing a network of participating religious institutions so that a different one is used each week (Fox 1985).

Zoning Issues

With regard to zoning, these ordinances pose a significant obstacle to siting a shelter in most suburban communities, even in those jurisdictions with laws favoring shelters. This is not to say that the legal battles cannot be won. The problem is that the battles must be fought on a case by case basis making the siting a long and tortuous process at best (Bourney 1986; Sciarra 1987).

Small residential shelters operated by nonprofit sponsors do exist in the suburbs but providers freely admit the problematic aspects of establishing them in resistant jurisdictions. They sketch out the process whereby the nonprofit sponsoring agency patiently goes through the motions of applying for a zoning permit for a shelter in a residential zone. The process becomes one of repeated delays and official obfuscation in the face of strong opposition by residents and nearby property owners. The next step involves a suit by the provider alleging illegal application of zoning authority. The provider is thus reduced to the status of petitioner asking for just application of local laws and is constrained from providing a service until the case is heard. The interminable nature of these proceedings effectively stymies any positive action regarding the actual operation of the shelter. As a result of the lessons learned from this experience, some suburban nonprofit providers have decided to take the initiative by reversing litigatory positions. In one case, this was accomplished by the simple stratagem of establishing the shelter first and then applying for zoning permission. When the expected denial was given, the provider applied for an injunction pending an appeal on the merits of the case. This was granted and the shelter is operating in a residential area while the legal arguments proceed. It is widely anticipated that the legality of this shelter will be upheld just as similar shelters have been in many jurisdictions (Knight 1987).

One successful approach to the problem has been developed in New York for group homes for the mentally ill. After encountering strong local resistance to the siting of such homes, the state legislature passed the Padavan law which allows decisions about group home siting to bypass local zoning so long as the homes meet state codes. Local input is restricted to questions of local over saturation and alternative sites in the same jurisdiction. Timetables for appeals were established, but such appeals cannot prevent the opening of the home. This legislation is credited with speeding the acceptance of group homes and with the successful implementation of a fair share approach to siting. A similar law governing the siting of homeless shelters is sorely needed (Winerip 1988a).

Wanted: A Shelter to Housing Continuum

Most local shelter advocates agree on the need for a spectrum of shelters designed to handle specific populations. Moreover, they see a need for a spectrum of housing that will allow those in emergency shelters to move into long-term housing. Transitional housing to bridge the gap between emergency shelter and long-term housing is an important part of this spectrum. The Philadelphia Coalition for the Homeless has espoused a sensible continuum of housing as the best local policy approach. Their continuum includes the following stages: initial contact, short-term shelter, case management, long-term placement, income, permanent housing, and further services. An important component of this program is the need for trained staff keyed into the service needs of particular shelters (Philadelphia Committee for the Homeless 1985). Another salient component is the need for a homelessness prevention program that seeks to help those about to lose their housing. Positive intervention with the mortgage company or landlord is the most cost effective strategy. New Jersey has a program that offers such bridging assistance (Governor's Task Force on the Homeless 1985).

Shelter Size

Clearly, there are many problems that must be overcome if we are to be able to provide shelter in our society for our homeless. But within the arguments over practical realities of shelter provision, there appears to be a major policy debate concerning what constitutes the best way to provide emergency shelter for the homeless. There is a strong feeling among some advocates for the homeless that small scale (25 bed) community-based facilities should be made available for the homeless rather than large institutional (100 bed and up) shelters. It is argued that policy should be directed toward normalization to the maximum extent possible and this means small home-style shelters with maximum privacy and support services. The aim of this approach is to minimize the trauma of homelessness which can easily push an individual into mental ill health from which his or her recovery is very problematic (Montgomery County Government 1985; Community Affairs 1987). Critics of this approach refer to the problems of cost factors and political realities that favor a centralized urban location as being most achievable. They characterize the small scale approach as naive given our sociopolitical power structure.

There are strong parallels between the rationale for small community-based shelters for the homeless and the long and profoundly reasoned history of the community living arrangements (CLA) for the mentally ill. Indeed, a significant proportion of the homeless exhibit some form of mental illness and significant numbers of homeless individuals are the very people deinstitutionalized from mental institutions. This is not the place to engage in a detailed history of the deinstitutionalization movement but suffice it to say that deinstitutionalization was based on a desire to "normalize" the living arrangements of as many mentally ill people as possible. This desire was rooted in the civil rights movement and the extension of this movement to all groups and classes of people. Often, mentally ill individuals had been incapable of maintaining proper standards of behavior that would allow them to function in the community. The advent of psychotropic drugs gave these individuals control over their deportment and allowed them to be reintroduced into the community. With this development, deinstitutionalization proceeded on the rationale that all people have a right to live in the least restrictive, most normal community setting possible rather than being helped in an institutional setting. It was argued that this rule should prevail unless there was a clear and compelling reason to believe that the patient posed a threat to himself or others (Botwinick and Weinstein 1985).

Clearly, this line of reasoning could be applied to the question of shelter policy for the homeless. Such reasoning would support the use of small residential-style shelters whenever possible, restricting the use of large institutional shelters to initial intake and observation and emergency use only. A more complete review of these issues is provided in the case study in Chapter 8.

Support Services

Many shelter programs provide a variety of counseling services. The number and variety of counseling services vary widely among shelter programs. Few can afford the full range of specialty services required. Most do stress services aimed at achieving independence for their clients given their individual needs and requirements. Most are well-connected to the local welfare services establishment and are able to ensure that their clients receive their entitlements. Some programs are able to marshal an impressive array of counseling and physical supports to assist clients in their reentry into society. Some nonprofit agencies such as the Volunteers of America frequently provide clients with donated vehicles and major appliances to lessen the start-up costs associated with establishing a new household (U.S. Department of Health and Human Services 1984; Public Technology Inc. 1985; Mayer and Shuster 1985).

Employment placement services are quite problematic. Many formerly homeless clients are first employed by their host agency or an affiliate. In this way they are able to reestablish a successful work record. Others who were made homeless for economic reasons may be able to make a more direct transition to the job market. Other clients have various physical or mental problems that are likely to prevent them from finding permanent employment. Others will be able to do so only if affordable day care services are available.

Needless to say, a major problem confronting many formerly homeless individuals is their lack of employment skills in an increasingly specialized job market. Job training programs may be of some help in these situations but these will be of little assistance to the older or low-skilled homeless clients. The fact is that much homelessness was created due to the loss of well-paying low-skill jobs in the manufacturing sector. Only the return of such job opportunities or their equivalent will suffice to reintroduce many of our homeless citizens to the workplace (Fox 1985; Harrington 1984).

SUMMARY OF LOCAL SHELTER POLICY

The list of local policy initiatives is an impressive testament to the generosity of spirit that prevails in our towns and cities across the country. Clearly, a tremendous amount of selfless dedication has gone into the development of this local system. Nonetheless, it must be pointed out that these efforts are not able to keep up with the rising numbers of homeless nor are they always able to provide an adequate level of service. These efforts are most successful at temporarily sheltering the homeless and less so in providing long term solutions to their plight. This is not to fault the efforts being made but rather to point out the unfair burden placed upon the local level. Recently, resentment over having to pay for increased services for the homeless surfaced during a budget hearing in Philadelphia and was a factor in the city council's unwillingness to fully fund the mayor's social services budget request. Many local officials point out that since homelessness results from forces beyond the control of any one locality or region, it requires a national response. The rest of this chapter will review the governmental response to homelessness.

THE GOVERNMENTAL RESPONSE

Recently, the number of the nation's emergency shelters and their capacities have been growing rapidly. Emergency shelter has traditionally been a service provided by private charities. Private nonprofit groups still operate over 90% of all shelters. Of this total, religious groups operate approximately 40%. It is only recently that any significant public monies have gone to fund these shelters. Public shelter operations began in New York City in response to the sheer size of the problem there. In 1983, public sources funded 37% of the cost of all shelter operations: some $80 million. Private sources contributed the remaining 63%. Volunteer labor for the year was estimated to be worth $31 million (Redburn and Buss 1986). Today, there is increasing pressure on federal, state, and local levels to do more to assist the homeless. The best way to ascertain the current level of aid is to review the response at each level of government as well as the private and nonprofit sectors.

The Federal Level

The Reagan administration's response to the existence of increasing numbers of homeless was colored by an attitude (alluded to earlier) which is dismissive of the problem and seeks to push responsibility for devising solutions onto local governments (U.S. H.U.D. 1984; Koch 1987). Accordingly, there was little in the way of concrete assistance forthcoming from Washington even as increasing evidence pointed to a major social problem. Pushed to respond by demonstrations and fasts by homeless advocates such as Mitch Snyder, the government reluctantly agreed to open up some federal facilities to the homeless in the Washington, D.C., area. In addition, it directed the Department of Defense to assess whether any disused buildings could be used as temporary shelters and HUD was directed to offer certain properties to local municipalities as shelters. Very few examples of such property transfers exist due to locational and structural problems with individual properties and problems with effective coordination between the federal and local levels (Partnership for the Homeless 1987).

For example, HUD has been authorized to make available, as transitional housing, single family homes that it has repossessed due to mortgage default. These units are to be leased for nominal rents but for short terms only. Only a handful of units have been made available to date. Indeed, the National Coalition for the Homeless is currently suing both HUD and the Veterans Administration (Lee v. Pierce; and National Coalition for the Homeless, et al. v. United States Veterans Administration) as a result of their inaction in this area (Safety Network 1988a). HUD has also encouraged local public housing authorities to move the homeless up on their public housing waiting lists. This policy is highly contentious in urban areas and does not enjoy the support of local public housing authorities. Few instances of such queue jumping have been processed because most urban areas have lengthy housing waiting lists and a major worry is that some families would make themselves homeless intentionally in order to qualify for a housing unit (Redburn and Buss 1986).

The Department of Defense (DOD) has also been encouraged to make available disused military facilities and housing units when possible. A central problem with such units is the remote location of most military facilities which makes it difficult to provide needed social services. For instance, in fiscal 1984 some $4 million was made available for such purposes but only $900,000 was obligated and this was spent on just two shelters. Four additional shelters have been opened at DOD facilities utilizing community and base funds. The Department of Defense has been more successful in donating surplus cots, tables, chairs, desks, and other items to existing shelters.

Beginning in 1983, Congress, by means of the Emergency Food and Shelter Program (EFSP), part of the jobs stimulus bill (PL 98-8), provided the Federal Emergency Management Agency (FEMA) with a series of individual appropriations for which municipalities could apply in order to support shelter services. In 1983, $140 million was appropriated; in 1984, $70 million; in 1985, $20 million; and in 1986, $70 million. Half of this money was to be disbursed by the states and half by a national board made up of representatives of private nonprofit charitable agencies (the national board program). This program was evaluated by the Urban Coalition which found that the national board program used $91 million in EFSP funds to distribute 85 million additional meals and 13 million additional nights of shelter. EFSP services included food vouchers, food banks and kitchens, shelter vouchers, mass shelters, and rent and mortgage assistance.

The Reagan administration rejected calls for a specific FEMA program for the homeless. It took the position that such programs are a state and local matter and that these levels of government should use their own and other federal funds for that purpose. Indeed, much of the current expansion of shelter services has been funded by the federal government via existing Community Development Block Grant (CDBG) funds. Since 1983, some $77 million in CDBG funds have been spent by localities to acquire and rehabilitate buildings for shelters, pay shelter operating costs and other related expenses. Needless to say, to the extent that localities are forced to so utilize their scarce CDBG funds, they are less able to maintain other program commitments (U.S. Committee on Government Operations 1985).

The remainder of the initial federal effort to assist the homeless has consisted of directives to diverse agencies to provide an array of in-kind services as well as obsolete furniture and equipment that might be utilized in shelter operations. In this regard, the Department of Health and Human Services (HHS) was assigned the chair of a new Inter-Agency Task Force on Food and Shelter for the Homeless in 1983. Its role is to provide technical assistance and to help local programs gain access to surplus federal buildings and equipment. The task force works with the National Citizen's Committee on Food and Shelter for the Homeless, a nonpartisan group that acts as a broker in the partnership between the government and the community in establishing a food or shelter project. The task force has been instrumental in securing a DOD-owned building and HHS funds in order to establish a 400-bed shelter in Washington, D.C. Aside from the DOD rehabilitation funds, the General Services Administration (GSA), DOD, and HUD have no money to pay for emergency shelter costs. Each agency has been instructed to lease available facilities at the lowest possible cost. The local leasing organization is responsible for organizing, administering, and financing the operation of the shelter. HHS Social Services block grants have been used to aid the homeless. It is not possible to identify the total amount of such funds spent on serving the homeless since these grants are disbursed by the states. In New Jersey, for instance, $1.9 million out of a total Social Services Block Grant of $4.9 million was used for the provision of emergency food and shelter. The Alcohol, Drug Abuse, and Mental Health Administration (ADAMHA) spent $5.6 million on thirty-seven projects designed to assist homeless persons with alcohol, drug, and mental health problems. The task force has also worked with state social service agencies in order to ease restrictions that prevent those with no fixed address from receiving entitlement benefits. Several states now allow the homeless to qualify by listing the address of a shelter. The Veterans Administration (VA) has developed an outreach program that entails visits to selected shelters in order to identify and accept applications from homeless veterans for VA disability benefits. HHS has a similar outreach effort seeking those elderly homeless who may not be receiving Social Security benefits. There is no information about the numbers of homeless affected by either effort. The ACTION agency has some 200 VISTA volunteers working in 50 projects for the homeless. The U.S. Department of Agriculture (USDA) dispenses food stamps to the homeless with no fixed address or length of residency requirement. It also makes surplus food available to nonprofit institutions including soup kitchens and shelters. It is not possible to ascertain the total funding that goes to the homeless under these programs (U.S. G.A.O. 1985).

Many members of Congress have been very concerned by the crisis of homelessness and a number of bills supporting increased spending for the homeless have been introduced. One has been passed and signed into law: the Stewart B. McKinney Homeless Assistance Act. This act provides funds for a number of new initiatives to help the homeless as well as additional funding for existing programs. This bill concentrates its funding on emergency services to the homeless. Appropriations under the Act already exceed $350 million and will likely reach $1 billion by the end of Fiscal Year 1988 if the promised appropriations are enacted by Congress. Funding under this program is triggered by the production of a Comprehensive Homeless Assistance Plan by the locality seeking funds. These plans must be approved by HUD. Funding would then be provided for emergency shelter grants, a supportive housing demonstration program, a supplemental assistance program, and an innovative demonstration program. Many of these programs require 50% local funding or an "in kind" match. Funding extensions for ongoing programmatic efforts provide for an increase in Section 8 rent subsidy certificates for SRO moderate rehabilitation, an increased effort to identify surplus property suitable for sheltering the homeless, and additional block grant funding for existing programs dealing with health care (HHS), mental health (HHS), community mental health services (HHS), alcohol and drug abuse treatment, emergency food and shelter programs (FEMA), emergency community services homeless grants (HHS), homeless children education grants (ED), adult literacy (ED), veterans job training, and additional domiciliary beds (VA) (Safety Network 1987).

Analysis

The McKinney Act is seen by advocates for the homeless as just an interim measure. They are currently concentrating their efforts on securing the passage of a $2 billion annual housing program designed to fund some 350,000 permanent low cost housing units. Such a program would be the first federal authorization for low cost housing in over five years. New units would be created through a combination of subsidized new construction and partly from additional rent subsidy certificates or vouchers (Safety Network 1988b).

Most of the federal efforts can be seen as supportive of local efforts to assist the homeless. These efforts are concentrated on the provision of temporary shelter services rather than addressing the lack of permanent low cost housing and adequate job opportunities.

The State Level

At the state level, responses to homelessness depend on the size of the problem and the vigor with which advocates for the homeless press their case. Some of the more active states are Massachusetts, New York, and New Jersey (Kaufman 1984; Cuomo 1987). Taking the example of New Jersey, the state had some 20,000 homeless individuals in 1983. In 1985, Newark alone reported some 8,500 homeless individuals. Currently, New Jersey has a shelter system consisting of some 54 shelters with a total of 700 beds. The response to the continuing increase in the numbers of homeless has been the establishment of a governor's commission to review the problem and to make recommendations. This group issued reports in 1983 and 1985. The 1985 report said:

Homelessness is fueled by major shortcomings in our society's safety net: the lack of sufficient affordable housing, the low level of public assistance payments, the lack of coordinated public and private efforts to deal with the problem. The root causes of homelessness lie in poverty, which is largely ignored by society. It is typified by the fact that in 1985 in New Jersey single unemployed individuals on General Assistance received $127.00 per month to meet their needs, that general assistance benefits have risen only 7% since 1974, and that AFDC welfare benefits for families are only 52% of the federal poverty guideline (Governor's Task Force, 1985).

Essentially, these reports called for greater coordination of existing services and for easier access of all homeless individuals to these services. The reports also called for increased spending for low income housing, boarding homes, and a system of small decentralized shelters. It is important to note that these reports called for these shelters to be established on a fair share policy, meaning that each community had to provide shelter for its own homeless. On the local level, each county was made responsible for establishing an oversight committee. This comprehensive emergency assistance system (CEAS) was made up of representatives of those public and private agencies responsible for providing services to the homeless (Governor's Task Force 1983, 1985). In addition, New Jersey provides the following programs and services to the homeless:

State Appropriations for the Homeless: The State Department of Human Services was granted additional funding over and above federal FEMA funds to assist the homeless. $2.85 million was appropriated in Fiscal Year 1986. These funds are for emergency services.

Social Services Block Grant Fund: The state designated $4.9 million in this fund for services to the homeless; of this, $1.9 million can be used for emergency food and shelter.

Aid to Families of Dependent Children and General Assistance Funds: A 7% increase in these funds was secured for eligible homeless.

Department of Youth and Family Services, Regional Shelters: Through a special bond issue, $600,000 was made available for the establishment of four shelters for eligible families in immediate need of shelter.

Rental Assistance Program: A $3.3 million rental assistance program was created to assist low income households with securing accommodation.

Centralized Shelter Licensing System and Uniform Shelter Standards: Legislation requiring a centralized shelter licensing system and uniform shelter standards has been enacted.

Study of New Jersey's Homeless: The Department of Human Services is conducting a study of homelessness in order to ascertain why individuals and families are rendered homeless.

Homelessness Prevention Program: New Jersey has a program of emergency short-term assistance to renters and homeowners who are experiencing difficulty with their housing payments.

The totality of these efforts place New Jersey among those few states which have fashioned a clear and comprehensive approach to the problem. This does not imply that all the needs of the homeless are being met—as can be seen from the review of local shelter policy in Chapters 8 and 9. A further assessment of the state's legislative efforts to assist the homeless are found in Chapter 9.

There are a host of national and local level advocacy groups, such as the National Coalition for the Homeless which coordinates services while exerting pressure on the political system for more resources. Allied with these groups are an array of private nonprofit service providers at the local level. They are funded from a variety of sources such as local governments, private foundations, religious denominations, and user fees (Cooper 1987; Stoner 1988). Many of the best programs for the homeless have been provided by these groups (Heskin 1987; Ritzdorf and Sharpe 1987; Vosburgh 1988). Some examples of their work are outlined in the following section.

Local Level Efforts to Assist the Homeless

As mentioned above, a sizable proportion of the homeless are housed not in homeless shelters but in local motels and hotels under the emergency assistance program. These housing arrangements are made on an emergency basis at the county level. This program is a joint federal, state, and county program that provides emergency shelter usually for a short term only. The system was set up to respond to the needs of those made homeless due to fire, flood, or other natural catastrophe. People who presented themselves as homeless for social or economic reasons had been routinely rejected for this program. A landmark court decision in New Jersey, now commonly referred to as the Matica case, enjoined all municipalities to provide such shelter to all who presented themselves as homeless, regardless of their ability to produce an address. This ruling has caused an increase of those being sheltered under the emergency assistance program. It is probably true that some of these people were housed prior to receiving emergency assistance program benefits but were in overcrowded conditions. The program has clearly functioned as a shelter resource of last resort and undoubtedly provides housing to some whose need is marginal. Nonetheless, most local officials agree that accommodations under the emergency assistance program are far from plush. As a result, there is broad agreement that the interest in the program is evidence of the degree to which many individuals are currently housed in unacceptable conditions and have no alternative paths open to them (Matica v. Atlantic City 1985).

Many of those accommodated are the working poor. Those working in service jobs that pay about $15–16,000 per annum cannot afford the median New Jersey rent of $500 per month. Thus, while the Matica decision has attracted some additional individuals into the emergency shelter system, this has been limited to those who were inadequately housed to begin with. Nonetheless, the overall trend indicates that many localities are confronting the reality that this short-term program needs to be recast as a long-term program until true low income housing resources are developed. Not surprisingly, the federal level is going in the opposite direction and has recently proposed that it will enforce the original thirty day limit on emergency assistance program payments which up until now have been commonly extended by court action (Safety Network 1988).

Examples of Local Shelter Programs

A good example of a small residential shelter that is part of a comprehensive approach to meeting the needs of the homeless is Prospect House in Springfield, Massachusetts (National Coalition for the Homeless, 1987a). This shelter with twenty beds for homeless families and individuals was established in 1983 by a coalition of over twenty human service and religious organizations. Shelter, food, and counseling services are provided. Prospect House functions on the basis of communal responsibility for shelter upkeep and maintenance. They established a private, nonprofit housing agency to run Prospect House. Funding comes partly from the state and from private and foundation sources. Volunteers are used to assist the small staff. In 1983, over 500 individuals were assisted.

A separate nonprofit, Service Providers Inc., is an umbrella agency that oversees policy with regard to homelessness in the greater Springfield area. It is concerned with unemployment, urban redevelopment, and housing policy. It has three divisions: the Affordable Housing Project, the Homeless Action Center, and Prospect House.

The Homeless Action Center was created in 1985 to provide centralized intake and referral services for individuals and families in need of emergency shelter. The center keeps track of all available shelter beds so as to be able to refer people to the appropriate shelter. They feel that this results in a more integrated, efficient shelter-finding process for agencies and individuals. The center helps people deal with the crisis of finding emergency shelter as well as working to secure long-term housing. It should be noted that this agency is not a provider of shelter services.

The Affordable Housing Project was established to assist individuals and groups to work on campaigns that generate a positive impact on affordable housing in the Springfield area. The aim was to preserve and upgrade the stock of low income housing in Springfield. Such a campaign was established to try to prevent the demolition of a local hotel which functioned as an SRO.

Kennett Square, Pennsylvania

Another example of a small shelter (thirty beds) in a residential setting can be found in Kennett Square, Pennsylvania. This shelter was an outgrowth of a feeding program for the homeless run by a faith community in the town. The faith community group purchased a fire damaged residential structure and renovated it with a mix of private and community development funding and with the aid of volunteer labor. This shelter has a pointedly noninstitutional style. It has some rooms for families and some dormitory style space for single women. A separate dormitory for men is in the basement. There are dining and sitting areas. The shelter is owned by a religious community which obviates possible zoning conflicts. The operating budget comes from the local United Way and the William Penn Foundation (M. H. Lang 1987).

Church Policy

A large proportion of the effort to assist the homeless has come from the various faith communities. These groups have been instrumental in providing both services and volunteer labor support. Many of these efforts stem from the desires of particular congregations. Others, such as the Volunteers of America and the Salvation Army, are a cross between traditional congregation-based religious groups and social service organizations. Some denominations have taken public stands in favor of increased funding for the homeless. For example, the official statement on homelessness of the Unitarian Universalist Association (1987) reads in part:

. . . Therefore be it resolved that the general assembly of the Unitarian Universalist Association affirms the provision of suitable non-transient housing as a just and achievable goal and it calls upon its member societies to:

1. Work on the establishment and continuation of programs to assist the homeless on the local, state and national levels;

2. Participate in community cooperative efforts to identify and support creative approaches in developing housing for persons receiving low incomes;

3. Encourage the development of appropriate community based housing for chronically mentally ill persons;

4. Work to provide not only short term shelter such as billeting in our homes and churches, but also intermediate term communal housing that will ensure privacy and dignity for persons in need, as well as long term housing for individuals and families, recognizing the wide range of needs among the homeless;

5. Explore and support preventative approaches to the problems of homelessness among families, the deinstitutionalized, the unemployed, the disabled, the elderly, runaways and victims of abuse; and

6. Advocate legislation at the state, provincial and national levels which will alleviate the immediate misery of homelessness while also addressing its precipitating and long term causes.

While it is clear from this review that many fine programs exist at the local level, much remains undone or is currently done poorly (U.S. H.H.S. [984; Public Technology Inc. 1985). To a large extent, this is due to the shortage of available funds, but it is also due to the host of barriers to effective program design and implementation that exist at the local level. The next chapter provides a case study of the problems that plagued one local community when it demonstrated a strong commitment to service the homeless.

8

Local Shelter Policy: A Case Study

This chapter will outline the attempts of one New Jersey community to respond to the growing problem of homelessness in its midst. The degree to which this community actively sought to fashion a workable solution to servicing the homeless is remarkable. Coincidentally, it can be seen as an early test of the proposed regional solution to homelessness advanced by Dear and Wolch (1987). However, what emerges from this narrative is the clear picture of a community unable to cope adequately with this problem. The reasons for this failure are multi-faceted but a central reason concerns the fact that the lack of a current federal policy initiative in this area has meant that localities are essentially alone in their battle to solve the problem of homelessness. The case study presented here serves to highlight the extraordinary efforts that some local authorities have brought to bear on solving the problem of homelessness. To a limited extent, it exhibits the dynamic community spirit that the Reagan administration's conservative agenda was supposed to unleash. Nonetheless, after all their efforts, the problem of homelessness continues to spiral out of control.

CAMDEN COUNTY, NEW JERSEY

Camden County, New Jersey, is in most ways a typical urbanizing county. Located across the Delaware River from Philadelphia, it has a total adult population of 334,213 living in suburban communities and in the older core City of Camden which has a population of 84,910. The suburban communities are overwhelmingly white and are relatively affluent. County per capita income is $10,499 while unemployment is 8.1% and the median house value is $42,300. In general, the New Jersey economy has made the transition from a postindustrial manufacturing base to one characterized by service and technology-related industries. Statewide, the unemployment rate of 5% in 1986 was considerably below the national average. Camden City, on the other hand, is the poorest city in New Jersey and one of the poorest in the country. Per capita income stands at just $3,966. Initially a blue collar industrial center, today some 33% of its inhabitants are below the poverty line. Its population is overwhelmingly Black and Hispanic. No new private housing has been built in the city for decades and the existing housing stock is very old, much of it in very poor condition. Between 1970 and 1980, the city demolished 6% of its housing stock. Current median values are about $15,800. One or two neighborhoods have experienced some limited renovation and gentrification but at present this amounts to a handful of buildings. Broadway, once a bustling commercial strip, now consists of a long array of vacant stores. Today, locals have very few of the services that most people take for granted. There is no movie house, few national chain stores, only one national chain food store. Many of Camden's neighborhoods appear only partly inhabited. Many are blighted by the effects of random housing demolition. As a result, trash strewn vacant lots predominate in some districts. The city suffers from the second highest reported crime rate in the state and a school district under threat of a state takeover due to the low achievement rate of its students. The city's finances are in perilous condition. Receipts from the high local property tax decline annually as residents increasingly are unable to pay. The state is forced to subsidize city services such as fire and police. The few remaining large private companies have been asked to contribute to a fund that is used to increase the salaries of city officials to a level sufficient to attract competent professionals. The local economy, initially based on heavy industry and manufacturing, declined rapidly after World War II. Countervailing growth in the service, health, and education sectors has only recently begun to create a new job base but most of these jobs require skills not possessed by the local workforce. Accordingly, official unemployment is at about 17% of the workforce (U.S. Dept. of Commerce 1983).

City revitalization plans call for the redevelopment of the shared waterfront with Philadelphia which will include an aquarium, office park, shops, marina, and middle income housing. Officials hope to capitalize on the city's proximity to Philadelphia's commercially redeveloped waterfront and prosperous downtown. A ferry service linking these two cities is planned. Important as this development is for Camden's future, there are serious questions as to whether it will produce the kind of economic revitalization that will result in direct or indirect benefits for Camden's poor. This problem has been often characterized as economic development without community development (Fainstein et al. 1986).

Current city development policy is aimed at rebuilding the tax base by attracting an economically balanced population that will allow the city to work its way out of receivership. In the administration's opinion the city is already overburdened with low income housing; it has chosen to put its limited dollars into a program designed for the more affluent. Accordingly, all available revenue has been spent to encourage the in-migration of middle income inhabitants: the new workers at the existing health, education, and service facilities in town. This is an understandable and even laudatory goal but unfortunately the city is so strapped for funds that it cannot simultaneously pursue this goal and continue to adequately service the existing low income population. Accordingly, as the city center glitters with new buildings built with state revenues, increasing numbers of homeless citizens fill the city's shelters to overflowing. This dichotomy is evidence of the failure of the Reagan administration to provide the level of assistance required to make the revitalization of our older cities possible. It is also evidence of the widening gap between the affluent suburbs and the impoverished inner city neighborhoods (Peterson, Lewis, and Carol 1986; W. J. Wilson 1987; Ellwood 1987; Hartman 1983).

In past years, the city funded nonprofit providers to operate a vacant housing rehabilitation program for low income people. This program was generally viewed as successful even if its overall output was too small to make much headway against the high rate of annual housing abandonment in the city. In 1980, with the advent of the new policy of attracting a middle class back into Camden, this program was eliminated. The city claimed at the time that it would carry out this housing program itself and would be able to do so more efficiently than the nonprofit providers. However, in five years it did not rehabilitate one house for low income households. This failure to deliver on a promise is not due to a callous disregard for the city's poor. Simply put, there are not enough dollars, particularly since the Reagan administration's cuts in the CDBG program, to carry out both programs simultaneously (Cinaglia 1985).

The declining level of affordable housing in Camden and the lack of entry level jobs paying sufficient income has combined to produce the increase in homelessness that is evidenced today. The city has chosen to respond by participating with the state and the county in establishing temporary shelters for the homeless.

HISTORY OF SHELTERING
THE HOMELESS IN CAMDEN

The approach that the City of Camden has followed in sheltering its homeless has centered on the reliance on a major private nonprofit provider, the Volunteers of America (VOA), to provide shelter, food, and counseling services. The city has provided a backup facility in the form of a large gymnasium (100 beds) to be used in the evenings only by single males bedded down on portable cots. Some limited specialized services for battered wives and substance abusers are also provided. A total of 250 beds are available. All told, some 75,716 shelter nights were provided in 1986.

Some shelter services were initially provided in renovated row houses in or near the central business district (CBD) in Camden City. This proved to be a less than optimal situation from a number of different perspectives. First, these shelters were located in a business zone. This brought the shelter and its inhabitants into conflict with the nearby merchants who increasingly demanded that the shelters be relocated. The city, after some initial hesitation, weighed in on the side of the merchants since the shelters were located in a sector of the CBD slated for revitalization under the city's ambitious redevelopment plan. In order to effect a change, a task force was assembled to look into the prospects for relocating these shelters. The task force was made up of a spectrum of representatives from local social agencies, local government, merchants, and community groups working under the aegis of the Emergency Housing Consortium of the Camden Planning and Advocacy Council/Human Services Coalition (CPAC/HSC), a coalition group empowered by the county to conduct all planning for human services. Utilizing a subcommittee structure, this task force worked diligently to solve both the problem of shelter location as well as the larger long-term problem of establishing shelter policy for the homeless. The former was addressed by a site selection subcommittee and the latter by the alternative housing subcommittee. A third subcommittee dealt with "the physical space needs of the emergency facilities population" (M. H. Lang 1987).

The consortium's first report of July 11, 1984 dealt with the issue of alternative housing. The thrust of the subcommittee's work concerned policy recommendations aimed at promoting the development of additional units of housing ". . . outside of a crisis centered facility such as the Volunteers of America operated shelters." The committee divided alternative housing into two broad categories: (1) temporary (longer term/transitional) and (2) permanent. It then established a definitional framework for a continuum of housing resources that included the following: emergency shelter, auxiliary emergency shelter, temporary housing, transitional housing, transitional housing I, transitional housing II, transitional housing III, and permanent housing (CPAC/HSC 1984; M. H. Lang 1987).

The report went on to review existing providers by category of housing supplied and it made recommendations with regard to future funding. The categories reviewed by the committee were boarding and rooming homes, subsidized housing, Section 8 certificates, shared housing, transitional housing, private development, and centralized information and referral. Needless to say, the committee recommended that all of these services be encouraged and expanded. No cost estimates were provided. Also included were a series of recommendations regarding new and existing programs that might help prevent homelessness. The committee provided a brief review of public assistance programs in order to dramatize the degree to which program recipients were unable to compete in the housing market (CPAC/HSC 1984).

All the recommendations made by this committee were based on a clear need. Many of their suggestions had been made before and will have to be made again by others. The problems remain because the solutions require funding over and above what is currently available at the local level. The nonprofit and charitable sectors cannot fill the vacuum left by the federal retreat from responsibility for housing the country's poor and needy.

This CPAC/HSC report, while correct in its call for additional resources for the homeless, sidestepped any discussion about where the homeless should be sheltered or housed. Not addressed was the issue of suburban responsibility for the 25% of the homeless who originate from these jurisdictions. This was to become an issue of some import in the county in a short time (CPAC/HSC 1984).

The second report, issued on July 27, 1984, dealt with the issue of where to relocate those shelters located in the CBD which were the target of complaints from local merchants. This committee had ". . . to identify potential sites for emergency housing shelters. The identification of potential sites has been conducted in order to recommend such sites for shelter location, to the mutual benefit of the countywide population to be housed and the redevelopment of the municipalities in which the potential sites are located." The report went on to discuss ten sites all in the City of Camden. The final recommendations narrowed this list down to three. Nowhere in the report is there mention of a suburban site nor of suburban responsibility for financing county shelters (CPAC/HSC 1984).

The third subcommittee dealt with "the physical space needs of the emergency facilities population." This subcommittee had as its purpose to:

1. Review the demographics of the population currently served by the VOA.
2. Describe the programs needed to assist the current population in the emergency housing facilities to locate housing.
3. Use the demographic and programmatic needs to describe the physical space requirements.
4. Describe the future needs of the homeless population.

This report included a list of programmatic initiatives that were deemed worthy of increased funding including additional employment opportunities, increased staffing, etc. This report was the only one to discuss the issue of centralized versus decentralized siting for shelter facilities. The report did not make clear whether or not decentralized siting included suburban jurisdictions. The report appeared to favor centralized sites due to cost savings from lowered transportation and other costs (CPAC/HSC 1984).

During 1985, there was much discussion about how to carry out the recommendations contained in the three reports compiled by CPAC/HSC. County Freeholder Joseph Carroll, a college professor, took an active part in the ongoing planning process. He formulated a plan that centralized shelter facilities for the county in a newly renovated shelter in Camden City. This shelter was to be placed in a residential area. It was based on three preexisting buildings that required extensive renovations. The result would be a complex that would allow all of the homeless in the county to be sheltered, fed, and serviced on one site. There would be a degree of segregation of client types both between and within buildings. Parking and open playground space was to be provided. The ultimate capacity was 250 individuals in mainly dormitory accommodations. Critics disparagingly labeled this facility a "super shelter" in reference to its large size and institutional nature. However, there was some evidence that other communities such as Philadelphia were moving toward similar developments which they preferred to call "campus style" shelters. The basic justification for this style of shelter is cost. Economies of scale can be realized in larger centralized facilities. Having one central shelter also eases siting problems and coordination of services (Manno 1985a).

A unique aspect of Carroll's plan was that it recognized that a significant portion of the homeless come from suburban jurisdictions. Accordingly, it suggested that all thirty-four suburban municipalities contribute to the establishment of the new $1.5 million central shelter. A funding formula was utilized based on each community's proportion of the population under the poverty line (Manno 1985a).

The shelter plan drew immediate opposition from residents of the Bergen Lanning neighborhood where it was to be located. A central point of concern was the lack of any participation by community leaders before the properties were acquired by the VOA. Strong protests were lodged before both the zoning board and city council but both bodies supported the plan. The residents then vowed to pursue the matter in court. The local paper, the Courier Post, reluctantly supported the plan, but wrote:

The City of Camden and the rest of the municipalities in Camden County have come to terms on a strategy for sheltering the county's homeless. The city will provide the site. The rest of the towns (with help from the state) will pay for it. The Volunteers of America, a charitable group, will operate the shelter. It is an arrangement that the city has grown accustomed to; it tends to get things that other communities do not want: the county jail, the county's sewage treatment plant, a state prison. We do not mean to equate the homeless with criminals or waste, only to suggest that they have not always been greeted with open arms. Too often they have been treated as someone else's problem and shunted aside usually to the cities (Courier Post 1985).

After going on to state their support for the central shelter, the editor added a final caveat:

Consolidation in one place also poses a problem, namely, the reluctance of some people, long time residents of a particular area, to leave it to seek help elsewhere. Under the laws of this state, municipalities still bear the ultimate responsibility for the homeless within their borders. They may not be able to buy their way out of that obligation completely. The center in Camden will help, but other municipalities, working with churches and other charitable organizations, may still find it necessary, legally if not morally, to provide their own smaller shelters for the homeless (Courier Post 1985).

This latter policy was one that an important group in the county supported. This group, the Camden Shelter Coalition, was to go on to develop this policy alternative into a strong opposition to the county's plan for a central shelter.

THE CAMDEN SHELTER COALITION

The homeless policy review process that was established under the aegis of CPAC/HSC appeared to be well conceived and included most of the major providers of service to the homeless. One major actor was not represented, however. This was the Camden Shelter Coalition (CSC), a group that is not a member of CPAC/HSC and is not a partner to its ongoing planning process. This lack of formal involvement stems from CSC's preference for participating in community affairs as an independent group rather than as an insider; in this way the broader problem of possible cooptation would be avoided. While CSC eschews day-to-day involvement with CPAC/HSC, it is not averse to joint participation in selected research projects and the like.

CSC became an important actor in the policy debate over shelter services for the homeless in Camden County. The group is based in North Camden, one of the city's poorest neighborhoods and site of the existing large city shelter. The group has worked in the field of low cost housing for a long period of time and has established several successful housing delivery programs in the area. An affiliate group, Leaven House, provides a daily free meal to the needy in the neighborhood. Over the years, CSC has been a sharp critic of VOA which has operated the county's shelter services. CSC has charged that some of these shelters are not providing an adequate level of service. The group was particularly critical of the larger shelters, a viewpoint that solidified when a baby died of neglect in one shelter and a homeless man was murdered in a dispute over a bed in another. In addition, CSC claimed that as many as ten to fifteen individuals were sleeping in front of the city police station each night and cited this as evidence of the reluctance of many homeless to go into VOA-run shelters.

CSC was not a participant in the CPAC/HSC planning process but it was aware of the progress of these plans and was opposed to the direction these plans were taking. In particular, it was opposed to the overall policy of centralization of homeless services and favored a policy of decentralization that would involve the siting of some small shelters in suburban districts under the aegis of a church-affiliated or private nonprofit provider. The group made these views known in repeated direct contacts with members of CPAC, the County Board of Freeholders, and Camden City Council. A memo sent to the freeholders in the spring of 1985 summarized their position. Their central contention was that the planning process never allowed for a realistic consideration of an alternative policy of decentralization of homeless shelters in Camden County (Camden Shelter Coalition 1985).

In particular, the memo outlined what were characterized as deplorable conditions at the large city run shelter. It went on to question the expenditure of funds for an even larger centralized facility then currently under development in the city. It outlined the position of the Shelter Coalition which favored a policy of decentralization, i.e., ". . . a wide range of private and public agencies providing a number of community based shelters (25 persons or less)." Furthermore, it suggested the establishment of a county level agency to carry out the intake of applicants for shelter. This agency would also have a recordkeeping and monitoring responsibility (Camden Shelter Coalition 1985).

Later in October of 1986, the group developed an outline of their proposal for decentralization. The outline was a more detailed treatment of the basic issues outlined in the memo. The first section presented a history of the Camden Shelter Coalition's involvement with shelter policy development. The development of the new shelter (referred to as the "supershelter" by CSC) at Line Street was outlined and their efforts to modify this development were cataloged. The second section of the outline listed the reasons decentralized shelters were preferable to large centralized shelters. These reasons appeared to be consonant with standard opinion among supporters of small community-based shelters and stressed the benefits of small, functionally distinct, noninstitutional community-based shelter environments. The third section dealt with the operation of a decentralized shelter network. It suggested utilization of a centralized intake and coordination facility that was not a shelter provider. Policy would be set by a representative board of providers and residents. Other points dealt with issues of transportation, resident support responsibilities (financial and labor), health services, day centers, and program costs. Cost assumptions included the use of existing buildings with capital costs for modifications only. Cost factors relative to purchase were not discussed (Camden Shelter Coalition 1986).

These direct overtures to elected and appointed county officials did not produce an immediately favorable response. Instead, county officials directed CSC to work through the CPAC process in attempting to affect shelter policy development. Surprisingly, the CSC followed the freeholders' advice and contacted CPAC. CPAC supported CSC's contention that decentralization never received adequate consideration during the planning process. Indeed, it was clear from informal conversations with members of the CPAC board that many felt such decentralization, while morally correct, was politically impossible and hence could be quickly dismissed. This helps explain why decentralization was not given any credence in the planning process: it was assumed to be impossibly idealistic because the suburban communities would refuse to participate and there was no way they could be encouraged or forced to do so. In addition, the VOA, which favored a centralized approach, had been a member of CPAC for a long time and was felt by many to be doing the best job it could in difficult circumstances and with a limited budget. CSC, on the other hand, was resented since its members refused repeated invitations to join CPAC and participate in its deliberations. In addition, there was a strong antipathy between particular members of the VOA and CSC resulting from broad and profound differences regarding the administration of services to the poor. Thus, the political climate surrounding the issue of centralization versus decentralization was highly charged.

However its members felt personally about each other, CPAC has always been supportive of an inclusionary and a deliberative approach to all social service planning in the county. Accordingly, its director, Cathy deCheser, was instrumental in persuading the County Board of Freeholders to fund a study that would evaluate the practical potential of a decentralization approach as well as other alternatives. It is somewhat surprising that this study was commissioned considering the fact that the shelter development process was as advanced as it was. Indeed, renovations on the first building in the Camden central shelter were already underway. While it reflected positively on CPAC and its commitment to an inclusionary planning process, it is important to note the degree of delay that is inherent in this localized approach to problem solving. It is also true that the lack of even a cursory evaluation of the decentralized approach during the initial planning process left CPAC and the freeholders vulnerable to charges of bias. Finally, the tortuous process by which the evaluation of a decentralized approach to the homeless was finally given consideration is evidence of the degree of opposition to suburban involvement in the provision of unpopular municipal services. This is a theme that shall be developed more fully in the conclusions to this chapter.

THE DECENTRALIZATION STUDY

The Camden Shelter Study was carried out at the request of two major social service agencies in Camden County, CPAC/HSC and CSC (M. H. Lang 1987). The request stemmed from a desire to review current county policy with regard to emergency shelter for the homeless. The purpose of the study was to attempt to ascertain whether or not it was possible to identify specific areas of agreement regarding broad and realistic policy for the provision of emergency shelter services (Gonzales 1987).

The central research issues established by CPAC/HSC and CSC were:

1. Whether emergency shelters should be centralized or decentralized;
2. The optimal size for emergency shelters;
3. The best organizational model for overall shelter operations;
4. A sample of emergency shelter policies in other areas;

5. The cost of various alternative emergency shelter systems;
6. The overall feasibility of various alternative emergency shelter systems;
7. The best type (e.g., residential, etc.) of shelter facility;
8. The best type (e.g., city, suburban, etc.) of location for a shelter facility.

In order to resolve some of the broad issues of shelter policy listed above, a Delphi panel was utilized as the central methodology. The panel was convened in order to bring disinterested expert opinion to bear on a sensitive issue. The panel did not rely on face-to-face contact so as to minimize the effects of powerful oratory or exhortations by a skillful panelist. The methodology was based on having the panel reach a consensus regarding solutions to the problems placed before them for consideration. The panel was "blind" in that panel members knew who their colleagues were at the outset, but all responses to questions were confidential, thereby further ensuring objectivity (Northeastern Illinois Planning Commission 1973, 108).

The specific final policy recommendations that came from the panel's deliberations were as follows:

1. Camden County should adopt a clear policy statement with regard to the siting and characteristics of all new temporary shelters.

2. This statement should emphasize, to the extent possible, that established new shelters be home-style small facilities preferably in or immediately adjacent to a residential community. These facilities should be organized so that each caters to a particular population group in need of services (e.g., families, female-headed households, single adults, etc.).

3. To minimize community concerns, some of these temporary shelters could initially operate during the evening hours only and make separate centralized day services available. This centralized center(s) should also maintain overflow bed capacity. Intake/referral/observation services should be provided at a separate site.

4. The county should affirm that all communities are responsible for sheltering their own homeless and are expected to participate in providing space for regional needs when available. It is recognized that most of the homeless originate from Camden City; nonetheless, shelters should be established according to the fair share principle to the extent possible.

5. In order to encourage the broadest possible community participation, and to ensure that a permanent shelter system is not established, these residential shelters should be based on and operated by faith communities and other nonprofit providers.

6. The county should continue to support development of adequate low income housing resources countywide and with particular emphasis on boarding home facilities, vacant housing rehabilitation, and SRO dwellings in the county's older urban areas. The aim of this policy is to make shelters unnecessary as soon as possible.

7. All agencies involved in siting such shelters should establish a joint agency/local resident/client oversight committee to monitor the functioning of each shelter and to provide input.

8. The county should be encouraged to promote activities to raise community consciousness and awareness concerning this issue and how to resolve it.

9. The county should move to fund an advocate for the homeless, based in a neutral organization. This advocate should be responsible for carrying out recommendations 1 through 8 and will work in cooperation with existing social service agencies. The advocate's work should be overseen by a broad-based supervisory committee. Responsibility for program evaluation should be established at the outset (M. H. Lang 1987).

POLICY RAMIFICATIONS

Were such a policy implemented by Camden County, one would expect to see most shelters continue to be located in Camden City, since it is the point of origin of the greatest number of homeless, but suburban shelters might also be established under this policy. Another effect of such a policy would be the siting of shelters in or adjacent to residential areas throughout the city. The effect of decentralization would be to lessen the impact of the homeless in any one site thereby leading to greater community acceptance. Decentralization provides greater normalcy in living arrangements thereby maximizing the client's potential to reestablish him or herself. This might reverse the trend toward longer shelter stays. A small shelter system would also tend to lessen the instances of conflict inherent in large shelters and thereby serve more of the truly needy who are currently afraid of such shelters. Finally, a small shelter system could be readily dismantled when increased employment and low cost housing opportunities lead to lowered demand.

The nine recommendations were presented to the full CPAC board which approved all of the recommendations. A few modifications in wording were made to individual items and the precise composition of the board which would oversee the work of the homeless advocate was spelled out. A major modification was the change in the initial recommendation calling for a separate agency to handle homeless issues. This was dropped by the board which was fearful of creating too many separate agencies. Instead, it was suggested that the staff function be given to an existing independent agency. Since all of the existing social service agencies had spent the last four years working on or supporting a policy of centralization and were only now willing to support decentralization, it was crucial to select an agency that had not participated in the promulgation of the earlier policy. The local community college eventually was selected. The revised recommendations were eventually approved and funded by the Camden County Board of Freeholders (Courier Post 1987). The chronology of the entire shelter location decisionmaking process follows. As of January 1989, no new decentralized shelters have been established pursuant to the new policy.

CHRONOLOGY OF THE HOMELESS ISSUE IN CAMDEN CITY AND COUNTY

—October 7, 1983. Establishment of a statewide Emergency Assistance System (CEAS). Statewide implementation of a county based network of public and private agencies which coordinate planning and services to the homeless.

—July 11, 1984. CPAC/HSC Emergency Housing Consortium Report on the Development of Alternate Housing.

—August 1984. Report of the Emergency Housing Consortium on their Relocation of the VOA Emergency Housing Facility.

—July 27, 1984. CPAC/HSC Emergency Housing Consortium Recommendations for Potential Sites for Emergency Housing Shelters.

—July 1984. Report on the Physical Space Needs and the Programmatic Space Needs of the Emergency Housing Facilities Population.

—May 9, 1985. City and county announce plans to establish centralized shelter facility in Camden City with suburban financial support.

—Spring 1985. Camden Shelter Coalition writes to Freeholders questioning whether full consideration had been given to policy of decentralization.

—October 2, 1985. City zoning board approves central shelter over strong opposition of local residents.

—June 1985. CEAS plan submitted, supports central shelter proposal for Camden City.

—May 1986. CEAS plan submitted, supports central shelter proposal for Camden City.

—September 1986. Camden Shelter Coalition officially approves concept of decentralization.

—October 1986. CSC releases proposal for decentralization.

—November 1986. CSC representation to the Freeholder board supporting decentralization. Told to work through CPAC planning process.

—March 1987. CPAC/HSC agree to support study of decentralization

—May 26, 1987. Consultant hired.

—December 1987. CPAC board approves all recommendations in report.

—January 1988. Freeholder director puts forward $500,000 proposal to fund several decentralized shelters throughout county.

—February 1988. Board of Freeholders meets to discuss new county policy favoring decentralization.

—February 29, 1988.   Letter and copy of policy statement sent to all mayors in the county from Freeholder director. Letter said in part, "First and foremost, I wish to stress that our policy is a policy of cooperation with municipalities. I will not support any homeless policy that does not include a provision that requires the consent of the municipal governing body before any homeless facility or housing rehabilitation takes place in a municipality."

—March 10, 1988.   Board of Freeholders passed resolution 81, accepting the recommendations contained in the study.

—June 23, 1988.   Board of Freeholders passed resolution No. 25, establishing the position of homeless advocate.

—July 8, 1988.   Letter from Executive Director of CPAC/HSC to Freeholder director suggesting protocols to be followed by Homeless Advocate and new Homeless Advisory Board.

—December 19, 1988.   Homeless Advisory Board (now named the Homeless Decentralization Committee) hires homeless advocate.

—January 1989.   Status: No new shelters established.

CONCLUSIONS

The results of this study are remarkable for several reasons. First, the study gives evidence that the localities have not been able to solve the problem of homelessness on their own. The simple fact that Camden County is struggling to articulate a coherent policy for servicing the homeless some eight years after the problem surfaced shows the degree to which solutions are not being found with sufficient dispatch. Clear, too, is the fact that with the multi-faceted problem of homelessness, no one local jurisdiction can hope to solve even its own problem.Indeed, there is a disincentive to do so since a successful program will attract the homeless from other jurisdictions all too happy to send their homeless to a model program elsewhere.

Just how effective the proposed homeless advocate will be in Camden remains to be seen. It is important to realize that what has been proposed here is far from optimal. A system of church-based shelters is not a long-term solution nor even the best temporary solution to the problem. What should have been proposed is a truly regional system of small community-based shelters. This system should have been established with the active involvement of all the local jurisdictions. The political impossibility of this otherwise rational solution is the Achilles' heel of all efforts to create a society that is desegregated in all senses. Thus, Camden is forced to try to put together a patchwork service system because of the stubbornness of suburban opposition to meaningful participation that would entail a full partnership with the city.

The results of the study also show a strong support for decentralized shelters, but acknowledge the strength of suburban opposition. The degree of this opposition is typified by the shelter provider mentioned earlier who suggested the legal subterfuge of opening a shelter without legal authority as the only way to gain access to the suburbs. Realistically, this is not the only way but it is also clear that only token shelters have been provided in the suburbs to date. Recently, a coalition of religious groups in Nassau County, New York, announced their willingness to shelter the homeless in the winter months. Such programs are testimony to a concern for the homeless that crosses jurisdictional lines. Regrettably, such efforts are not sufficient to meet the needs of the homeless nor are they ever likely to become so regardless of optimistic proposals based on a complex process of rewards, trade-offs, and community bargaining such as those recently suggested by Dear and Wolch (1987).

The simple truth is that today the suburbs see themselves as having to fight off the incursions of urban-style problems. The fact that many of these problems emanate from within their own jurisdictions does not matter. Whether it is low income housing, a regional incinerator, or a shelter for the homeless, the suburban response is to put it in the city. The final CPAC/HSC shelter report skirted this issue to some extent since it did not call upon the suburban municipalities to take responsibility for their own homeless. Instead, it called on suburban churches and other religious groups to provide these services. This was seen as the only way to open up the suburbs to shelters without provoking a major confrontation. Religious organizations can provide shelter under the common law tradition that allows anyone to seek sanctuary in a religious building. Thus, the myriad problems associated with local zoning laws can be neatly sidestepped. Church-based facilities and services are apt to be temporary in nature, an important point for suburban officials. The fact that this less than optimal approach must be used is further evidence of the strength of suburban opposition to municipal sharing of regional responsibilities. The suburbs are not about to take their "fair share" of anything if they can help it and so far they have been remarkably successful at doing just that.

While the final recommendations include a call for a fair share approach to housing the homeless to the extent possible, the central recommendation calls for the utilization of church-based providers and thereby largely absolves municipalities of any requirement to take specific action to be in compliance with local fair share policy.

The concept that the city receives all the social problems that are excluded from more affluent suburban areas is not a new one. Seventeen years ago in a classic essay entitled "The Unwalled City," Norton Long

(1972) outlined a process whereby the city was treated almost like a reservation that served to isolate our urban society's problem individuals and groups from contact with the prevailing suburban society. This essay was one of the first to assess the strong anti-urban impact of our suburban-oriented land use development process. As an urbanist, Dr. Long was well aware that other industrialized countries had in place policies that specifically prevented such suburban sprawl and its resultant negative impact on urban areas. Only time would tell which policy was the better.

Today, we are experiencing the full range of problems that arise from this choice. We are seeing increasingly impoverished cities that are wracked with multiple social problems to which they cannot fully respond. In the increasingly segregated suburbs there is a strong reaction against sprawl and the resultant loss of open space, environmental degradation, and traffic congestion. Repeated attempts to solve these problems at the local or state level have proved fruitless. The local planning process is effectively impotent. It serves only to issue an array of impact statements and permits that increase the cost of development, but do little or nothing to really control it. Planners' attempts to guide development have proven futile as there are no laws giving them the authority to do so. They have the authority to make plans, not to implement or enforce them. Not surprisingly, development is guided by the free market process. As a result, many localities have closed their planning departments to save costs. In effect, local development is out of control. There is no level of governmental authority overseeing the development of our communities so as to ensure that they are open to all and do not injure other jurisdictions. Without such a governmental policy role, we will continue to see the uneven, dysfunctional pattern of development that has prevailed for the last eighteen years. We will see regions unable to devise an effective response to social problems because the whole process is politicized by parochial suburban interests that reject community responsibilities that are potentially difficult or offensive to them. It is no way to maintain strong local communities that are the basis of a democratic society.

The next chapter will examine the potential for one national approach to housing policy which may benefit the homeless.

Part V

REAL POLICY REFORM
—THE IMPOSSIBLE
DREAM?

9

Toward a National Right to Housing

Homelessness in the United States is a national crisis of significant proportions which has been met with an insufficient public and private response. Four avenues of response—voluntary assistance, legislative initiative, pressure by organized social movements, and judicial review—have provided the basis for sporadic attempts to address the plight of the homeless. The failure to develop national legislative and judicial remedies which effectively combat this problem mirrors the lack of societal commitment to guaranteeing shelter to needy citizens. In contrast, Great Britain codified a national policy of sheltering vulnerable citizens in the form of the Housing (Homeless Persons) Act 1977 (Hoath 1983; Donnison and Ungerson 1982). The lack of an equivalent comprehensive measure in the United States has forced state governments to confront this dilemma individually. Scattered legislation, sporadic funding, and appeals to the state judiciary on the grounds of a state "right to shelter" have achieved only limited success (Governor's Task Force on the Homeless 1985; Matica v. Atlantic City 1985; Stolarski 1988).

New Jersey has been in the forefront of state-level attempts to grapple with these issues. Accordingly, this chapter will examine its response to the homelessness crisis with particular emphasis on the attempt to establish a state constitutional right to shelter. The first part will briefly examine the national legislative and judicial constructions of remedies. The second part will analyze New Jersey's statutory and judicial policies, the practical ramifications these provisions have for homeless persons, and the need for a more comprehensive legislative solution. A proposal for the structure of such state legislation will follow in the third part in the form of an examination of Britain's Housing (Homeless Persons) Act, its successes and failures, and its possible relevance to New Jersey's situation.

AN OVERVIEW OF ATTEMPTED LEGISLATIVE AND JUDICIAL REMEDIES

Congressional response to homelessness has been minimal and oriented to emergency services (Werner 1984, 1985). The lack of significant national legislation and appropriation of funds specifically directed at the alleviation of homelessness has a dual result: (1) the onus of responding to the needs of the homeless is placed on state and local governments, and (2) the absence of articulation of precise duties or administrative guidelines prevents the implementation of any consistent national policy (although several states have enacted specific statutes governing adult protective services for the homeless) (Ford. Urb. L. J. 1981). However, such state statutes are often vague and incomprehensive, drawn to meet the needs of homeless vagrants and not those of the diverse contemporary homeless population. Where the responsibility is not given to each municipality to care for its own homeless population, inner cities are often forced to absorb the burdens of all of a state's destitute citizens. National or state legislation defining municipal duties is needed to prevent this and to ensure systematic response to the homeless population's needs.

In the absence of satisfactory legislation, litigation has become a preferred tool of homeless advocacy (Brooklyn L. Rev. 1984; Fabricant and Epstein 1984). The homeless as a coalition are too poor and unorganized to wield sufficient political clout and thereby affect policy (Werner 1985; Jenkins 1983). In their place, a social movement of local public and nonprofit advocacy agencies has emerged and become an effective tool for securing basic rights for the homeless often through the utilization of judicial appeal (Stolarski 1988). Indeed, as a result of the initial victory in a New York Supreme Court (Callahen v. Carey 1979) the right to shelter has been pursued by such agencies in many localities (McCain v. Koch 1984; Hodges v. Ginsberg 1983; Lubetkin v. Hartford 1983).

Several legal strategies have been utilized in homeless litigation. First, constitutional due process arguments have been advanced to prevent the discontinuance of existing entitlements. This argument has met with limited success. A federal district court enjoined the city of Washington, D.C., from closing a public shelter on the theory that the closure deprived the city's homeless of their property interest in an entitlement. However, the court of appeals held that continuing shelter facilities is a judicially nonreviewable, political question. The court required the city only to give notice of the closure and an opportunity for citizens to make written comments. In the court's view, the actual decision to discontinue the shelter's services was a legislative not judicial decision (Williams v. Barry 1980, 1983).

A second litigatory theory challenging barriers to assistance for the homeless has met with more success. New Jersey and Illinois courts have ruled that general assistance benefits cannot be denied to a homeless person because he or she does not have a permanent address (Matica v. Atlantic City 1985). Efforts to secure voting rights for the homeless have also met with success in several localities (Pitts v. Black 1984; Committee for Dignity and Fairness for the Homeless v. Tartaglione 1984). In addition, the right to establish a shelter and the right to community after care for state mental patients represent alternative grounds for court challenges by homeless advocates (Brooklyn L. Rev. 1984; St. John's Evan. Lutheran Church v. Hoboken 1983).

The Right to Shelter

A final legal strategy in homeless litigation pursues the right to housing as a constitutional guarantee. On the federal level, "nowhere in the United States Constitution is such a right (to shelter) even implied" (Brooklyn L. Rev. 1984). The United States Supreme Court rejected the assertion that the federal Constitution provides any guarantee of access to dwellings or assurance of housing. The Court specifically stated that "the Constitution does not provide judicial remedies for every social and economic ill" (Lindsey v. Normet 1972). Its ruling reinforced the concept that as a federal matter housing needs and policies are legislative not judicial functions (Stolarski 1988).

A statutory basis for a right to housing appears to be lacking as well, despite the extent of federal low cost housing legislation. While it can be said that the federal commitment to a "decent home for every American family" is not merely a commitment to freedom of economic opportunity, neither is it yet the declaration of an enforceable legal claim. Michelson has said, "It remains the statement of a welfare ideal, a general guide to administration and interpretation of the housing statutes—but not an enforceable promise by the government to the public to tax and appropriate as heavily as would be required to satisfy the ideal" (Mandelker et al. 1981, 31).

The right to shelter is an elusive concept. Even if explicitly adopted by a state court, its practical enforcement requires legislative and administrative endorsement and funding (Mandelker et al. 1981). A state constitutional challenge has been most successful when targeted at particular government practices denying due process and equal protection of the law to anyone who is homeless (Callahen v. Carey 1979). However, such success has been limited, and a right to shelter per se has not been recognized by a high court of any state. The issue is currently the subject of pending litigation in New Jersey where the State Public Advocate has posed the existence of a state right to shelter and municipal duty to provide the same (Matica v. Atlantic City 1985).

NEW JERSEY'S POLICIES
ON THE HOMELESS PROBLEM

The New Jersey legislature has addressed the problem of homelessness throughout the state in four separate and unconnected legislative acts. This legislation includes laws governing financial assistance to needy persons, a 1983 temporary act allocating funds for emergency food and shelter to the homeless, the Prevention of Homelessness Act, and an act governing emergency shelter provision (Governor's Task Force on the Homeless 1985). The passage of this legislation indicates political recognition of the desperate situation which exists in the state. The laws also provide a basis for court intervention in individual situations where a party or agency violates the substance or intent of any given provision. As can be gleaned from the Camden case study, these laws established an emergency-oriented service system that is currently overtaxed since it is being used for long-term problem resolution.

General Assistance laws often form the core of homeless advocacy challenges to the actions of municipal agencies. New Jersey Statute 44:8–120 (1986) requires that "immediate public assistance" be given to "any needy person" by the welfare office in "the municipality where the person is found." After reasonable inquiry, aid must be rendered ensuring that the individual "not suffer unnecessarily from cold, hunger, sickness, or be deprived of shelter" (N.J. Stat. 44:8–122 1986). The process consists of two steps: first, emergency assistance must unconditionally be provided until an eligibility determination for general assistance is made; second, once eligibility has been determined, appropriate benefit assistance must be given. Homeless persons can receive $133 per month, or if they are disabled, $209 per month (Philadelphia Inquirer 1986).

Problems concerning this statute have arisen. In some instances, homeless persons have been denied benefits because of their lack of a verifiable address (Matica v. Atlantic City 1985). Municipalities have also failed to comply with the requirement to provide immediate emergency assistance. While municipalities are required to provide immediate assistance, state aid for emergency shelter facilities has not been equitably distributed throughout the state (Philadelphia Inquirer 1986). Finally, because most New Jersey suburban municipalities do not have shelters, the shelter and welfare offices of poverty-stricken cities have become inundated with the homeless from both cities and suburbs.

The Prevention of Homelessness Act declared a state policy "that no person should suffer unnecessarily from cold or hunger, or be deprived of shelter" (N.J. Stat. Ann. 52:27D-281 1986). This act designates the Department of Community Affairs as the appropriate agency to assist the homeless or those in imminent danger of homelessness. Such a broad policy statement and responsibility charge is deceiving given the intricacies of the act. For example, temporary assistance will only be extended when the failure of resources is beyond an applicant's control. Which events constitute failures within one's control is amorphous. Presumably, persons who become homeless due to eviction, domestic problems, or other unfortunate circumstances do not qualify for temporary assistance. Still, their situation may indeed be beyond their control and just as horrendous as one whose homelessness is covered under the act. It appears strange that when reconciled with the act's purpose, such adversity falls outside the designation of unnecessary suffering.

A statute governing emergency shelter for the homeless became effective on February 13, 1985. This act articulates a public concern for safe and habitable shelters, and it charges the Department of Community Affairs with providing technical assistance to the operators of shelters. However, the statute does not impose any responsibility on municipalities to provide a shelter (N.J. Stat. Ann. 55:BC-1 to 55:BC-6 1985).

New Jersey's legislation provides a first step toward a coherent state policy, but it does not propose a sufficient response to the plight of the state's homeless. Homeless litigation, initiated in four different New Jersey townships, indicates the need for more carefully drawn and integrated legislation (Matica v. Atlantic City 1985; Algor v. County of Ocean 1984; SCOPE v. Vineland 1984; Rodgers v. Newark 1984). This litigation has utilized the policy statements in current legislation, statements of the Governor's Task Force, as well as the specific language in the state constitution to assert that New Jersey law provides a right to shelter for all citizens. A comprehensive codification of this right could integrate the current laws, articulate specific municipal responsibilities, and eliminate the need for judicial intervention in state policy. One unified act admittedly would not solve the homeless problem, but it would create a more accessible mechanism for obtaining adequate shelter. Such a mechanism would replace the current emergency-oriented programs with a comprehensive policy approach to homelessness.

Judicial Finding: A Right to Shelter

Assertions of a federal constitutional right to shelter have been unsuccessful in the United States Supreme Court (Lindsey v. Normet 1972). As state constitutions can provide a broader basis of rights for citizens, advocates for the homeless in New Jersey have begun to contend that the New Jersey Constitution ensures each citizen a right to enjoy adequate and safe shelter. When a court recognizes a fundamental and important state constitutional right, implementation of its protections can be directly enforced by that court. Arguments advancing the right of homeless persons to emergency and long-term shelter generally rest on three primary principles. First, the state constitution provides that the citizens of New Jersey possess a general right to life and the pursuit of safety and happiness. Second, New Jersey courts have historically recognized the central importance of sanitary housing to the preservation of each citizen's health. Finally, the New Jersey Supreme Court has developed an extensive body of law recognizing the fundamental importance of housing. Augmenting these central principles is the assumption that the New Jersey Legislature has repeatedly recognized the right to shelter in the policy formation of current legislation (Robinson v. Cahill 1973; Southern Burlington County NAACP v. Township of Mount Laurel 1975, 1983; Right to Choose v. Bryne 1982).

The textual basis for a state constitutional right to shelter allegedly exists in Article I, paragraph I of the New Jersey Constitution. This provision states:

All persons are by nature free and independent, and have certain natural and inalienable rights, among which are those of enjoying and defending life and liberty, of acquiring, possessing, and protecting property, and of pursuing and obtaining safety and happiness.

Establishing whether or not a fundamental right exists requires identifying "the traditions and collective conscience" of the citizens of New Jersey (King v. So. Jersey Nat. Bank 1974). This is the traditional federal approach to identifying fundamental rights which are not explicitly stated in the Constitution's text. While New Jersey adopted this approach, it is not clear that the "collective conscience" of the citizens of the United

States is the same as that of the citizens of New Jersey. Advocates for finding a right to shelter assert that the two traditions of conscience are vastly different. However, in litigation the State of New Jersey has posed that Article I, paragraph I "creates no duty on the part of any public entity to provide shelter to homeless individuals" (Matica v. Atlantic City 1985). This proposition supports a similarity between federal and state traditions which refuse to acknowledge the right to shelter as fundamental (Lindsey v. Normet 1972).

In the past, the New Jersey Supreme Count has interpreted federal and state "collective consciences" to be different. The United States Supreme Court refused to reach a finding of a fundamental right of women to Medicaid funds for abortion (Harris v. McCrae 1980). Nonetheless, the New Jersey Supreme Court interpreted the state constitution to be more expansive than its federal counterpart (Right to Choose v. Bryne 1982). The Court acknowledged the traditional "high priority historically accorded to the preservation of health in this state" (Pollock 1983). It is possible this same health priority can be analogized to the need for safe and healthy shelter for all state citizens.

The third component of the right to shelter rests on New Jersey's fair share housing mandate. Depending on one's perspective, this element of the argument represents either the cornerstone of the right to shelter argument or its tragic flaw. Proponents interpret the court mandate to municipalities to provide a realistic opportunity for low income housing as the construction of a municipal obligation to provide shelter. Those who contend that the right to shelter is a legislative, not judicial, function maintain that "access to adequate housing . . . as a fundamental part of decent living" and a "constitutional obligation to give the poor a fair chance for housing" are not directives to localities to provide shelters (Southern Burlington County NAACP v. Township of Mount Laurel 1983). The complexity of this argument as the basis for a right to shelter is indicated by the refusal of all state courts currently reviewing homeless litigation to rule on this constitutional issue.

Practically, the need for a constitutional ruling is crucial only where the effects of current legislation have fallen short of an effective response. If the New Jersey Legislature were to specifically articulate a state and municipal duty to shelter the homeless, the constitutional finding would not be necessary. The right to shelter rationale is a plausible one given the arguments stated above; however, the niceties of judicial procedure and the nightmare of Mount Laurel litigation leaves the finding of a state constitutional right to shelter a dubious proposition.

Two Homeless Challenges

Two examples of recent litigation challenging inadequate compliance with homeless laws and asserting a state constitutional right to shelter are Matica v. Atlantic City and Algor v. County of Ocean. Both suits were successful in obtaining emergency injunctive relief for homeless plaintiffs.

Filed on behalf of six homeless people, Matica alleged a violation of 44:8–120 of New Jersey Statutes Annotated. Pursuant to this statute, a person seeking the aid of a local welfare office must receive immediate food, shelter, and clothing pending an eligibility determination for general assistance. The New Jersey Public Advocate brought suit against Atlantic City and the State Department of Human Services alleging that this emergency assistance was not provided to the plaintiffs. When defendant Atlantic City failed to meet the discovery demands of the plaintiffs, the New Jersey Superior Court entered a default judgment against Atlantic City. Judge Michael Connors ruled that the statute had been violated and ordered emergency injunctive relief to the plaintiffs. In addition, the judge held that upon a determination of eligibility, assistance benefits could not be denied to any person because of their lack of a verifiable address. Finally, the judge ordered the defendants to draft a comprehensive plan detailing Atlantic City's proposal for sheltering 200–300 homeless persons (N.J. Law Journal 1985).

In January of 1986, the parties again appeared in court over a dispute involving the comprehensive plan. The plan articulated measures for servicing an estimated population of 800 homeless persons in Atlantic City (Atlantic City Comprehensive Homeless Plan 1985). In this proceeding, Judge Connors refused to uphold the plaintiffs' proposal for distributing the $1.5 million in state aid to the homeless. Judge Connors stated that any changes in such procedures had to originate in the legislature (Philadelphia Inquirer 1986). Because the allegations in this proceeding went beyond the scope of the original complaint, the judge ordered the Public Advocate to amend the complaint before continuation of the litigation. More centrally, the judge refused to address any claim on a state constitutional right to shelter (Donnolly 1986).

The Matica case illustrates the limitations judicial proceedings pose for homeless advocacy. The initial victory of emergency injunctive relief merely obtained for the plaintiff's compliance with a current legislative mandate (N.J. Stat. Ann. 44:8–120, 1986). The Public Advocate's attempt to enforce a more thorough relief measure was thwarted by a standard judicial deference to legislative authority. It seems unlikely, absent a finding of a right to shelter, that the judiciary can enforce a comprehensive response to the homeless problem. The outcome of the Matica case reinforces the message that funding for shelters or low income housing as well as an imposition on each state and municipality to provide these facilities, must come in the form of a legislative mandate.

Algor represents the family counterpart to the Matica case. The office of legal services brought suit against Ocean County on behalf of seven families in the county who were denied emergency shelter pursuant to the regulations governing Aid to Families with Dependent Children. The suit challenged a general county policy of relinquishing any support obligation once a family has exhausted emergency benefits. While refusing to reach any constitutional issue, Superior Court Judge Kaplan ordered preliminary injunctive relief housing for each of the plaintiff families. The plaintiffs are seeking a long-term right to be afforded shelter by county services (Pascale 1986).

The plaintiffs in Matica and Algor all experienced the frustration and indignity of being without adequate shelter for an extended period of time. Adding to their frustration and that of thousands of other homeless people in New Jersey is an uncertainty of what emergency aid is available and where to acquire it. A more comprehensive and accessible system of emergency aid would probably not remedy their long-term situation. Unfortunately, the absence of low income housing or subsidies will continue to exacerbate their problems. However, the presence of an integrated societal response such as that considered in the next section, might begin to alleviate this situation.

A MORE COMPREHENSIVE STATE LEVEL RESPONSE TO HOMELESSNESS

British policy toward homelessness is quite distinct from ours. The best illustration of this difference is the presence of Britain's Housing (Homeless Persons) Act of 1977 (Hoath 1983; Donnison and Ungerson 1982). To some extent this is indicative of the general differences between the two nations; Britain's traditional welfare state ideology stands in contrast to the United States' which is strongly free market in orientation. Similarly, the central control of Parliament contrasts with the high degree of autonomy enjoyed by the American states and localities. Nevertheless, shortages of low income rental housing stock, an overemphasis on stimulating the production of owner-occupied housing for the affluent, and decreases in central government funding for public housing have left both countries with a sizable homeless population (Bailey 1973; Prichard 1981; Waites and Wolmar 1980; Shelter 1984).

The most significant contemporary achievements on behalf of the homeless in Britain were accomplished in the 1970s. The government spearheaded a campaign to transfer responsibility for the homeless situation from social services to local housing departments. The difficulty in ascertaining an accurate count of the homeless rendered identification of the magnitude of the country's problem a difficult task (Shelter 1982). A weakened economy and the severe housing crisis occasioned by the obvious shortage of low income housing led Parliament to pass a comprehensive act governing administration of the problem.

The Housing (Homeless Persons) Act of 1977 "defines homelessness and gives statutory responsibility for the homeless to the local housing authority." The purpose of the Act was to clarify the law governing homelessness and impose duties on local municipalities to carry out the law. The following four conditions must be met in order for one to fall within the purview of the Act:

1. An applicant must be "homeless" or "threatened with homelessness."
2. He or she must have a priority need.
3. The applicant cannot be "intentionally homeless."
4. A "local connection" must exist between the homeless person and the local authority providing aid (Hoath 1983).

If one has no accommodation or cannot secure accommodation, one is considered to be homeless. If one is deemed likely to be homeless within twenty-eight days, one is considered to be threatened with homelessness. These basic definitions cut across all profiles of homeless persons and do not target only one specific homeless group such as older alcoholic vagrants. This aspect of the Act interjects needed flexibility and coverage (Werner 1984).

A crucial provision of the Act establishes the categorization of priority needs among homeless persons. First among persons to receive aid are homeless households with dependent children. Other priority need classifications include those persons who are homeless as a result of an emergency "such as flood, fire or any other disaster," and people who are vulnerable due to old age, mental illness, disability or pregnancy (Hoath 1983).

A substantial amount of litigation which resulted in Britain involved the concept of intentional homelessness (Shelter 1982; Hoath 1983). If a person does or fails to do something which causes the loss of a home, he or she receives a lesser assistance from the local authority. The burden lies with the authority to establish the homelessness as intentional before providing a lesser degree of help. Finally, an authority must establish a local connection between an applicant and the housing authority where he or she seeks assistance. A local connection means the applicant normally resides in the locality, he or she was employed there or has family there. Aid to the applicant must be received from the locality to which he or she is connected (Hoath 1983; Shelter 1982).

The Act articulates specific duties to be undertaken by each housing authority. Initial inquiry as to the facts of the situation and available accommodations must first be made. Then it remains the authority's duty to notify the applicant of its determination. For those who are homeless with a priority need, permanent housing must be secured. One who is threatened with homelessness may apply to the authority for preventative aid and advice. To those who do not have a priority need or who are intentionally homeless, the authority must give advice and limited assistance (Hoath 1983; Shelter 1982).

The impact of the Act, which became effective on December 1, 1977, indicated the great need for government assistance to the homeless in Britain. The government experienced a large increase in the numbers for whom the housing council now had a duty to provide. Prior to the Act, 32,000 persons were admitted into temporary accommodation, and less than half were rehoused into a permanent accommodation. This number has been steadily increasing (Shelter 1982, 1984; Hoath 1983).

While Britain's Act provides a codified delineation of the government's responsibility to the homeless, it is not without its problems. Budgeting changes in the past few years have resulted in unsatisfactory resolution of many homeless situations. Fewer accommodations are available; and in 1984, 139,000 persons were housed in "ordinary board and lodging accommodations," or bed and breakfasts (Conway and Kemp 1985). This practice is both expensive and undesirable. In April of 1985, two new provisions were enacted which drastically affected the homelessness of young people. For individuals under twenty-six years of age, the length of time allowed for staying in accommodations has been limited. In addition, the government placed a maximum ceiling on payments to boarders which is on the average lower than 80% of the previous local authority allocations (Shelter 1985).

Despite its problems, the Act provides a framework for housing/homeless policy throughout Britain. The role of the courts is to properly enforce the Act. The courts do not provide appeals from local authority decisions, but they can intervene when the authority makes an arbitrary or unreasonable decision (Shelter 1982). Were New Jersey to have such legislation, the courts could then approach individual problems with the knowledge of a state plan allocating responsibility to local townships. The assertion of complicated and philosophical claims to a right to shelter could be eliminated through the codification of this right—a policy which already appears to be the implicit position of the state government (Governor's Task Force on the Homeless 1985).

CONCLUSION

Britain's national homeless policy exemplifies the commitment of a government to shelter its indigent citizens. Nothing short of a concerted financial commitment to the provision of long-term low income housing within a supportive socioeconomic community can alleviate the core of the homeless problem. However, the Housing (Homeless Persons) Act operates as a starting point for providing for basic needs. The current litigation and growing statistical evidence of the magnitude of this same problem in the United States prompts comparisons between American and British policies. States such as New Jersey which have an apparent commitment to housing their poor would do well to devise comprehensive legislation. Construction of a state act not unlike that of Great Britain would be an advantageous state policy. The state could then ensure that all its localities provide a meaningful response to homelessness in order to facilitate the proper disbursement of what little subsidies are available. Even where inadequate funding exists for ideal solutions, the presence of a cohesive act would serve to dispense what few resources are available on a just basis.

Examples of right to shelter laws do exist in this country but only on the local level where close examination often shows them to have limited application. Philadelphia, for example, has a right to shelter ordinance (Phila. Ord. No. 1962 1982), while Washington, D.C., passed Initiative 17 which directed the city government to institute a right to shelter policy (Stolarski 1988). In the former instance, this right has proved to be effective. Indeed, subsequent litigation has limited the city's discretion in providing shelter. An applicant can only be turned away if known to set fires, is in possession of a deadly weapon, or is showing signs of a contagious disease or condition (Committee for Dignity and Fairness for the Homeless v. Tartaglione 1984). In point of fact, the shelter provided is often less than adequate which leads to the necessity of further legal action. This situation prompted one observer to say, "Apparently, the battle is only begun with a favorable court ruling" (Stolarski 1988). For example, in Washington, D.C., subsequent court action has rolled back or limited the impact of its right to shelter policy (District of Columbia v. District of Columbia Board of Elections and Ethics 1985; Robbins v. Reagan 1985).

The application of this analysis to the federal level appears germane. Indeed, much of the utility of Britain's act comes from the fact that it is a national law establishing a clear national policy. To pursue a similar policy in this country on a state by state basis immediately raises the oft encountered problem of policy fragmentation. However, it must be recognized that the policy process in this country frequently results in progressive domestic policies which had initially emerged from states grappling with the issue at hand (Stolarski 1988). The eventual adoption of such policies at the federal level remains an option.

The final chapter will assess the likelihood that this or any other national policy for assisting the homeless will be successful.

10

Summary and Conclusions: Toward a Policy of Balanced Community Development

The preceding chapters described the efforts that have emerged over the past few years to shelter the homeless. The chief characteristic of these efforts is their essentially local and piecemeal nature. Much of the analysis in this book has been directed at assessing whether or not our local free market housing can produce sufficient units of low cost housing based on a fair share principle to meet the needs of the poor and homeless. The answer that has emerged is a qualified negative in the recognition of the strength of the local forces arrayed against local fair share housing providers. Indeed, it is extremely difficult for localities and providers to deliver adequate short-term shelters; the additional burden of producing sufficient amounts of transitional and permanent low cost housing for the inner city poor is likely to be too great for our disjointed low cost housing delivery system to bear.

Evidence was also provided that suggested that a strong national level policy approach might prove more efficacious because uniform national policies can sometimes cut through the tangle of conflicting parochial and business interests that dominate the local policy process. Indeed, strong national policies occasionally have been established in this country in defiance of negative business pressures.

But it must be asked if such an approach is realistic with regard to homelessness. To answer this question one must recall the discussion about policymaking in Chapter 2 that suggested that national public policy formation is anything but rational. The point was also made that its pro-business orientation is public policymaking's salient characteristic. Accordingly, this final chapter will discuss why it is highly unlikely that any coherent housing policy based on a right to housing will emerge as a result of the public scrutiny of the problem of homelessness.

The efficacy of this national level approach to the problem was broached in some of the earlier chapters. A number of programs and mechanisms for implementing this approach were suggested based on an analysis that holds that many of the problems surrounding low cost housing provision can be traced to the unequal application of local policy initiatives. It was suggested that a national policy that ensures the right to low cost housing based on a fair share allocation might successfully avoid the problems inherent in a more localized approach. Although not subject to the same amount of analysis, it was also suggested that this housing policy would need to be coupled with an income policy based on a national full employment/minimum income program that encourages individual independence within strong families and households. In short, under such a comprehensive policy, government would ensure that all people have the necessary income to rent or purchase adequate shelter and have enough left over to purchase food and other basic necessities. Such income may come from work or welfare payments or some combination of both. It might come in the form of a government-supported jobs program that ensures that the less skilled will have meaningful long-term career possibilities. Such work can be designed to be meaningful while avoiding competition with the private sector. In principle, this system could be relatively simple to comprehend and operate (Thurow 1980). Needless to say, the difficult part would be to fund such an effort. It would require a shifting of national spending priorities if we are not to add to our national debt. There are no simple solutions here, but domestic tranquility cannot be assured without a better approach to welfare and inner city joblessness (Shelby County Culture of Poverty Think Tank 1987; Thurow 1980; Gilbert 1986; Dear and Wolch 1987). Such reform would require a bold espousal of a more egalitarian social policy based upon significant income redistribution (Harrington 1980; Titmuss 1963; Crossman 1952; Gans 1968). If enacted, it would constitute the first comprehensive reform of the welfare system since the New Deal (notwithstanding the recent "workfare" modifications sponsored by Senator Moynihan).

DISCUSSION

There are indications that we are approaching a point where the failings of the private market as allocator can no longer be denied. Certainly the anticipated surge in long-term economic investment—as a result of Reagan's tax cuts for the wealthy and spending reductions for social programs—has not lived up to expectations. While the economy has experienced a long period of growth, many economists feel that this expansion has been fueled by extraordinary public spending on the military over and above our means. The effects of this approach can be seen in our growing deficit. We have been treating the national economy as if it were a gigantic Ponzi or pyramid scheme: continuing to buy short-term prosperity by putting the costs onto the shoulders of the succeeding generations who will be unable to pay it off. Reagan appears to have pulled off this stunt so that the hard choices will not have to be made on this "watch." Perhaps the next president can put it off a bit longer. No one knows for sure since short-term prosperity can be occasioned by a host of unpredictable factors such as the development of new technology and new markets. But the growing vulnerability of our postindustrial service-based economy is a real problem that will not go away. Increasingly, the jobs that are being created are characterized by low wages, low security, and low potential for advancement. Given an economic downturn, unemployment may rise faster and affect more areas than heretofore.

We first faced the need to regulate markets during the Great Depression, and we blinked. The nation went on to build a postwar prosperity on a free market approach with disjointed entitlements for the poor (Dellums 1986). In the future it is likely we will not have that luxury. Should there be another economic crisis, we will need to devise new national social and economic policies that reform our system of entitlements or else risk serious social upheaval. How to pay the cost of this approach is a real problem. We have never faced the fact that, in order to devise and deliver a truly just society that protects the interests of all of its citizens, we all will have to pay the cost (Thurow 1980; Harrington 1980; Crossman 1952).

Others who have grappled with these issues have advocated various forms of national or regional social and economic planning capable of counterbalancing the preponderant business-oriented interests in our society (Alperovitz and Faux 1980, 1984; Etzioni 1983; Carnoy, Shearer, and Rumberger 1983; Danziger and Weinberg 1986; Burt and Pittman 1986; Harrington 1980). All of the economic democrats who have argued this position admit that they have no clear idea how such a national planning process can be built into our system of disjointed governmental regulations (Medcalf and Dolbeare 1985; Dear and Wolch 1987; Popper 1981; Graham 1976). Many bemoan the lack of a clear policymaking process rooted in strong and distinct political parties. Today we even lack the prod of serious third party presidential candidates such as Norman Thomas of the Socialist Party. Thomas advocated strong redistributive social welfare and market interventionist policies that stopped short of expropriating all private property interests. In this regard, his policies were similar to Britain's Labor party. Today the closest equivalent figure of national stature is Michael Harrington, the head of the Democratic Socialist Organizing Committee which unfortunately has little public visibility. Nonetheless, there remains the possibility that the failure of the Democratic party to develop a viable post-New Deal identity may induce a faction of the party to embrace more radical social democratic policies which, in turn, may influence the development of more egalitarian social and economic policies by both political parties (Harrington 1980; Thurow 1980; Crossman 1952; Gans 1968).

It is possible to envision an alternative scenario whereby such policies might be operationalized. The core of such a scenario would be the growth of a new or existing national social democratic political party whose central policies would embrace the theme of individual socioeconomic rights within a context of strong support for existing neighborhoods and communities. At present, the low level of political participation in this country, coupled with the dissatisfaction with the existing dominant political parties, raise the possibility of the development of a new third party fueled by various social movements—much as earlier socioeconomic ills fomented the rise of the Progressive party (A. Davis 1967). But, although an attractive scenario, current socioeconomic realities impede such an effort. Simply put, today's poverty, while no less grinding than before, is a more limited phenomenon (Ellwood 1987). In addition, both history and current political wisdom do not offer much hope for third party efforts. Thus, while income inequality continues and even has expanded of late, there is no widespread political consciousness or concern about this phenomenon. To the contrary, as Harrington has pointed out, there is a perverse need to preserve such individual economic distinctions in our society, a need often shared by the poor themselves. The veneration of the entrepreneur Donald Trump supports Harrington's point: "This nation is psychologically individualistic, more so than any other advanced country, for many historic and cultural reasons. The outrageous differentials in income and wealth . . . are the stuff of hopeful daydreams, not the object of angry resentment" (Harrington 1980).

While the Republicans and their free market policies appear to be ascendant for the moment, there is an increasing feeling that we have weathered an important experiment in conservative approaches to government and have emerged the wiser. There is a widespread perception that the experiment was a failure. The phenomena of extensive homelessness, farm bankruptcies, rising infant mortality rates, and ghetto violence underscore this. Eight years after the inauguration of a strongly conservative president with a mandate to pursue a conservative policy agenda, we have witnessed the foundering of this agenda on the shoals of real world socioeconomic problems (Aronson and Hilley 1986). Whether in the area of crime, the urban underclass, urban enterprise zones, the sale of public housing, regional economic competition, etc., the agenda has not solved any of our pressing urban, social, and economic problems—indeed, in many instances, it has made them worse (Abramovitz 1986).

As a result, many now speak of a return or a cycle that will bring the Democratic party with an alternative agenda to the fore at the national level (Schlesinger 1986; Eisenstadt and Ahimeir 1985; Quigley and Rubinfield 1985). There are many problems inherent in this belief. Such reactive cycles often offer a return of sorts but never a return to familiar territory; instead, the next cycle builds upon the old and creates the new. As a result, Schlesinger and others suggest the image of a spiral rather than a pendulum (B. Lang 1939). In the United States, too much has changed since the Democrats were last in power to hope for a simple taking up from where they left off. Rather, if we are to be able to cycle back to a stronger central governmental role in urban social and economic policy, this role must be distinct from earlier Democratic approaches which appear to have little following (Magill 1986). Many contend that we will need strong central planning that results in clear and enforceable laws that serve to establish the basic parameters of a just society (Reich 1983). What we do not need is a Marshall Plan for the cities or another "War on Poverty" since both these approaches entail a return to the flawed federally funded, locally implemented policies of the past (Lekachman 1982; Hayden 1980). What is needed is the commitment to a national policy of guaranteed social, economic, and civil rights and the implementation of those governmental programs necessary to secure their delivery.

PROBLEMS WITH CENTRALIZED PLANNING

The postwar era saw many democratic countries embrace the principles of an egalitarian welfare state. Many European countries, in particular, have been quite successful in applying such principles to issues of public policy for some time (de Schweinitz 1943; A. Davis 1967). Britain and the Scandinavian countries are often thought of in this regard. Britain, with its nationalized health care system, land use planning system, public housing, and New Towns program, possesses a spectrum of exemplary programs that form the core of an egalitarian welfare state. Yet no example of a problem-free welfare state exists, since all are in various stages of development and are continuously responding to changing circumstances. National planning cannot be expected to solve all problems nor be problem-free in its operation (neoconservatives have been all too happy to point out its problems) (Medcalf and Dolbeare 1985; Haar 1984).

The experience of Britain is instructive in this regard. In its search for economic democracy, it attempted serious national economic planning. In one notable example, the Labor government tried to forestall a population shift from the north of England to the more prosperous and expanding south (similar to this country's migration to the Sunbelt). The results were not strongly positive yet the attempt to even out the disequilibrium caused by the market did serve to lessen the negative impact on the declining regions (McCone 1969). In particular, the British were quite effective in guiding the location of industry and workers who were lured to the south—something not attempted in the Sunbelt (Hall et al. 1973). It is also true that rising costs and program inefficiency dog the national health system and other social services. Whether such problems are endemic to nationalized services or are a function of larger macroeconomic market forces continues to be a point of sharp partisan debate. Nonetheless, the lesson of reduced expectations is clear: so long as society wishes to retain a mixed economy, the market can be highly regulated but not completely controlled. The important point here is the need for government to be willing and able to respond to market changes while keeping paramount its responsibility to promote the interests of the citizenry over those of capital. Those who support this principle need to become more adept at defending it from conservative charges of inefficiency and waste; the ammunition is there if they would care to look (Clawson and Hall 1973; Eversley 1973; Titmuss 1963; Crossman 1952).

CONCLUSIONS

We may well be entering a period when this country will confront the necessity of adopting components of a national planning system. The simultaneous crisis of homelessness, structural unemployment, open space depletion, toxic waste disposal, and other environmental problems all signal the true end of America's privatistic frontier consciousness. We are witnessing multiple demonstrations of the "era of limits" notion first broached in the 1970s. While we were able to shrug off this political message and all it implied for a short period under the expansion-at-all-costs policies of Reagan, its consequences have simply been postponed for most of us. For the unemployed and homeless, it is here today; for those millions existing on insecure low wage jobs, it will arrive in due time. The United States is entering the community of mature developed nations and must be ready to plan with them for mutual benefit. The only other choice left is to await some significant and undeniable crisis and hope that last minute policy adjustments will forestall catastrophe; given our policymaking structure and our strong individualist tendencies, such a choice is a real and very stark possibility.

It would be convenient, after suggesting that the recent trend toward local control of urban policy has failed to adequately assist the poor and the homeless, to simply call for a rededication to national or regional level policymaking and implementation. Presumably, a more analytic and scientific policymaking process would then lead to more egalitarian policies (Dear and Wolch 1987). Yet achieving rational policies at the national level is very difficult because national level policymaking is so constrained. There is little likelihood of achieving the adoption of a policy for the homeless that includes the elements discussed above because of the cleavages inherent in our approach to public policy. Lindblom (1980, 12) has explained the problem succinctly:

In short, a deep conflict runs through common attitudes towards policymaking. On the one hand, people want policy to be informed and well analyzed. On the other hand, they want policymaking to be democratic, hence necessarily political. In slightly different words, on the one hand they want policymaking to be more scientific; on the other, they want it to remain in the world of politics.

Many democratic theorists and political leaders have tried to resolve this conflict. They assure us that open political interchange in a democratic society—a "competition of ideas"—is the best road to truth, that democratic politics offers the best chance for informed and reasoned policymaking. But we cannot be sure. Even if it is the best road, it looks perilous. Many people distrust democratic politics because they believe that the competition of ideas generates less reason than contentiousness in policymaking. Thus the conflict between reason, analysis, and science on the one side, and politics and democracy on the other, remains. If society wants more reason and analysis in policymaking, perhaps it must surrender some aspects of democracy.

The application of this analysis to the problem of homelessness and the lack of good quality low cost housing is germane. Simply put, those interests that want policymaking to remain accessible via the political process are predominant in our society. This can clearly be seen in the case of a fair share low cost housing policy where access to the local political process imparts a veto power to local communities over the siting of such housing. This veto power will not be surrendered easily. There are too many interests that would be threatened by a national or regional fair share low cost housing program and too few who would feel that they might benefit. It is not just that major interest groups would oppose these policies but the average citizen too would oppose them. It is worth examining why this is the case.

A National Fair Share Low Cost Housing Program

A national fair share housing program would offend the interests of individual citizens as it would be frequently perceived as a threat to the continued appreciation in value of their real estate investment in their homes. Some 70% of American citizens are homeowners; there are few such salient characteristics that are shared by so many and aspired to by a good proportion of the rest of the population. Homeownership is based on the two functions that it provides: shelter and personal investment. This latter function serves to explain why 70% of the population is predisposed to oppose any housing policy that can be viewed as threatening their investment. For the vast majority, any form of low cost housing in their community falls into this category (Perin 1977; Medcalf and Dolbeare 1985; Lukas 1985).

In some less affluent suburban areas resistance to low cost housing may emanate from those local residents who are barely better off than the program recipients. They feel that there is little difference in their economic situations but that they had to work to pay the full market rent or mortgage while the low cost housing recipients will receive a helping hand. This attitude, often associated with the New Right, has fueled much of the local opposition to low cost housing in such areas as Philadelphia, Pennsylvania, and Yonkers, New York (Medcalf and Dolbeare 1985; Lukas 1985).

In addition, in most communities there exists a sense that assistance should freely be given on an emergency basis but that long-term or permanent benefit programs are inherently unfair to those whose success was achieved by unassisted struggle. This sense or ethic holds that one must earn one's way into a community and not attempt to gain entry by government fiat. While it is claimed that this ethic only amounts to simple justice, it is based upon a weak understanding of structural economic and social realities. All told, this body of opinion is perhaps the largest single obstacle to meaningful housing policy reform.

Since the policy would have limited impact on them directly, some business interests might not be so negatively disposed. To a limited extent, they might be expected to support it as it may bring lower cost labor closer to suburban job centers. However, business interests are oriented toward ensuring the highest returns on their investments. Low cost housing would be seen as exerting a potentially negative force on some local business investments and might therefore be opposed. The better utilization of modern transportation systems might be suggested by business leaders as a less contentious means of achieving improved access to labor. In addition, realtors, builders, developers, and financial institutions—the whole apparatus that currently undergirds the production of private market housing—would be threatened with the possibility that successful government-supported housing might begin to attract meaningful political support which, in turn, could lead to lessened government support for the private market system. As a result, business interests would not be likely to support a fair share low cost housing policy and their support would be crucial to the passage of any national level legislation.

Labor unions are taking an increasingly progressive stance in relation to programs promoting economic democracy which affect the well-being of their members (Carnoy, Shearer, and Rumberger 1983). Low cost housing is an issue that has occasioned the active involvement of a number of local and statewide unions. Of course, many elements within the building trades have a longstanding relationship with the prevailing private housing delivery system and can be expected to continue to support it. This is a new area of endeavor for many unions which might be expected to view housing policy as beyond their frame of reference. Nonetheless, their support would be an important element in any effort to promote a fair share housing program (Nenno and Brophy 1982).

Local officials would be very hesitant to support a fair share low income housing policy in their community. As was seen during the Nixon administration, local officials might be among those who would perceive low cost housing as a threat to their political futures (Polikoff 1978; Lukas 1985). The best that could be hoped for is that they would opt out of the process leaving the issue to federal officials who could be expected to carry out a fair share housing program. Indeed, there are occasions when federal officials have successfully carried out low cost housing projects in the face of vehement local opposition (Nenno and Brophy 1982).

Interest groups will fall on both sides of this issue depending upon their orientation. Homeowners associations, taxpayer groups, and the like can be expected to oppose a fair share housing policy on the grounds that it imposes the federal government on local matters and increases the cost of services that could result from the development. Other socially oriented interest groups might be expected to support a fair share program. There are numerous groups, some affiliated with religious denominations, which have an interest in housing and related social issues. Many have already sponsored the construction of low cost housing developments. Clearly, many such groups can be expected to support a fair share housing program.

Many diverse political interest groups would also oppose a national fair share housing policy. Neoconservatives would deride it as quixotically egalitarian and dependent for its implementation on a cumbersome and costly public bureaucracy. The New Right would see it as another elitist attack on the hard working blue collar communities. This response might be mitigated if the program were to place some low cost housing in all communities. Traditional conservatives would oppose the program as an unwarranted intrusion into the private market in housing. Many neoliberals might also oppose a fair share policy on the grounds that it represents an overemphasis on an idealistic and unattainable social policy by government that should instead focus its limited energies on ensuring the nation's economic competitiveness in the face of mounting global challenges.

On the other hand, there are a host of political groups that might be expected to support a national fair share program to some extent. Social democrats, economic democrats, reform liberals, and some mainstream liberals might be expected to support efforts to achieve a national fair share policy. Most of these groups would see such a policy as a manifestation of the economic democracy that forms the core of their beliefs (Hochschild 1984; Lukas 1985). However, given the politicized policy process as described by Lindblom (1980) and the fact that the forces opposed to large scale governmental socioeconomic programs are currently ascendant in a polity where a central role is ceded to the highly organized New Right, the outlook for supporters of a fair share policy appears bleak indeed (Medcalf and Dolbeare 1985).

Cutting the Gordian Knot

Clearly, a national or regional planning system with real powers would be helpful as it would provide a means to develop a national housing policy along the lines suggested here. Indeed, there is broad agreement among housing activists about the need for a national fair share low cost housing policy. What eludes them is how to get it passed into law and implemented.

In reality, it is highly unlikely that national planning will be adopted unless there is another business crisis on the scale of that the nation suffered during the Great Depression. Only if the business sector is directly affected will the government be able to get sufficient support for such an approach (Medcalf and Dolbeare 1985). Even then, national planning and market intervention would be justified as temporary measures aimed at job creation or business stimulation (as occurred in the World War I and New Deal eras). Such measures would have to be cloaked in the proper terms. No one would be able to call things as they are but would be forced to play word games much like the Queen of Hearts did in "Alice in Wonderland." How long programs created under such subterfuge can be expected to survive is highly speculative. All this notwithstanding, we may well be poised for just such an experiment since the conservative Reagan revolution has apparently run its course. But it must be cautioned that while such an experiment might begin to utilize some of the rhetoric of national planning, policymakers almost certainly will pull back from establishing a system based on specific powers of federal or regional intervention in local affairs—which is a basic requirement for a comprehensive policy approach (Burt and Pittman 1986).

This situation is exasperating for those who wish to see a substantive response to the crisis of homelessness. Indeed, they may well ask, what is left for housing advocates who must work within a market-oriented democratic policymaking framework? What remains is recognition of the odds against achieving meaningful national reforms while continuing to advocate for such reforms. Equally important is continuing to work at the local policy level since it is there that there is an increasingly impressive record of successful local programs. Needless to say, this is a long-term strategy and in many senses suboptimal, yet it is based on a recognition of how the policy process works and how change proceeds. The United States has always been a country that has venerated local entrepreneurs who achieved financial success however banal the means; likewise, it has often denigrated successful public sector employees no matter how grand their accomplishments. It is no different in the area of housing reform.

Housing reform began in the slums of New York and with few exceptions, has remained a largely local level activity with few rewards. The names of important local housing activists that quickly come to the mind of politically active citizens—Jane Addams, Dorothea Dix, Stanley Milgram, Alice Liscomb, Maggie Kuhn, Paul Davidoff, Chester Hartman, Harry Hopkins, and others—are all part of the pantheon of local social and housing reformers known to the small coterie of housing activists in this country. That the reformers are not better known is due in part to the local nature of the housing development process but also because we do not value such activities highly in this political economy. With the exception of Mr. Hopkins, few were given a chance to bring their expertise into play at the national level. In this, our social policy history is distinct from that of the British, since local activists such as Beatrice and Sidney Webb eventually were able to have a singular impact on the development of a major political party and national level public policies (Cole 1946). Despite the optimism of some advocates for the homeless, there is little reason to expect this situation to change in the near future (Dolbeare 1983; Dear and Wolch 1987). In the meantime, the homeless shall remain dependent upon the vitality and good work done by the thousands of local housing activists in our towns and cities across America.

Mixed Scanning Revisited

If centralized socioeconomic policy planning is impossible in the short term, it may be possible for social organizations to promote a version of Etzioni's mixed scanning paradigm, combining aspects of centralized rational planning and decentralized incremental decisionmaking. While there is little hard evidence of this development, there are reasons to expect that such an approach would be more possible than in the past and may achieve limited success in some regions of the country; the location of community-based mental health facilities is a case in point (Winerip 1988a; Goldstein, Goodrich, and Brown 1987).

From a historical perspective, there are some reasons to foresee the evolution of such an approach. Specifically, it is possible to divide postwar U.S. urban and housing policy into three epochs. The Democratic epoch from 1933 to 1968 had the strongest aspects of centralized planning. To be sure, much of this central planning was vague and unenforceable; nonetheless, the federal level was in an activist mode, often working closely with cities due to their orientation to the Democratic party. The second period was the Republican incrementalist epoch from 1968 to the present. This period was characterized by the devolution of power from the federal level to the largely Republican-oriented states and suburban localities. The emergence of a third epoch is purely hypothetical, yet is based on the reasoned arguments that foresee the need for new policy mechanisms after the twin failures of the first two epochs. Briefly, the Democratic epoch was characterized as a failure because its social programs failed to produce the promised results (Levitan 1969). Increasingly, the Republican epoch is seen as a failure because the locally based approach, while providing exemplary individual programs and projects, is uneven in its application and insufficient in overall output (Hanson 1983; Meyers 1986; Peterson, Lewis, and Carol 1986). These twin failures may provide the impetus for a new hybrid approach fueled by emerging political pressure from disparate social organizations and movements. In response, certain policy areas of fundamental importance would be seen as appropriate for strong federal level intervention, while others of a more local impact would be left to the local level. For example, right to housing legislation might be proposed as a policy area requiring a strong federal or regional response due to the national economic forces contributing to the current low cost housing crisis. Such a proposal would not preclude an ongoing role for local policy input and control. Local applications might center around nonprofit housing corporations which build low cost housing with low interest funds from a national development bank as was proposed by the Carter urban policy initiative. Such an approach is not dissimilar to the regional fair share approach put forward by Dear and Wolch (1987). Clearly, there would be much overlap and compromise but it is possible that what might emerge would be a good approximation of Etzioni's mixed scanning paradigm.

A Proposal for a Council of Social Policy Advisors

Mixed scanning suggests a framework by which policies may be reviewed in order to determine whether their implementation should proceed incrementally or comprehensively, but it does not specify how this process will be administered. Indeed, with the current fluidity between levels of governmental authority and weak political party structure, there does not appear to be an obvious existing agency or branch of government in which to place this function (Reagan and Sanzone 1981). Dear and Wolch (1987) foresee a mixed scanning oriented regional fair share plan for the homeless evolving out of a somewhat ad hoc local/regional community development process. Something along this line has already occurred in several areas, but this process might become more widespread if the process were given further support and encouragement at the national level. One way to promote this would be for social organizations to press for a new national council of social advisors. This new agency might provide sufficient visibility and authority to accomplish the task of promoting a mixed scanning approach on a national basis.

An executive level council of social policy advisors appears to offer a strong base for conducting the type of policy review required by the mixed scanning approach. It could function as a companion agency to the existing Council of Economic Advisors. As such, it would be advisory to the chief executive who would have to carry any policy initiatives to Congress for action. The council could conduct a monitoring of social policy issues that would arise through the normal political and administrative channels. The council would allow for the articulation of professional views, the development of policy position papers, and an annual report outlining the costs and benefits of proposed courses of action. Central to its mission would be consideration of the best locus for the proposed policy mechanisms: national, state/regional, or local. Staff services might include training and facilitation for a mixed scanning/fair share approach to social services.

Yet, the lack of clear authority to pursue a national or regional policy orientation remains a problem and the inherent weakness in the mixed scanning approach (Burt and Pittman 1986; Danziger and Weinberg 1986). The bottom line is that this proposed structure can only suggest and encourage a particular approach; it cannot require a particular response. Given the intense local opposition to low cost housing in many suburban and nonmetropolitan areas, there is little likelihood of achieving strong support for a fair share low income housing policy regardless of how this issue is approached. Simply put, the policymaking process in the United States is not easily mobilized to pursue any particular policy, especially if the policy is not one of universal entitlement (as is the case with low cost housing). Attempts to promote the fair share principle with regard to the siting of community-based mental health facilities has met with some success. However, there is evidence to suggest that the success rate falls off when the facility to be sited is seen as unwelcome (Goldstein, Goodrich, and Brown 1987). In short, it is likely that voluntary fair share will result in a "creaming off" of the less controversial facilities leaving the unpopular facilities in the urban areas.

Thus, it is one thing to say that as the result of the public outcry over widespread homelessness Congress and the president will produce some additional resources to address the problem, and quite another to say that this effort can be channeled into a well-conceived national or regional housing/income policy by means of a mixed scanning or other particular approach. A diffuse, voluntary, low cost housing program coupled with strong local controls is attainable because it threatens the fewest interests; a specific national or regional policy is most likely unattainable as it threatens the most interests.

Given this understanding of the policymaking process in this country, what outcomes can be realistically expected? Simply that more resources for low cost housing will be made available such as proposed in the Community Housing Partnership Act. By and large, these resources will be made available to nonprofit organizations that currently bear most of the burden for sheltering the homeless (Atlas and Dreier 1988). Some national level housing programs may well be funded, but these programs will be made available to states and localities on a voluntary basis. The result of this approach will be to ensure that the poor and homeless are sheltered and housed in the older urban areas, an outcome which is often defended as providing access for the poor to social services (Goldstein,

Goodrich, and Brown 1987). Simultaneously, they will continue to be denied access to those more affluent communities which contain the bulk of the job and educational opportunities. Indeed, New York City is currently embarked on a major effort to rehabilitate apartment buildings for low and moderate income households. While this represents a major improvement over the use of homeless shelters, it does little to ensure that the poor and homeless will be housed in communities that have sufficient social and economic resources to enable them to rebuild their lives. By continuing to house the poor in the city, it perpetuates the ghetto and sentences thousands of children to lifelong poverty and dependence. This approach ensures the continued isolation of the poor from the mainstream of American society (Dear and Wolch 1987; W. J. Wilson 1987; Ellwood 1987). It is a housing policy destined to fail; yet when it does, it will be the poor who will be blamed. This approach is regrettable because it squanders the opportunity to utilize these new resources to build a network of open, balanced communities throughout the country.

Implications for Urban Areas

If homelessness is dealt with solely on the local level, it will have profound implications for our urban areas that already have a preponderance of the poor. Cities will be the most likely recipients of federal and state housing funds for low cost housing and they can be expected to greet this largess with something less than total enthusiasm. City officials feel that they are always expected to shoulder society's burdens and can be expected to plan the expenditure of these funds in such a manner as to not jeopardize ongoing private revitalization efforts. The risk is that this motivation may lead to the redevelopment of low cost housing in less than optimal locations thereby continuing the cycle of segregation and restricted opportunities associated with many previous housing programs. Indeed, some observers are concerned that our current shelter-based approach to homelessness is recreating the old urban centered punitive workhouse and asylum system for the "deficient poor" (Dear and Wolch 1987).

Even in the face of structural impediments, there is a real need for housing activists to continue to advocate that low cost urban housing be made available under a low density, scattered site program that offers opportunities for program beneficiaries to participate in all types of urban neighborhoods (Dear and Wolch 1987; Orfield 1983; Diamond 1985). This policy advocacy must be tied to a guaranteed jobs/incomes program to ensure meaningful work for all able members of society. The point must be made that only by striving to ensure the inclusion of the poor and homeless in viable communities with publicly provided social and economic services can the homeless have a chance to succeed in rebuilding their lives so that they can live in security and dignity. Only in this way will succeeding generations avoid the pain and embarrassment of living in an affluent society that accepts the existence of a permanent urban underclass. The means to this end are far from clear. Several have been offered here with an awareness of their utopian aspects as well as their potential ineffectiveness. Still, efforts to craft a workable and just solution must go forward; not to make the attempt would be unthinkable.

Bibliography

Aaron, H. 1981. Policy implications: A progress report. In *Do housing allowances work?* *See* Bradbury and Downs 1981.

Abramovitz, M. 1986. The privatization of the welfare state: A review. *Social Work* 31(4):257–64.

Abrams, C. 1946. *The future of housing.* New York: Harper & Row.

Achtenberg, E. P., and P. Marcuse. 1983. Toward the decommodification of housing: A political analysis and a progressive program. In *America's housing crisis: What is to be done. See* Harman 1983.

Ahlbrandt, R. S., and P. Brophy. 1975. *Neighborhood revitalization.* Lexington, Mass.: D. C. Heath.

Aiken, C. 1985. New settlement patterns of rural blacks in the American south. *The Geographical Review* 75(4):383.

Algor v. Ocean County. 1984. Docket No. L-37425-85 (Ocean County Law Division).

Allen, G., J. Fitts, and E. S. Glatt. 1981. The experimental housing allowance program. In *Do housing allowances work? See* Bradbury and Downs 1981.

Alperovitz, G., and J. Faux. 1980. Conservative chic: Reindustrialization. *Social Policy* (Dec.):6–9.

Alperovitz, G., and J. Faux. 1984. *Rebuilding America: A blueprint for a new economy.* New York: Pantheon Books.

Anderson, M. 1964. *The federal bulldozer: A critical analysis of urban renewal.* Cambridge, Mass.: MIT Press.

Anderson, N. 1923. *The hobo: The sociology of the homeless man.* Chicago: University of Chicago Press.

Apgar, W. C., and H. J. Brown. 1988. *The state of the nation's housing.* Boston: Joint Center for Housing Studies of Harvard University.

Arnstein, S. 1972. A ladder of citizen participation. In *The city in the seventies. See* Yin 1972.

Aronson, J. R., and J. Hilley. 1986. *Financing state and local governments.* Washington, D.C.: Brookings Institution.

Atlantic City. 1985. *Comprehensive plan for emergency shelter services for homeless persons*. Atlantic City, N.J.

Atlas, J., and P. Dreier. 1988. Not the American dream Part II: Ingredients for a housing action agenda in '88. *Shelterforce* X(6):7.

Auletta, K. 1982. *The underclass*. New York: Random House.

Badcock, B. 1984. *Unfairly structured cities*. New York: Basil Blackwell.

Bahr, H.M. 1973. *Skid row: An introduction to disaffiliation*. New York: Oxford University Press.

Bailey, R. 1973. *The squatters*. Middlesex, England: Penguin Books.

Baldassare, M., ed. 1983. *Cities and urban living*. New York: Columbia University Press.

Barbanel, J. 1987. Cycles of concern: Societies and their homeless. *New York Times*. Nov. 29.

Baxter, E., and K. Hopper. 1981. Private lives/public spaces: Homeless adults on the streets of New York City. New York: Community Service Society.

Beauregard, R. 1984. Structures, agency and urban redevelopment. In *Cities in transformation. See* M. P. Smith 1984.

Belcher, J., and J. Singer. 1988. Homelessness: A cost of capitalism. *Social Policy.* 18(4):44–48.

Bellush, J., and M. Hausknecht. 1973. Public housing: The contexts of failure. In *Housing urban America. See* Pynoos, Schafer, and Hartman 1973.

Bensman, J. 1978. Marxism as a foundation for urban sociology. *Comparative Urban Research* 6(23):69–75.

Bingham, R., R. E. Green, and S. B. White. 1987. *The homeless in contemporary society*. Beverly Hills, Calif.: Sage.

Birch, D. 1972. Toward a stage theory of urban growth. In *The city in the seventies. See* Yin 1972.

Bisgaier, C. 1984. Plaintiff's Brief. Superior Court of New Jersey, Law Division, Jurisdiction Docket No. L-061299-84.

Blaesser, B. 1984a. Local government liability under the Fair Housing Act and under state anti-exclusionary zoning doctrines. Part I. *Land Use Law and Zoning Digest* 36(Jan.):3.

Blaesser, B. W. 1984b. Local government liability under the Fair Housing Act and under state anti-exclusionary zoning doctrines. Part II. *Land Use Law and Zoning Digest* 36(Feb.):9.

Blocker, G., and E. H. Smith, eds. 1980. *John Rawl's theory of social justice*. Athens, Ohio: Ohio University Press.

Bluestone, B., and B. Harrison. 1982. *The deindustrialization of America: Plant closings, community abandonment, dismantling of basic industry*. New York: Basic Books.

Bogue, D. 1986. An introduction to Chicago's skid rows—survey results. In *Housing the homeless. See* Erickson and Wilhelm 1986.

Bottomore, T. B. 1966. *Elites and society*. Middlesex, England: Penguin Books.

Botwinick, G., and E. Weinstein. 1985. *Community/residential alternatives to institutionalization*. Princeton, N.J.: Mental Health Association of New Jersey.

Bourney, J. 1986. Cleburne Living Center v. City of Cleburne: The irrational relationship of mental retardation to zoning objectives. *John Marshall Law Review* 19:469.

Bowser, B. 1985. Race relations in the 1980's. *Journal of Black Studies* 15(3):307.

Boyea, J. A. 1982. *A critical analysis of neighborhood housing services.* Richmond, Va.: Dept. of Planning and Community Development.

Boyer, M. C. 1986. *Dreaming the rational city.* Cambridge, Mass.: MIT Press.

Bradbury, K., and A. Downs. 1981. *Do housing allowances work?* Washington, D.C.: Brookings Institution.

Bradbury, K., A. Downs, and I. Small. 1981. Forty theories of urban decline. *Urban Affairs Papers* 3:13–20.

Bratt, R. G., C. Hartman, and A. Meyerson. 1986. *Critical perspectives on housing.* Philadelphia: Temple University Press.

Brooklyn Law Review. 1984. Establishing a right to shelter for the homeless. 50(8):939–40.

Bruner, S. J., and J. W. Cosby. 1985. The homeless in Atlantic County: A multi-dimensional analysis. Atlantic City, N.J.: Atlantic County Department of Social Services.

Burchell, R. W., and D. Listoken. 1983. *After Mount Laurel II, Challenge and delivery of low cost housing.* New Brunswick, N.J.: Center for Urban Policy Research.

Burke, E. 1968. Citizen participation strategies. *Journal of the American Institute of Planners* 34(5):288.

Burns, L. 1987. Third World solutions to the homeless problem. In *The homeless in contemporary society. See* Bingham, Green, and White 1987.

Burt, M. A., and K. Pittman. 1986. *Testing the safety net.* Washington, D.C.: Urban Institute Press.

Callahen et al. v. Carey et al. 1979. Index No. 42582/79, Supreme Court of the State of New York.

Camden Planning and Advocacy Council/Human Services Coalition. 1984. Emergency Housing Consortium. Camden, N.J.

Camden Shelter Coalition. 1985. Memo sent to Camden County Board of Freeholders. Camden, N.J.

Camden Shelter Coalition. 1986. Decentralization of the homeless in Camden County. Camden, N. J.

Campi, M. 1985. Building a home of legal rights: A plea for the homeless. *St. John's Law Review* 59:530.

Caputo, D. 1985. American cities and the future. *Society* 22(2):59.

Caputo, D. A., and R. L. Cole. 1974. *Urban politics and decentralization: The case of general revenue sharing.* Lexington, Mass.: Lexington Books.

Caputo, D.A., and R. L. Cole, eds. 1976. *Revenue sharing.* Lexington, Mass.: Lexington Books.

Carliner, M. 1987. Homelessness: A housing problem? In *The homeless in contemporary society. See* Bingham, Green, and White 1987.

Carnoy, M., D. Shearer, and R. Rumberger. 1983. *A new social contract: The economy and government after Reagan.* New York: Harper & Row.

Castells, M. 1977. *The urban question: A marxist approach.* Cambridge, Mass.: MIT Press.

Castells, M. 1984. Space and society: Managing the new historical relationships. In *Cities in transformation. See* M. P. Smith 1984.

Center on Budget and Policy Priorities. 1986. Falling behind: A report on how blacks have fared under Reagan. *Journal of Black Studies* 17(2):148–72.

Cibulskis, A., and C. Hoch. 1985. *Homelessness: An annotated bibliography.* Chicago: Council of Planning Librarians.

Cinaglia, R. 1985. Camden's vacant housing rehabilitation program: An evaluation. Unpublished research project, Graduate Program in Public Policy, Rutgers University. Camden, N.J.

Clawson, M., and P. Hall. 1973. *Planning and urban growth: An Anglo-American comparison.* Baltimore: Johns Hopkins University Press.

Clay, P. 1978. *Neighborhood revitalization: The recent experience of large American cities.* Cambridge, Mass.: MIT Press.

Clay, P. 1987. At risk of loss: The endangered future of low income rental housing resources. Washington, D.C.: Neighborhood Reinvestment Corporation.

Cole, M. 1946. *Beatrice Webb.* New York: Harcourt Brace.

Coleman, J. 1986. Diary of a homeless man. In *Housing the homeless. See* Erickson and Wilhelm 1986.

Coll, B. D. 1971. *Perspectives in public welfare.* 2d ed. Washington, D.C.: Department of Health, Education, and Welfare.

Collins, S. M. 1983. The making of the Black middle class. *Social Problems* 30(4):369.

Collins-Parker, J. 1986. Hunger in Camden. Unpublished monograph, Department of Urban Studies, Rutgers University. Camden, N.J.

Columbia Law Review. 1966. Citizen participation in urban renewal. 66(3):527.

Committee on Banking, Housing and Urban Affairs. 1987. *A new national housing policy.* Washington, D.C.

Committee for Dignity and Fairness for the Homeless v. Tartaglione. 1984. (Eastern District Court of Pennsylvania).

Community Affairs. 1987. Emergency shelter program: New outlook for the homeless. Dec. 1.

Congressional Budget Office. 1979. *The long term costs of lower income housing assistance programs.* Washington, D.C.

Conway, J., and P. Kemp. 1985. *Bed and breakfast: Slum housing of the eighties.* London: Shelter Housing Action Committee.

Cooper, M. 1987. The role of religions and nonprofit organizations in combating homelessness. In *The homeless in contemporary society. See* Bingham, Green, and White 1987.

Costa, F., J. L. Dustin, and J. L. Shanahan. 1987. Transforming a manufacturing city: Akron's readjustment plans. In *The future of winter cities. See* Gappert 1987.

Coughlin, E. 1988. Studying the homeless: The difficulty of tracking a transient population. *Chronicle of Higher Education* XXXV(8):6.

Council on Affordable Housing. 1986. *Newsletter* 1:2. Trenton, N.J.

Courier Post. 1987. Fairshare help for the homeless. Cherry Hill, N.J. Dec. 21.

Courier Post. 1985. A promising plan to help the homeless. Cherry Hill, N.J. May 11.

Crosland, C. A. R. 1952. The transition from capitalism. In *New Fabian Essays. See* Crossman 1952.

Crossman, R. H. S., ed. 1952. *New Fabian Essays.* New York: Praeger.

Cunningham, J. 1972. Citizen participation in public affairs. *Public Administration Review* 32:595.

Cuomo, M. 1987. The state role: New York State's approach to homelessness. In *The homeless in contemporary society. See* Bingham, Green, and White 1987.

Dahl, R. 1961. *Who governs.* New Haven, Conn.: Yale University Press.

Danielson, M. N. 1976. *The politics of exclusion.* New York: Columbia University Press.

Danziger, S., and D. Weinberg. 1986. *Fighting poverty: What works and what doesn't.* Cambridge, Mass.: Harvard University Press.

Davidoff, P. 1967. Advocacy and pluralism in planning. In *Taming megalopolis. See* Eldridge 1967.

Davis, A. 1967. *Spearheads for reform.* New York: Oxford University Press.

Davis, R. 1984. Tricia Meadows: A manufactured home community. Mt. Laurel, N.J.: Rodger Davis Enterprises Marketing Information.

Dear, M., and J. Wolch. 1987. *Landscapes of despair: From deinstitutionalization to homelessness.* Princeton, N.J.: Princeton University Press.

Dellums, R. 1986. Welfare state v. warfare state. *The Black Scholar* 17(5):38–51.

Department of Community Affairs. 1988. *The Housing Advocate* 1:2. Trenton, N.J.

de Schweinitz, K. 1943. *England's road to social security.* New York: Barnes.

Dewey, J. 1963. *Liberalism and social action.* New York: Capricorn Books.

Diamond, P. R. 1985. *Beyond busing: Inside the challenge to urban segregation.* Ann Arbor: University of Michigan Press.

District of Columbia v. District of Columbia Board of Elections and Ethics. 1985. Civil Act No. 12280-84 (DC Superior Court, July 19) (Appeal pend.).

Dolbeare, C. N. 1983. The low income housing crisis. In *America's housing crisis. See* Hartman 1983.

Dolbeare, C. N. 1985. *Federal housing assistance: Who needs it? Who gets it?* Washington, D.C.: National League of Cities.

Dolbeare, C. N. 1987. *Low income housing needs.* Washington, D.C.: National Low Income Housing Coalition.

Domhoff, W. 1967. *Who rules America?* Englewood Cliffs, N.J.: Prentice-Hall.

Dommel, P. R. 1974. *The politics of revenue sharing.* Bloomington, Ind.: Indiana University Press.

Donnison, D., and C. Ungerson. 1982. *Housing policy.* New York: Penguin Books.

Donnolly, D. 1986. Interview with attorney, New Jersey Office of the Attorney General. April 14.

Downs, A. 1973. *Opening up the suburbs.* New Haven, Conn.: Yale University Press.

Downs, A. 1977. Competing claims of neighborhoods. In *Justice and the city,* by P. Levy. Philadelphia: Institute for the Study of Civic Values.

Downs, A. 1983. *Rental housing in the 1980's.* Washington, D.C.: Brookings Institution.

Downs, A., and K. Bradbury. 1981. Conference discussion. In *Do housing allowances work? See* Bradbury and Downs 1981.

Dye, T. 1983. *Who's running America?* Englewood Cliffs, N.J.: Prentice-Hall.

Economist. 1988. A worthy capital. 307(16):13.

Edwards, R. C., M. Reich, and T. E. Weisskopf. 1986. *The capitalist system.* Englewood Cliffs, N.J.: Prentice-Hall.

Eichler, R., and M. Kaplan. 1967. *The community builders.* Berkeley: University of California Press.

Eichler, E., and M. Kaplan. 1973. New communities. In *Housing urban America. See* Pynoos, Schafer, and Hartman 1973.

Eisenstadt, S. N., and O. Ahimeir. 1985. *The welfare state and its aftermath.* Totowa, N.J.: Barnes and Noble.

Eldred, W. 1985. Making Mount Laurel II work: Three approaches. *New Jersey Munic-ipalities* 62:37.

Eldridge, H. 1967. *Taming megalopolis: How to manage an urbanized world.* New York: Doubleday.

Ellwood, D. T. 1987. *Divide and conquer.* New York: Ford Foundation.

Erickson, J., and C. Wilhelm, eds. 1986. *Housing the homeless.* New Brunswick, N.J.: Center for Urban Policy Research.

Etzioni, A. 1983. *An immodest agenda.* New York: McGraw-Hill.

Eversley, D. 1973. *The planner in society.* London: Faber.

Fabricant, M. 1988. Empowering the homeless. *Social Policy* 18(4):49.

Fabricant, M., and I. Epstein. 1984. Legal and welfare rights advocacy: Complementary approaches in organizing on behalf of the homeless. *Urban and Social Change Review* 17(1):15.

Fainstein, S. S., N. I. Fainstein, R. C. Hill, D. Judd, and M. P. Smith. 1986. *Restructuring the city.* 2d ed. New York: Longman.

Faludi, A. 1973. *Planning theory.* New York: Pergamon.

Ferrell, F. 1985. *Trevor's place.* San Francisco: Harper & Row.

Firey, W. 1947. *Land use in central Boston.* Cambridge, Mass.: Harvard University Press.

First, R., D. Roth, and B. D. Arewa. 1988. Homelessness: Understanding the dimensions of the problem of minorities. *Social Work* 33(2):120.

Fishman, R. 1977. *Urban utopias in the twentieth century.* New York: Basic Books.

Fordham Urban Law Journal. 1981. Homelessness in a modern setting. 10(8):749.

Forrester, J. F. 1969. *Urban dynamics.* Cambridge, Mass.: MIT Press.

Fox, E. 1985. *Homelessness in Philadelphia: People, needs, services.* Philadelphia: Philadelphia Health Management Corporation.

Friedlen, R. 1983. The politics of profit and the geography of growth. *Urban Affairs Quarterly* 19(1):41.

Friedman, L. 1973. Public housing and the poor. In *Housing urban America. See* Pynoos, Schafer, and Hartman 1973.

Friedman, R. 1983. Housing for the elderly. Unpublished monograph, Graduate Program in Public Policy and Administration, Rutgers University. Camden, N.J.

Gans. H. 1962. *The urban villagers.* New York: Free Press.

Gans, H. 1965. The failure of urban renewal: A critique and some proposals. *Commentary* 31:29.

Gans, H. 1968. *More equality.* New York: Pantheon Books.

Gappert, G., ed. 1987. *The future of winter cities.* Beverly Hills, Calif.: Sage.

Gilbert, N. 1986. The welfare state adrift. *Social Work* 31(4):251.

Gilder, G. 1981. *Wealth and poverty.* New York: Basic Books.

Gilder, G. 1984. *The spirit of enterprise.* New York: Simon & Schuster.

Gioglio, G., and R. J. Jacobsen. 1986. *Homelessness in New Jersey.* Trenton,N.J.: Department of Human Services.

Glazer, N. 1971. The limits of social policy. *Commentary* 37:51.

Glazer, N. 1973. The bias of American housing policy. In *Housing urban America. See* Pynoos, Schafer, and Hartman 1973.

Godschalk, D. R., D. J. Brower, L. D. McBennett, B. A. Vestal, and D. C. Herr. 1979. *Constitutional issues of growth management.* 2d ed. Washington, D.C.: Planners Press.

Goering, J. M., ed. 1986a. *Housing desegregation and federal policy.* Chapel Hill: University of North Carolina Press.

Goering, J. M. 1986b. Minority housing needs and civil rights enforcement. In *Race, ethnicity, and minority housing in the United States. See* Momeni 1986.

Goldstein, M., E. J. Goodrich, and C. A. Brown. 1987. Where group homes are: A descriptive analysis. *Sociology and Social Research* 1(1):55.

Gonzales, P. 1987. Study recommends decentralizing Camden County homeless shelters. *Courier Post,* Cherry Hill, N.J. Dec. 18.

Goodman, R. 1979. *The last entrepreneurs.* New York: Simon & Schuster.

Gottdiener, M. 1977. *Planned sprawl.* Beverly Hills, Calif.: Sage.

Gottdiener, M., ed. 1986. *Cities in stress.* Beverly Hills, Calif.: Sage.

Governor's Task Force on the Homeless. 1983. Trenton, N.J.: Department of Human Services.

Governor's Task Force on the Homeless. 1985. Trenton, N.J.: Department of Human Services.

Graham, O. 1976. *Toward a planned society.* New York: Oxford University Press.

Gray, G. E., G. G. Shelton, and K. T. Gruber. 1980. *The relevance of manufactured housing to the needs of low income families.* Greensboro: North Carolina A & T State University Press.

Green, C. 1967. *Negative taxes and the poverty problem.* Washington, D.C.: Brookings Institution.

Greer, N. R. 1986. *The search for shelter.* Washington, D.C.: American Institute of Architects.

Gregorio, L. 1988. An analysis of New Jersey's fair share housing plan. Unpublished thesis, Rutgers University, Graduate Department of Public Policy and Administration. Camden, N.J.

Grigsby, W. G. 1963. *Housing markets and public policy.* Philadelphia: University of Pennsylvania Press.

Grigsby, W. G. 1973. Housing markets and public policy. In *Housing and community development.*

Grigsby, W. G., et al. 1977. *Re-thinking housing and community development policy.* Philadelphia: University of Pennsylvania.

Grigsby, W. G., and T. Carl. 1983. Declining neighborhoods: Problem or opportunity. In *Annals of the American Academy of Political and Social Science* 465:87–97.

Haar, C. 1984. *Cities, law and social policy: Learning from the British.* Lexington, Mass.: D. C. Heath.

Haar, C., and D. Iatrides. 1974. *Housing the poor in suburbia: Public policy at the grass roots.* Cambridge, Mass.: Ballinger.

Hagen, J. L. 1987. Gender and homelessness. *Social Work* 32(4):312.

Hager, T. 1988. The "Mad Housers": Young Atlantans build shelter huts for the homeless. *Safety Network* 7:4.

Hall, P., H. Gracey, R. Drewett, and R. Thomas. 1973. *The containment of urban England.* London: Allen and Unwin.

Hallman, H. 1970. *Neighborhood control of public programs.* New York: Praeger.

Hamby, A. L. 1985. *Liberalism and its challengers.* New York: Oxford University Press.

Hanley, R. 1988. Affordable housing in Jersey is still an elusive goal. *New York Times.* Oct. 24.

Hanson, R., ed. 1983. *Urban policy: Urban development in an advanced economy.* Washington, D.C.: National Academy Press.

Harkins, J. 1987. The Mt. Laurel decision. Unpublished monograph, Graduate Program in Public Policy, Rutgers University. Camden, N.J.

Harrington, M. 1980. *Decade of decision.* New York: Simon & Schuster.

Harrington, M. 1984. *The new American poverty.* New York: Penguin Books.

Harris v. McCrae. 1980. 448 U.S. 297.

Harrison, R. 1982. *Ecological change among urban, suburban, and rural municipalities: Black suburbanization and residential segregation in New Jersey.* Camden, N.J.: Rutgers University Forum for Policy Research and Public Service.

Harrison, R. 1984. *Zoning laws and wealth segregation in South Jersey: Trends before Mount Laurel II.* Camden, N.J.: Rutgers University Forum for Policy Research and Public Service.

Hart, D. 1972. Theories of government related to decentralization and citizen participation. *Public Administration Review* 32:615.

Hartman, C. 1973. The politics of housing. In *Housing urban America.* See Pynoos, Schafer, and Hartman 1973.

Hartman, C. 1974. *Yerba Buena; Land grab and community resistance in San Francisco.* San Francisco: Glide.

Hartman, C. 1975. *Housing and social policy.* Englewood Cliffs, N.J.: Prentice-Hall.

Hartman, C. 1983. *America's housing crisis: What is to be done.* Boston: Routledge and Kegan Paul.

Hartman, C., D. Keating, and R. LeGates. 1982. *Displacement: How to fight it.* Berkeley, Calif.: National Housing Law Project.

Hawley, W., and F. Wirt. 1968. *The search for community power.* Englewood Cliffs, N.J.: Prentice-Hall.

Hayden, T. 1980. *The American future: New visions beyond old frontiers.* Boston: South End Press.

Herbers, J. 1986. *The new heartland.* New York: Time Books.

Herington, J. 1984. *The outer city.* London: Harper & Row.

Heskin, A. 1987. Los Angeles: Innovative local approaches. In *The homeless in contemporary society.* See Bingham, Green, and White 1987.

Hill, R. 1984. Urban political economy: Emergence, consolidation and development. In *Cities in Transformation.* See M. P. Smith 1984.

Hinshaw, M., and K. J. Allott. 1973. Environmental preferences of future housing consumers. In *Housing urban America.* See Pynoos, Schafer, and Hartman 1973.

Hoath, D. 1983. *Homelessness.* London: Sweet and Maxwell.

Hobbs-Fernie, L. 1986. Consideration of New Jersey's homeless policy; A comparison to Britain's national policy. Unpublished monograph, Rutgers University, Graduate Program in Public Policy and Administration. Camden, N.J.

Hoch, C. 1987. A brief history of the homeless problem in the United States. In *The homeless in contemporary society.* See Bingham, Green, and White 1987.

Hochschild, J. L. 1984. *The new American dilemma: Liberal democracy and school desegregation.* New Haven, Conn.: Yale University Press.

Hodges v. Ginsberg. 1983. 303 S.A. 2d 245 (W. Va.)

Holcomb, B., and R. A. Beauregard. 1981. *Revitalizing cities.* Washington, D.C.: Association of American Geographers.

Hombs, M. E., and M. Snyder. 1982. *Homelessness in America: A forced march to nowhere.* Washington, D.C.: Community for Creative Non-Violence.

Hope, M., and J. Young. 1986a. *The faces of homelessness.* Lexington, Mass.: Lexington Books.

Hope, M., and J. Young. 1986b. The politics of displacement: Sinking into homelessness. In *Housing the homeless. See* Erickson and Wilhelm 1986.

Hopper, K., and J. Hamberg. 1984. *The making of America's homeless: From skid row to new poor.* New York: Community Service Society of New York.

Housing and Community Research Groups. 1973. *Community housing development corporations: The empty promise.* Cambridge, Mass.: Urban Policy Aid Inc.

Hughes, J. W., and G. Sternlieb. 1987. *The dynamics of America's housing.* New Brunswick, N.J.: Center for Urban Policy Research.

Hunter, F. 1953. *Community power structure.* Chapel Hill: University of North Carolina Press.

Hyson, J. M. 1984. Pennsylvania exclusionary zoning law: A single alternative to Mt. Laurel II? *Land Use and Zoning Digest* 36:6.

Jackson, K. 1985. *The crabgrass frontier.* New York: Oxford University Press.

Jahiel, R. 1987. The situation of homelessness. In *The homeless in contemporary society. See* Bingham, Green, and White 1987.

Jefferson, A. 1986. Black America in the 1980's: Rhetoric vs. reality. *The Black Scholar* 17(3):2.

Jenkins, J. C. 1983. Resource mobilization theory and the study of social movements in America. *Annual Review of Sociology* 9:527.

Joe, T., and C. Rodgers. 1985. *By the few: The Reagan welfare legacy.* Lexington, Mass.: D. C. Heath.

Johnson, P. W. 1986. Summary of the homeless program. Boston, Mass.: Executive Office of Human Services.

Johnston, R. J. 1982. *The American urban system.* New York: St. Martin's Press.

Judd, D., and R. Ready. 1986. Entrepreneurial cities and the new politics of economic development. In *Reagan and the cities. See* Peterson, Lewis, and Carol 1986.

Kantor, P. 1987. The dependent city. *Urban Affairs Quarterly* 22(4):493.

Kasinitz, P. 1986. Gentrification and homelessness: The single room occupant and the inner city revival. In *Housing the homeless. See* Erickson and Wilhelm 1986.

Kates, B. 1985. *The murder of a shopping bag lady.* San Diego, Calif.: Harcourt Brace Jovanovich.

Kaufman, N., and J. L. Harris. 1983. *Profile of the homeless in Massachusetts.* Boston: Governor's Office of Human Resources.

Kaufman, N. K. 1984. Homelessness: A comprehensive policy approach. *Urban and Social Change Review* 17(1):21.

Kearns, K. 1980. Urban squatting: Social activism in the housing sector. *Social Policy* 10:21.

Keefe, W. J. 1988. *Parties, politics and public policy in America.* Washington, D.C.: Congressional Quarterly Inc.

Kennedy, M. 1984. The fiscal crisis of the city. In *Cities in transformation. See* M. P. Smith 1984.

Keyes, L. C. 1973. The role of nonprofit sponsors. In *Housing in America. See* Mandelker 1973.

King v. South Jersey National Bank. 1974. 66 N.J. 161, 178.

Knight, J. H. 1987. Interview with Attorney for the Westchester Committee for the Homeless. White Plains, New York.

Koch, J. 1987. The federal role in aiding the homeless. In *The homeless in contemporary society. See* Bingham, Green, and White 1987.

Kondratas, S. A. 1985. *A strategy for helping the homeless.* Washington, D.C.: The Heritage Foundation.

Kozol, J. 1988. *Rachel and her children.* New York: Crown.

Lake, R. 1981. *The new suburbanites.* New Brunswick, N.J.: Center for Urban Policy Research.

Lamb, H. R. 1984. Deinstitutionalization and the homeless mentally ill. *Hospital and Community Psychiatry* 35:899.

Lang, B. 1939. *SPIROGRAM.* Unpublished monograph. Westport, Conn.

Lang, M. H. 1982. *Gentrification amid urban decline.* Cambridge, Mass.: Ballinger.

Lang, M. H. 1985a. *Availability of mortgage funds in Camden, New Jersey.* Camden, N.J.: Rutgers Forum for Policy Research and Public Service.

Lang, M. H. 1985b. *Urban squatting programs in two cities.* Camden, N.J.: Rutgers Forum for Policy Research and Public Service.

Lang, M. H. 1987. Shelter policy for Camden County: A report to CPAC/HSC and CSC. Camden, N.J.: Camden Planning and Advocacy Coalition.

Lang, M. H. 1989. Gentrification. In Lisa Taylor, ed. *Housing.* New York: Cooper Hewitt Museum.

Lansing, J. B., C. Clifton, and J. N. Morgan. 1973. New homes and poor people: A study of the chain of moves. In *Housing in America. See* Mandelker 1973.

Laska, S., and D. Spain, eds. 1980. *Back to the city: Issues in neighborhood renovation.* New York: Pergamon.

Lehman, H. J. 1989. Private groups make up deficit in federal low cost housing program. *Philadelphia Inquirer.* April 30, p. 2-I.

Lekachman, R. 1982. *Greed is not enough.* New York: Pantheon.

Lenkowsky, L. 1986. *Politics, economics, and welfare reform.* Lanham, Md.: University Press of America.

Lentini, C. 1985. Lawsuits build up around Mt. Laurel II ruling. *Courier Post,* Cherry Hill, N.J., March 3.

Levi. 1973. Focal leverage points in problems relating to real property. In *Housing in America. See* Mandelker 1973.

Levine, R. A. 1970. *The poor ye need not have with you.* Cambridge, Mass.: MIT Press.

Levitan, S. 1969. *The Great Society's poor law.* Baltimore, Md.: Johns Hopkins Press.

Levitan, S. 1984. *Beyond the safety net.* Cambridge, Mass.: Ballinger.

Levy, P. 1978. *Queen Village: The eclipse of community.* Philadelphia: Institute for the Study of Civic Values.

Lichter, D. 1986. Convergence in White and Black population redistribution in the U.S. *Social Science Quarterly* 67(1):21.

Lindblom, C. E. 1970. The science of muddling through. In F. Cox, *Strategies of community organization.* Itasca, Ill.: Peacock.

Lindblom, C. E. 1977. *Politics and markets.* New York: Basic Books.

Lindblom, C. E. 1980. *The policy making process.* Englewood Cliffs, N.J.: Prentice-Hall.

Lindsey v. Normet. 1972. 405 U.S. 59.

Lipton, G. 1980. The future central city: Gentrified or abandoned? *Urban Affairs Papers* 2:1.

Loeb, V. 1987. 42 city homeless die in 2 years. *Philadelphia Inquirer.*

Logan, J. 1983. The disappearance of communities from national urban policy. *Urban Affairs Quarterly* 19(1):75.

London, J. 1977. *The people of the abyss.* 2d ed. London: Journeyman Press.

Long, N. E. 1972. *The unwalled city.* New York: Basic Books.

Lowi, T. J. 1969. *The end of liberalism.* New York: Norton.

Lowi, T. J. 1971. *The politics of disorder.* New York: Basic Books.

Lowry, I. 1960. Filtering and housing standards: A conceptual analysis. *Land Economics* 36:362.

Lubetkin v. Hartford, 1983. In *Legal and welfare rights advocacy. See* Fabricant 1984.

Lukas, J. 1985. *Common ground: A turbulent decade in the lives of three American families.* New York: Knopf.

Magill, R. 1986. Social welfare policies in urban America. *Social Work* 31:5.

Main, T. 1983a. The homeless of New York. *The Public Interest* 72(3):28.

Main, T. 1983b. New York City's lure to the homeless. *Wall Street Journal.* Sept. 12.

Mallach, A. 1988. Opening the suburbs: New Jersey's Mt. Laurel experience. *Shelterforce* XI(2):12.

Mandelker, D., and R. Montgomery. 1973. *Housing in America: Problems and Perspectives.* Indianapolis, Ind.: Bobbs-Merrill.

Mandelker, D., et al. 1981. *Housing and community development.* Indianapolis, Ind.: Bobbs-Merrill.

Manno, R. 1985a. Group acquires property for city homeless shelter. *Courier Post,* Cherry Hill, N.J. May 10.

Manno, R. 1985b. Towns sharing cost to house the homeless. *Courier Post,* Cherry Hill, N.J. May 5.

Marcuse, P. 1988. Neutralizing homelessness. *Socialist Review* 1:69.

Massachusetts Department of Public Welfare. 1987. *Sheltering the homeless: A guide to establishing a shelter.* Boston: Department of Public Welfare.

Mastro, A. 1984. Mt. Laurel II and municipal home rule. *New Jersey Municipalities* 61:34.

Mathers, M. 1973. *Riding the Rails.* Boston: Gambit.

Matica v. City of Atlantic City. 1985. Superior Court of New Jersey, Law Division, Atlantic County. No. L-8306-84E.

Mayer, R., and T. Shuster. 1985. *Developing shelter models for the homeless: Three program design options.* New York: Community Service Society of New York.

McCain v. Koch. 1984. 127 Misc. 2d, 23 (Sup. Ct. Spr. Term, NY Cov).

McCone, G. 1969. *Regional policy in Britain.* London: Allen and Unwin.

McFadden, R. 1988. Derelict shell becomes co-op for homeless. *New York Times.* Nov. 15.

McJimsey, G. 1987. *Harry Hopkins: Ally of the poor and defender of democracy.* Cambridge, Mass.: Harvard University Press.

Medcalf, L., and K. Dolbeare. 1985. *Neopolitics: American political ideas in the 1980's.* New York: Random House.

Mental Health Association in New Jersey. 1985. *Community/residential alternatives to institutionalization.* Trenton, N.J.

Meyers, E. M. 1986. *Rebuilding America's cities.* Cambridge, Mass.: Ballinger.

Milgram, M. 1979. *Good neighborhood: The challenge of open housing.* New York: Norton.

Mills, C. W. 1956. *The power elite.* New York: Oxford University Press.

Minogue, K. R. 1963. *The liberal mind.* New York: Vintage Books.

Momeni, J. A., ed. 1986. *Race, ethnicity, and minority housing in the United States.* New York: Greenwood Press.

Montgomery County Government. 1985. *Emergency shelter services.* Rockville, Md.: Department of Family Resources.

Moynihan, D. P. 1969. *Maximum feasible misunderstanding.* New York: The Free Press.

Moynihan, D. P. 1986. *Family and nation.* San Diego, Calif.: Harcourt Brace Jovanovich.

Muller, P. O. 1981. *Contemporary suburban America.* Englewood Cliffs, N.J.: Prentice-Hall.

Murphy, T. P., and J. Rehfuss. 1976. *Urban politics in the suburban era.* Homewood, Ill.: The Dorsey Press.

Murray, C. 1984. *Losing ground.* New York: Basic Books.

Murray, H. 1986. Time in the streets. In *Housing the homeless. See* Erickson and Wilhelm 1986.

Nathan, R. R. 1987. Will the underclass always be with us? *Society* 24(3):57.

Nathan, R. R., and C. F. Adams, Jr. 1977. *Revenue sharing: The second round.* Washington, D.C.: Brookings Institution.

National Coalition for the Homeless. 1987a. *America's homeless: Strategies for '88.* New Haven, Conn.

National Coalition for the Homeless. 1987b. *Pushed out: America's homeless Thanksgiving.* Washington, D.C.

National Commission on Excellence in Eduction. 1983. *A nation at risk.* Washington, D.C.

National Commission on Urban Problems. 1968. *Building the American city.* Washington, D.C.: U.S. Government Printing Office.

National Housing Task Force. 1988. A decent place to live. Washington, D.C.

Needleman, M., and C. Needleman. 1974. *Guerrillas in the bureaucracy.* New York: Wiley.

Nenno, M., and P. Brophy. 1983. *Housing and local government.* Washington, D.C.: International City Management Association.

Netzer, D. 1973. Income strategy and housing supply. In *Housing urban America. See* Pynoos, Schafer, and Hartman 1973.

Neuman, O. 1972. *Defensible space.* New York: Macmillan.

New Jersey Department of Community Affairs. 1982. *Affordable housing handbook.* Trenton, N.J.

New Jersey Department of Community Affairs. 1988a. *Summary of division housing programs.* Trenton, N.J.

New Jersey Department of Community Affairs. 1988b. New Jersey housing advocate: Program description. Trenton, N.J.

New Jersey Department of Human Services. 1986. *Homelessness in New Jersey.* Trenton, N.J.

New Jersey Law Journal. 1985. Court orders help for Atlantic City homeless. 115:28.

New Jersey Public Law, 1985. *Fair Housing Act.* Trenton, N.J. P.L. 1985, Chapter 222.

New Jersey Statute Ann. 1985. 55:BC-1 to 55:BC-6, Ch. 48.

New Jersey Statute Ann. 1986. 44:8-120 to 44:8-122 (West Supp. 1986).

New Jersey Statute Ann. 1986. 52:27D-280 to 287 (West Supp. 1986).

Northeastern Illinois Planning Commission. 1973. *Public participation in the regional planning process.* Vol. 1. Chicago, Ill.

Norton, R. D. 1979. *City life cycles and American urban policy.* New York: Academic Press.

O'Connor, P., and R. Shaffer. 1988. Interview with Peter O'Connor and Robert Shaffer of Fair Share Housing Development Inc. Cherry Hill, N.J. Oct. 21.

Olsen, E. 1973. A competitive theory of the housing market. In *Housing urban America. See* Pynoos, Schafer, and Hartman 1973.

Orfield, G. 1983. *State housing policy and urban school desegregation.* Denver, Colo.: Education Commission of the States.

Orwell, G. 1933. *Down and out in Paris and London.* New York: Harcourt Brace Jovanovich.

Oser, A. S. 1988. Program for homeless picks up its pace. *New York Times,* June 19.

Ostrum, E. 1983. The social stratification–government inequality thesis explored. *Urban Affairs Quarterly* 19(1):91.

Pagano, M. A., and R. J. T. Moore. 1985. *Cities and fiscal choices.* Durham, N.C.: Duke University Press.

Partnership for the Homeless. 1987. *National funding to assist the homeless.* New York.

Pascale, C. 1986. Interview with Attorney, Ocean County Office of Legal Services. April 14.

Pateman, C. 1970. *Participation and democratic theory.* New York: Cambridge University Press.

Perin, C. 1977. *Everything in its place.* Princeton, N.J.: Princeton University Press.

Peroff, K. 1987. Who are the homeless and how many are there? In *The homeless in contemporary society. See* Bingham, Green, and White 1987.

Perry, D. 1984. Structuralism, class conflict and urban reality. In *Cities in transformation. See* M. P. Smith 1984.

Peterson, G., E. Lewis, and W. Carol, eds. *Reagan and the cities.* Washington, D.C.: The Urban Institute.

Peterson, P. E., ed. 1985. *The new urban reality.* Washington, D.C.: Brookings Institution.

Peuquet, S. W., and P. J. Leland. 1988. *Homelessness in Delaware.* Newark, Del.: College of Urban Affairs and Public Policy, University of Delaware.

Philadelphia Committee for the Homeless. 1985. *Homeless to housed continuum.* Philadelphia.

Philadelphia Health Management Corporation. 1985. *Homelessness in Philadelphia: People's needs, services.* Philadelphia.

Philadelphia Inquirer. 1986. Judge won't tell state not to distribute homeless funds. Jan. 25.

Philadelphia Ordinance No. 1962. 1982. Nov. 10.

Phillips, K. P. 1969. *The emerging Republican majority.* New Rochelle, N.Y.: Arlington House.

Phillips, M. H., D. Kronenfeld, and V. Jeter. A model of services to homeless families in shelters. In *Housing the homeless. See* Erickson and Wilhelm 1987.

Pickvane, C. G. 1984. The structuralist critique in urban studies. In *Cities in transformation. See* M. P. Smith 1984.

Pierce, N. 1988. Now New Jersey is busting out all over. *Philadelphia Inquirer*. April 18.

Pitts v. Black. 1984. (Unrep) S. Supp (SCNY).

Piven, F. F., and R. Cloward. 1971. *Regulating the poor: The functions of public welfare*. New York: Vintage.

Polikoff, A. 1978. *Housing the poor*. Cambridge, Mass.: Ballinger.

Pollock, S. 1983. State constitutions as separate sources of fundamental rights. *Rutgers Law Review* 37(4):707.

Popper, F. J. 1981. *The politics of land use reform*. Madison, Wis.: The University of Wisconsin Press.

Porter, P. 1976. *The recovery of American cities*. New York: Sun River.

President's Commission for a National Agenda for the Eighties. 1980. *A national agenda for the eighties*. Washington, D.C.: Library of Congress.

President's Commission on Housing. 1982. Washington, D.C.: Library of Congress.

President's Committee on Urban Housing. 1968. *A decent home*. Washington, D.C.: United States Government Printing Office.

President's National Urban Policy Report. 1980. Washington, D.C.: Department of Housing and Urban Development.

Presthus, R. 1974. *Elites in the policy process*. New York:Cambridge University Press.

Price, D. E. 1984. *Bringing back the parties*. Washington, D.C.: Congressional Quarterly, Inc.

Prichard, A. M. 1981. *Squatting*. London: Sweet and Maxwell.

Public Technology Inc. 1985. *Caring for the hungry and homeless: Exemplary programs*. Alexandria, Va.: Emergency Food and Shelter National Board Program.

Pyle, L. 1985. The land market beyond the urban fringe. *The Geographical Review* 75(1):32.

Pynoos, J., R. Schafer, and C. Hartman, eds. 1973. *Housing urban America*. Chicago: Aldine.

Quigley, J. M., and D. L. Rubinfield. 1985. *American domestic priorities: An economic appraisal*. Berkeley: University of California Press.

Rainwater, L. 1973. The lesson of Pruitt Igoe. In *Housing urban America. See* Pynoos, Schafer, and Hartman 1973.

Reagan, M., and J. Sanzone. 1981. *The new federalism*. New York: Oxford University Press.

Redburn, F. S., and T. F. Buss. 1986. *Responding to America's homeless*. New York: Praeger.

Reich, R. 1983. *The next American frontier*. New York: New York Times Books.

Rein, M., and P. Marris. 1968. Poverty and the community planners mandate. In *Urban planning and social policy*, by B. Frieden and R. Morris. New York: Basic Books.

Reitman, B. 1937. *Sister of the road*. New York: Harper & Row.

Ricci, D. 1971. *Community power and democratic theory: The logic of political analysis*. New York: Random House.

Richman, W. 1987. Government policies and Black progress: The role of social research in public policy debates. *Social Work* 32(4):353.

Right to Choose v. Bryne. 1982. 91 NJ 287.

Ritzdorf, M., and S. Sharpe. 1987. Portland, Oregon: A comprehensive approach. In *The homeless in contemporary society. See* Bingham, Green, and White 1987.

Robbins v. Reagan. 1985. 616 F.Supp. 1259:780; F.2d 37.

Robinson v. Cahill. 1973. 62 NJ 473, 495 cert. denied 414 U.S. 976.

Rodgers, H. 1986. *Poor women, poor families: The economic plight of America's female headed households.* Armonk, N.Y.: M. E. Sharpe.

Rodgers v. Newark. 1984. Docket No. L-17401-84 (Essex County Law Div.).

Roske, M. D. 1983. *Housing in transition.* New York: Holt.

Rossi, P. H. 1981. Residential mobility. In *Do housing alternatives work? See* Bradbury and Downs 1981.

Rust, E. 1975. *No growth: Impacts on urban areas.* Lexington, Mass.: D. C. Heath.

Safety Network. 1987. Stewart B. McKinney Homeless Assistance. 5(1):2. Washington, D.C.: National Coalition for the Homeless.

Safety Network. 1988a. Stewart B. McKinney Homeless Assistance Act, appropriations reported to authorizations. 6(4):3. Washington, D.C.: National Coalition for the Homeless.

Safety Network. 1988b. Two new homeless bills are introduced in Congress. 7(5):1. Washington, D.C.: National Coalition for the Homeless.

Safety Network. 1988c. First federal agencies sued under Homeless Assistance Act. 7(7):1. Washington, D.C.: National Coalition for the Homeless.

Saint John's Evangelical Lutheran Church v. Hoboken. 1983. 195 N.J. Sup. Ct. 414, 479A, 2d 935 (Law Division).

Salins, P. 1987. *Housing America's poor.* Berkeley: University of California Press.

Saltman, J. 1982. *Neighborhood stabilization strategies as social inventions.* Kent, Ohio: Kent State University Press.

Sassen-Koob, S. 1984. The new labor demand in global cities. In *Cities in transformation. See* M. P. Smith 1984.

Sawyers, L. 1978. Cities and countryside in the Soviet Union and China. In *Marxism and the metropolis. See* Tabb and Sawyers 1978.

Sawyers, L., and W. K. Tabb. 1984. *Sunbelt/Snowbelt: Urban development and regional restructuring.* New York: Oxford University Press.

Schafer, R., and C. Field. 1973. Section 235 of the National Housing Act: Homeownership for low income families? In *Housing urban America. See* Pynoos, Schafer, and Hartman 1973.

Schlesinger, A. 1986. *The cycles of American history.* New York: Houghton Mifflin.

Schmitt, Eric. 1987. Suburbs struggle to shelter the homeless. *New York Times.* Sept. 8.

Schneider, J. C. 1986. Skid Row as an urban neighborhood 1880–1960. In *Housing the homeless. See* Erickson and Wilhelm 1986.

Schoenberg, J. 1984. Interview with former Bedminster Township Assistant Administrator and J. Harkins. Bedminster, N.J., March 21.

Schorr, A. L. 1986. *Common decency.* New Haven, Conn.: Yale University Press.

Schultze, W. A. 1985. *Urban politics.* Englewood Cliffs, N.J.: Prentice-Hall.

Schutt, R. 1987. *Shelters as organizations: Full fledged programs or just a place to stay?* Boston: University of Massachusetts.

Schwartz, E. 1977. Political development: An alternative to triage. In *Justice and the city,* by P. Levy. Philadelphia: Institute for the Study of Civic Values.

Sciarra, D. 1987. Interview at N.J. State's Advocate office. New Haven, Conn., Sept. 1.

S.C.O.P.E. Inc. v. the Zoning Board of Adjustment of Vineland, et al. 1984. Docket No. L-053018-84 P.W., Cumberland County Law Division.

Scott, M. 1971. *American city planning since 1890*. Berkeley: University of California Press.

Sheffman, Y., and N. Foxworthy. 1985. *Producing low income housing in New York City*. New York: Community Service Society of New York.

Shelby County Culture of Poverty Think Tank. 1987. *Free the children: Breaking the cycle of poverty*. Memphis, Tenn.: Shelby County Government.

Shelter. 1982. *Ordinary people: Homeless in the housing crisis*. London: National Campaign for the Homeless.

Shelter. 1984. *Looking forward 1984: A shelter progress report*. London: National Campaign for the Homeless.

Shelter. 1985. *Shelter news*. London: National Campaign for the Homeless.

Sidel, R. 1986. *Women and children last: The plight of poor women in affluent America*. New York: Penguin Books.

Siegal, H. 1978. *Outposts of the forgotten*. New Brunswick, N.J.: Transaction Books.

Smith, M. P. 1979. *The city and the social theory*. New York: St. Martin's Press.

Smith, M. P., ed. 1984. *Cities in transformation: Class, capital, and the state*. Beverly Hills, Calif.: Sage.

Smith, M. P., and D. Judd. 1984. American cities: The production of ideology. In *Cities in transformation. See* M. P. Smith 1984.

Smith, N., and P. Williams, eds. 1986. *Gentrification of the city*. Boston: Allen and Unwin.

Smith, P. 1987. *National growth in homelessness: Winter 1987: Broken promises/Broken lives*. New York: The Partnership for the Homeless.

Smith, R. A., and D. Cozad. 1976. Patterns of revenue sharing expenditure from the actual use reports. In *Revenue sharing. See* Caputo and Cole 1976a.

Smith, W. 1975. Filtering and neighborhood change. In *Readings in social geography*, by Emrys Jones. London: Oxford University Press.

Snow, D., et al. 1986. The myth of pervasive mental illness among the homeless. *Social Problems* 33(5):407.

Solomon, A. 1973. Housing and public policy analysis. In *Housing urban America. See* Pynoos, Schafer, and Hartman 1973.

Sonnenberg, L. 1984. Cherry Hill can't buy its way out of Mt. Laurel II dilemma. *Courier Post*, Cherry Hill, N.J. Dec. 21.

Southern Burlington County NAACP v. Township of Mount Laurel. 1975. 336 A.2d 717 N.J.

Southern Burlington County NAACP v. Township of Mount Laurel. 1978. 161, NJ Sup. 317 (Law Division 1978):11.

Southern Burlington County NAACP v. Township of Mount Laurel. 1983. 92 N.J. 158.

Spiegel, Hans. 1968. *Citizen participation in urban development*. Washington, D.C.: N.T.L. Institute.

Sprague, J. F. 1986. *A manual on transitional housing*. Boston: Women's Institute for Housing and Economic Development.

Stanback, T. M., Jr., and R. V. Knight. 1976. *Suburbanization and the city*. Montclair, N.J.: Allanheld, Osmun & Co.

Staples, R. 1987. *The urban plantation: Racism and colonialism in the post Civil Rights era.* Oakland, Calif.: The Black Scholar Press.

Starr, R. 1978. Making New York smaller. In *Revitalizing the Northeast,* by G. Sternlieb and J. Hughes. New Brunswick, N.J.: Center for Urban Policy Research.

Stearns, L. B., and J. Logan. 1986. The racial structuring of the housing market and segregation in suburban areas. *Social Forces* 65(1):28.

Stefl, M. 1987. The new homeless: A national perspective. In *The homeless in contemporary society. See* Bingham, Green, and White 1987.

Sternlieb, G., and J. Hughes. 1980. The changing demography of the central city. *Scientific American* 243:27.

Sternlieb, G., and J. Hughes. 1983. Housing the poor in a post-shelter society. *The Annals of the American Academy of Political and Social Science* 465:109–122.

Stolarski, L. 1988. Right to shelter: History of the mobilization of the homeless as a model of voluntary action. *Journal of Voluntary Action Research* 17(1):36.

Stone, C. W., R. K. Whelen, and W. J. Murin. 1986. *Urban policy and politics in a bureaucratic age.* Englewood Cliffs, N.J.: Prentice-Hall.

Stone, I. 1965. *Jack London.* New York: New American Library.

Stone, L. H. 1986. Shelters for battered women: A temporary escape from danger: The first step toward divorce? In *Housing the homeless. See* Erickson and Wilhelm 1986.

Stone, M. 1973. Federal housing policy: A political economic analysis. In *Housing urban America. See* Pynoos, Schafer, and Harman 1973.

Stoner, M. 1986. The plight of homeless women. In *Housing the homeless. See* Erickson and Wilhelm 1986.

Stoner, M. 1988. The voluntary sector leads the war in delivery of health care to the homeless ill. *Journal of Voluntary Action Research* 17(1):24.

Strong, A. L. 1979. *Land banking.* Baltimore, Md.: The Johns Hopkins University Press.

Struyk, R., N. Mayer, and J. Tuccillo. *Federal housing policy at President Reagan's midterm.* Washington, D.C.: Urban Institute Press.

Stucker, J. 1986. Race and residential mobility: The effects of housing assistance programs in household behavior. In *Housing desegregation and housing policy. See* Goering 1986a.

Sullivan, P., and S. Damrosch. 1987. Homeless women and children. In *The homeless in contemporary society. See* Bingham, Green, and White 1987.

Summers, G. 1976. *Industrial invasion of nonmetropolitan America.* New York: Praeger.

Tabb, W., and L. Sawyers. 1978. *Marxism and the metropolis.* New York: Oxford University Press.

Taggert, H. T. 1974. How the banks starve the cities to feed the suburbs. *Planning* 10:14–16.

Taggert, H. T., and K. W. Smith. 1981. Redlining: An assessment of the evidence of disinvestment in metro Boston. *Urban Affairs Quarterly* 17:91–107.

Teitz and Rosenthal. 1973. Housing code enforcement in New York City. In *Housing in America. See* Mandelker 1973.

Terrell, P. 1976. *The social impact of revenue sharing.* New York: Praeger.

Thurow, L. C. 1980. *The zero-sum society.* New York: Basic Books.

Titmuss, R. 1963. *Essays on the welfare state.* Boston: Beacon Press.

Tomer, J. 1980. The mounting evidence on mortgage redlining. *Urban Affairs Quarterly* 15:488–501.

Turner, J. F. C. 1976. *Housing by people*. New York: Pantheon Books.

Turner, J. F. C. and R. Fichter 1975. *Freedom to build*. New York: MacMillan.

Unitarian Universalist Association. 1987. Official statement on homelessness. Boston, Mass.

U.S. Committee on Banking, Housing, and Urban Affairs. 1987. *A new national housing policy*. 100th Congress, 1st Session.

U.S. Committee on Government Operations. 1985. *Federal response to the homeless crisis*. 3d Report. Washington, D.C.: U.S. Government Printing Office.

U.S. Conference of Mayors. 1988. *The federal budget and the cities*. Washington, D.C.

U.S. Department of Commerce. 1983. *County and city data book*. Washington, D.C.

U.S. Department of Health and Human Services. 1984. *Helping the homeless: A resource guide*. Washington, D.C.

U.S. Department of Housing and Urban Development. 1975. *HUD guide to evaluating affirmative fair housing marketing plans*. Washington, D.C.: Office for Policy Development and Research.

U.S. Department of Housing and Urban Development. 1984a. *A report to the Secretary on the homeless and emergency shelters*. Washington, D.C.: Office for Policy Development and Research.

U.S. Department of Housing and Urban Development. 1984b. *Fair housing USA*. Washington, D.C.: Office of Fair Housing and Equal Opportunity.

U.S. General Accounting Office. 1985. *Homelessness: A complex problem and the federal response*. Washington, D.C.: U.S. Government Printing Office.

Vosburgh, W. 1988. Voluntary associations, the homeless and hard to serve populations—Perspectives from organizational theory. *Journal of Voluntary Action Research* 17(1):10.

Waites, N., and C. Wolmar. 1980. *Squatting: The Real Story*. London: Bay Leaf Books.

Ward, P. 1982. *Self help housing: A critique*. London: Mansell.

Warner, S. B. 1968. *The private city: Philadelphia in three stages of growth*. Philadelphia: University of Pennsylvania Press.

Weber, M. 1958. *The Protestant ethic and the spirit of capitalism*. New York: Scribners.

Webber, M. 1965. The role of intelligence systems in urban systems planning. *Journal of American Institute of Planners* 31:289.

Weicher, J. C., ed. 1984. *Maintaining the safety net*. Washington, D.C.: American Enterprise Institute for Public Policy Research.

Welfeld, I. 1973. Toward a new housing policy. In *Housing urban America. See* Pynoos, Schafer, and Hartman 1973.

Werner, F. 1984. On the streets: Homelessness causes and solutions. *Clearinghouse Review* 18(1):11.

Werner, F. 1985. Homelessness: A litigation roundup. *Clearinghouse Review* 18(11):1255.

Wiegand, G. 1988. 130 meet to discuss housing options for the homeless. *Phila-delphia Inquirer*. May 18.

Wiegard, R. B. 1985. Counting the homeless. *American Demographics* 7:34–37.

Wilber, C. K. 1983. *An inquiry into the poverty of economics*. Notre Dame, Ind.: University of Notre Dame Press.

Wilhelm, S. 1986. The economic demise of Blacks in America: A prelude to genocide. *Journal of Black Studies* 17(2):201.

Williams v. Barry. 1980. 490 F. Supp. 941. Washington, D.C., Circuit Court.

Williams v. Barry. 1983. 708 F 2d 789. Washington, D.C., Circuit Court.

Williams, W. 1972. *The struggle for a negative income tax.* Institute of Governmental Research, University of Washington, Seattle.

Wilson, J. Q. 1966. *Urban renewal: The record and the controversy.* Cambridge, Mass.: MIT Press.

Wilson, W. J. 1987. *The truly disadvantaged.* Chicago: University of Chicago Press.

Winerip, M. 1988a. Group homes: A law works ever so quietly. *New York Times.* Nov. 4.

Winerip, M. 1988b. Money is tight, but for a pool, HUD says yes. *New York Times.* Dec. 2.

Wisnosky, E. 1988. The New Jersey Housing and Mortgage Finance Agency's housing assistance program: Incentive or illusion? Unpublished thesis. Department of Public Policy and Administration, Rutgers University. Camden, N.J.

Wolfe, T. 1970. *Radical chic or mau mauing the flack catchers.* New York: Farrar, Straus, & Giroux.

Wright, J. 1988. The worthy and the unworthy homeless. *Society* 25(5):64.

Yago, G. 1983. Urban policy and national political economy. *Urban Affairs Quarterly* 19(1):113.

Yin, R. 1972. *The city in the seventies.* Itasca, Ill.: Peacock.

Young, E. 1978. The Philadelphia plan: An approach to neighborhood preservation. *Real Estate Review* 8:66–69.

Index

ABOUT THE AUTHOR

MICHAEL H. LANG is Associate Professor of Urban Studies and Public Policy at Rutgers University in Camden, New Jersey. Educated at Drew University, he holds two advanced degrees in urban planning from the London School of Economics and Political Science. He is the author of many published articles and research monographs dealing with international aspects of low cost housing policy and homelessness. His book *Gentrification Amid Urban Decline* was published by Ballinger Publishing Company, Cambridge. Recently, he was selected to write the chapter on gentrification for a book on housing published by the Cooper-Hewitt Museum of the Smithsonian Institution. As past director of the Rutgers Forum for Policy Research and Public Service, he authored or coauthored numerous applied urban policy research studies. He is currently conducting research into comparative aspects of private land tenure and squatting in Britain and America. A former Peace Corps Volunteer, he worked in less developed countries with international community development and housing agencies responsible for rehousing former urban squatters. Recently he helped establish a joint Peace Corps/Rutgers graduate program in international development policy on the Camden campus.